W0008858

NT Server 4
in the Enterprise

The Cram Sheet

This Cram Sheet contains the distilled, key facts about Windows NT Server 4 in the Enterprise. Review this information last thing before you enter the test room, paying special attention to those areas where you feel you need the most review. You can transfer any of these facts from your head onto a blank sheet of paper before beginning the exam.

DISK MANAGEMENT

1. Review Disk Administrator menus and options.

2. Only primary partitions can be active: Select Mark Active from the Partition menu in Disk Administrator.

3. When working with Disk Administrator, one important command is the Commit Changes Now option in the Partition menu. This command instructs Windows NT to make your requested changes to the affected storage devices.

4. To be active, a partition must be a primary partition. A primary partition can be made active by using the Mark Active command on the Disk Administrator's Partition menu.

FAULT TOLERANCE

5. NT Backup features and functions:

   • Do not back up temp files.

   • Back up the Registry on PDC and all BDCs.

   • NT Backup cannot back up the Registry across the network.

6. About disk striping with parity:

All partitions in set are equal sizes (or close). Partitions must be on different physical disks. Must use NTFS 3 drives minimum; 32 drives maximum. Slower than striping without parity, faster than mirroring.

7. If one drive in a set fails, missing data can be rebuilt from remaining devices and parity info.

8. If you lose a member of a volume set or stripe set without parity, everything is lost!

9. Neither boot nor system partitions can reside on a volume set or disk stripe set, even with parity.

10. RAID levels, speeds, and details:

   • RAID 0; not fault tolerant; fastest; includes disk striping without parity, volume sets

   • RAID 1; fault tolerant; slowest; includes disk mirroring (slower), disk duplexing (faster)

   • RAID 5; fault tolerant; intermediate; includes disk striping with parity

11. When dealing with Directory Replication, all data placed in an export server's export directory will be duplicated to all import servers' import directories. By default, the

WINS	DNS
Flat database name space	Uses FQDN's hierarchical structure
Used on MS clients and networks	Used on TCP/IP-based hosts and networks
Only one entry per client	Each host can have multiple aliases
Enables domain functions such as logon and browsing	N/A

NETWARE

34. NWLink default Frame Type Auto Detection usually works okay, but some Ethernet adapters won't work with this setting. To communicate with older NetWare versions, manually enter all frame types.

35. Always consider frame type mismatch when NT and NetWare (v3.12 and older) can't interact.

36. To give NetWare clients NT access, install GSNW and NWLink. NWLink works without NetWare, too.

37. GSNW lets MS network clients (Windows 3.x, 95, NT Workstation/Server) access NetWare resources.

38. Use NT utility NWCONV.EXE to migrate NetWare users, groups, and resources to Windows NT.

39. WINS maps computer names to IP addresses and reduces broadcast traffic on network.

RAS

40. Important RAS facts:

- RAS only supports PPP dialup clients (not SLIP) RAS supports up to 256 incoming connections

- NetBIOS gateway on server sustains standard NT network operations for PPP-attached clients.

- RAS supports IP and IPX routing.

- RAS supports PPTP and Multilink PPP

- RAS supports NetBIOS, NetBEUI gateway, and Windows Sockets applications.

41. RAS connection security settings are managed using Security tab of Phonebook entry for outbound links, Network Protocol Configuration dialog box for inbound links.

42. Put LMHOSTS files on RAS clients, entries use **#PRE** tag to cache IP addresses locally, speeds access.

43. RAS maintains list of WAN resources. When it is referenced, it attempts AutoDial to regain connection.

PERFORMANCE MONITORING

44. Performance Monitor displays server characteristics. All data is viewable in Chart, Alert, and Report views.

45. Define administrative alerts using Alert selection from Options menu in Performance Monitor.

46. Look at Memory: Pages/Second to decide whether more RAM is needed.

47. Performance Monitor Log option collects data to file to view later.

48. The Network Monitor is only able to capture as much information as will fit in the available system memory. Capture information accumulates rapidly. If you attempt to gather all data points over an extended period of time, you'll have a difficult job isolating (or even locating) any one element. It is, therefore, a good idea to limit the extent of the network capture. Through the use of filters, you can limit and fine-tune your gathering range to focus on one type of packet or data to and/or from one machine. A capture filter acts much like a database query. It specifies the results you want without dumping everything in your lap. Once you create a capture filter, it can be saved and reused later.

Certification
Insider™ Press

Replaces BIOS functions with software driver. Resides in root directory of system partition.

20. ARC name information:

- **scsi(*) or multi(*)** Most ARC names begin with multi(*); scsi(*) appears only when SCSI has BIOS disabled. Multi(*) applies to IDE, EIDE, ESDI, and SCSI (where BIOS enabled). (*) indicates address of hardware adapter. Numbers start at zero, with controller seated closest to slot 0 in PC.

- **disk(*)** Applies only when scsi(*) keyword appears. Then, value of (*) indicates SCSI bus ID, starting with zero, for drive where files reside. If multi(*) appears, disk(*) is always disk(0).

- **rdisk(*)** Applies only when multi(*) keyword appears, indicates SCSI logical unit number (LUN) for the drive. Numbering begins with zero, so first drive in chain named rdisk(0), second rdisk(1), and so on.

- **partition(*)** Indicates disk partition that contains designated files. Unlike other ARC numbering, partition numbers start at one, so first partition is partition(1), second partition(2), and so on.

- **\path** Indicates directory on partition for OS files. Default path for Windows NT is \winnt.

21. The ERD process often corrects boot sector problems. Otherwise, replace NTLDR, or repair NTOSKRNL.

DOMAIN CONTROLLERS, TRUSTS, LOGONS, PROFILES, POLICIES

22. Know the features of and differences between the following: single domain model, master domain model, multiple master domain model, and complete trust domain model.

23. Understand how trusts between domains work, and the difference between a trusted and trusting domain.

24. Understand the process of domain synchronization.

25. Trusts work only when a user from a trusted domain attempts to access resources in a trusting domain. If users don't log on to a domain where they have true user accounts, they can only function as Domain Guests in the domains they do log on to.

26. Trusts between domains are one-way only. Two-way trust = two one-way trusts between domains.

27. The logon system looks for system policies in the NETLOGON share. All policies are stored in a single file called NTCONFIG.POL.

28. User profiles are located in Winnt\Profiles\ <username>\Desktop directory.

29. The initial default settings of all newly created shares is Full Control to the Everyone group.

30. In addition to the Master Browser, there are Backup Browsers and Potential Browsers. The Backup Browser maintains a duplicate list of the resources and acts in a similar way within the Browser Service, as does the BDC within domain control. The Backup Browser can serve lists of resources to clients. A Potential Browser is any machine capable of becoming a Backup or Master Browser.

PROTOCOLS AND SERVICES

31. Windows NT can be a dynamic IP router or a static IP router. Dynamic routers share routing information with other routers to automatically build routing tables. Static routers employ manually configured routing tables.

32. Enabling RIP For IPX is just as simple as it is for IP—just add the RIP For IPX service on the Services tab of the Network applet of the Control Panel. An additional configuration tab for the NWLink protocol, named "Routing," contains a checkbox labeled "Enable RIP Routing." This checkbox must be marked.

33. Differences between WINS and DNS:

WINS	DNS
Maps IP addresses to NetBIOS names	Maps IP addresses to fully qualified domain names (FQDNs)
Automatic client data registration	Manual configuration

(continued)

direcory for the export server is: \%winntroot%\System32\Repl\Export\. Also, Directory Replication will not work if any application is accessing or viewing the export or import directories. The Application log of the Event Viewer displays error messages from the replication service.

12. Boot floppies should contain the following files: BOOT.INI, NTLDR, NTDETECT.COM, NTBOOTTDD.SYS (only if you are using a SCSI controller with BIOS translation disabled or missing), and BOOTSECT.DOS (only if you need to boot into MS-DOS or another operating system present on your system).

USERS AND GROUPS

13. Access tokens are created when a user logs on, and are not changed until the user logs off and logs on again. Therefore, any changes to a user or a group to which that user belongs will not affect those currently logged on. The changes will only affect him the next time he logs on.

14. There are two types of groups: local and global. Local groups are only available on local domains; global groups are available across domains. Local groups can contain users and global groups, global groups contain users only. You can't place groups within global groups, nor can you place local groups within other local groups.

15. For group permissions, the least restrictive right takes precedence, except No Access always wins! When combining NTFS and share permissions, the least restrictive wins for each kind (except No Access), when combining resulting NTFS and share permissions, the most restrictive wins.

16. You can perform the following in User Manager For Domains:

- Produce, change, duplicate, and remove user and group accounts

- Enable account policies (assign defaults for passwords, account lockouts, disconnect status, and so on)

- Create user rights and audit policies

- Establish trust relationships

BOOT FACTS

17. Boot and system partitions can reside on the primary disk in a disk mirror or duplex set. If the primary fails, you must handedit the BOOT.INI file on the boot drive to point to the ARC name for the remaining mirror or duplex drive instead.

18. Boot files—NTLDR, BOOT.INI,NTDETECT.COM, and so forth—reside on the system partition, Windows NT OS files—including NTOSKRNL.EXE—reside on the boot partition. BACKWARDS!

19. Most important Windows NT boot process components:

- **BOOT.INI** Boot initialization file: Describes Windows NT boot defaults, plus OS location, settings, menu selections. It resides in the root directory of the system partition. (Required for NT boot floppy.)

- **BOOTSECT.DOS** MS-DOS boot sector file: Used if NTLDR permits boot to some other Microsoft OS, like DOS or Windows 95. It resides in the root directory of system partition. (Not required.)

- **NTDETECT.COM** PC hardware detection: Reads device and config info before Windows NT boots. It resides in root directory of system partition. (Required for NT boot floppy.)

- **NTLDR** OS loader program: Loads Windows NT, or other designated OS. Relinquishes control once loading completes. Resides in the root directory of a system partition. (Required for NT boot floppy.)

- **NTOSKRNL.EXE** Executable file for Windows NT OS: Includes all basic capabilities and items necessary to establish runtime environment. Resides in \Winnt_root\system32 on boot partition.

- **OSLOADER.EXE** RISC OS loader: Provides services and info equal to NTDETECT.COM, BOOTSECT.DOS, NTDETECT.COM, and NTLDR on PCs. Resides in RISC boot PROM area.

- **NTBOOTDD.SYS** Used when system or boot SCSI drive has BIOS disabled.

Are You Certifiable?

That's the question that's probably on your mind. The answer is: You bet! But if you've tried and failed or you've been frustrated by the complexity of the MCSE program and the maze of study materials available, you've come to the right place. We've created our new publishing and training program, *Certification Insider Press*, to help you accomplish one important goal: to ace an MCSE exam without having to spend the rest of your life studying for it.

The book you have in your hands is part of our *Exam Cram* series. Each book is especially designed not only to help you study for an exam but also to help you understand what the exam is all about. Inside these covers you'll find hundreds of test-taking tips, insights, and strategies that simply cannot be found anyplace else. In creating our guides, we've assembled the very best team of certified trainers, MCSE professionals, and networking course developers.

Our commitment is to ensure that the *Exam Cram* guides offer proven training and active-learning techniques not found in other study guides. We provide unique study tips and techniques, memory joggers, custom quizzes, insights about trick questions, a sample test, and much more. In a nutshell, each *Exam Cram* guide is closely organized like the exam it is tied to.

To help us continue to provide the very best certification study materials, we'd like to hear from you. Write or email us (craminfo@coriolis.com) and let us know how our *Exam Cram* guides have helped you study, or tell us about new features you'd like us to add. If you send us a story about how an *Exam Cram* guide has helped you ace an exam and we use it in one of our guides, we'll send you an official *Exam Cram* shirt for your efforts.

Good luck with your certification exam, and thanks for allowing us to help you achieve your goals.

Keith Weiskamp

Keith Weiskamp
Publisher, Certification Insider Press

NT Server 4
in the Enterprise

Ed Tittel

Kurt Hudson

J. Michael Stewart

Certification Insider™ Press

An imprint of

 **CORIOLIS GROUP BOOKS**

an International Thomson Publishing company I**T**P®

Albany, NY • Belmont, CA • Bonn • Boston • Cincinnati • Detroit • Johannesburg • London
Madrid • Melbourne • Mexico City • New York • Paris • Singapore • Tokyo • Toronto • Washington

MCSE NT Server 4 in the Enterprise Exam Cram

Copyright © The Coriolis Group, 1998

The Coriolis Group, Inc.
An International Thomson Publishing Company
14455 N. Hayden Road, Suite 220
Scottsdale, Arizona 85260

602/483-0192
FAX 602/483-0193
http://www.coriolis.com

Printed in the United States of America
ISBN: 1-57610-191-6
10 9 8 7 6 5 4 3

Publisher
Keith Weiskamp

Project Editor
Jeff Kellum

Production Coordinator
Kim Eoff

Cover Design
Anthony Stock

Interior Design
Jimmie Young
April Nielsen

(From L. to R., Ed Tittel, J. Michael Stewart, Kurt Hudson)

About The Authors

. . . .

Ed Tittel

Ed Tittel recently worked as an instructor and course developer for American Research Group, where he developed and taught from a set of materials on Windows NT 4, both Workstation and Server. Ed is also a regular contributor to *Windows NT* magazine and an instructor for Softbank Forums at its Interop and NT Intranet tradeshows. Prior to going out on his own in 1994, Ed worked at Novell for six years, starting as a field engineer and departing as the director of technical marketing.

Ed has written over 40 computer books, including *HTML for Dummies* (with Stephen N. James, IDG Books Worldwide, 3rd ed., 1997); *Networking Windows NT 4.0 for Dummies* (with Mary Madden and Dave Smith, IDG Books Worldwide, 1996); and a variety of titles on Windows NT, NetWare, networking, and Web-related topics.

Ed has written over 200 articles for publications such as *Byte, InfoWorld, LAN Magazine, LAN Times, The NetWare Advisor, PC Magazine*, and *WindowsUser*. At present, Ed also writes a biweekly column for *Interop Online*. You can reach Ed by email at etittel@lanw.com or on the Web at http://www.lanw.com/etbio.htm.

Kurt Hudson

Kurt Hudson is a technical author, trainer, and consultant in the field of networking and computer-related technologies. For the past six years, he has focused his energy on learning and teaching technical skills. He has written several training manuals and books for government and private industry on topics ranging from inventory control to network administration.

As a former trainer for the U.S. Air Force, Kurt worked on high-security government projects employing technologies most people see only in the cinema. During his six-year engagement with the military, he earned three medals for improving systems efficiency, training excellence, and increasing national security. After departing the U.S. Air Force, he worked for a variety of private corporations, including Unisys and Productivity Point International, where he continued to learn and teach technical topics.

Since achieving Microsoft Certified Systems Engineer (MCSE) and Microsoft Certified Trainer (MCT) ratings, he has been writing books and conducting training sessions that have helped many individuals succeed in their pursuit of professional certification. You can reach Kurt on the Internet at kurtlh@onr.com or on the Web at www.onr.com/user/kurtlh.

James Michael Stewart

James Michael Stewart is a full-time writer focusing on Windows NT and Internet topics. In addition to working on the *Exam Cram* series, he has recently co-authored the *Intranet Bible* (IDG Books Worldwide, 1997) and the *Hip Pocket Guide to HTML 3.2* (IDG Books Worldwide, 1997). He also contributed to *Windows NT Networking for Dummies* (IDG Books Worldwide, 1997), *Building Windows NT Web Servers* (IDG Books Worldwide, 1997), and *Windows NT, Step by Step* (Microsoft Press, 1995).

Michael has written articles for numerous print and online publications, including C|Net, *InfoWorld*, *Windows NT* magazine, and *Datamation*. He is also the moderator for a Softbank online forum focusing on NT, located at http://forums.sbexpos.com/forums-interop/get/HOS_3.html and a former leader of an NT study group at the Central Texas LAN Association. He is currently an MCP for Windows NT Server 4, Workstation, and Windows 95.

Michael graduated in 1992 from the University of Texas at Austin with a bachelor's degree in Philosophy. Despite his degree, his computer knowledge is self-acquired, based on almost 14 years of hands-on experience. Michael has been active on the Internet for quite some time, where most people know him by his nom de wire, McIntyre. You can reach Michael by email at michael@lanw.com or through his Web pages at http://www.lanw.com/jmsbio.htm or http://www.impactonline.com/.

Acknowledgments

Ed Tittel

To begin with, I'd like to thank Keith Weiskamp at The Coriolis Group for understanding, and then championing, our idea for the Exam Cram series. I'd also like to thank the whole Coriolis team who helped turn the idea into a workable proposition, including Shari Jo Hehr, Lynn Guy, Josh Mills, Brad Grannis, and many others. Finally, I want to thank Paula Kmetz and Jeff Kellum for working out a design and a philosophy for these books that makes as much sense to its authors as we want it to make to our readers.

Closer to home, the whole LANWrights team pitched in and made good on some truly savage deadlines. Starting with my co-authors, Kurt Hudson and James Michael Stewart, the work never stopped. But we couldn't have made this book happen without the stalwart efforts of Dawn Rader, who, as a part-time contributor and full-time editor and project manager, coordinated all the many bits and pieces that must go into a book. Likewise, Mary Burmeister, our Jill of all trades, and Natanya Pitts, Webmistress and HTML Goddess without compare, produced screen shots, graphics, tables, and the Glossary. Thanks a million to each and every one of you. Thanks most of all to my dear, departed Labarador retriever, Dusty. You gave me the best 10 years of my life; I'd gladly have given you some of mine to have kept you around longer. Rest in peace, old friend.

Kurt Hudson

I want to first thank all of the employees at LANWrights (including Ed and Michael) for their help, encouragement, and hard work. I also want to thank Ed Tittel and the people at The Coriolis Group for sharing my vision of producing a line of training materials for the general public. Thanks to the Marcinkiewicz and Smit families for offering their unfailing support all these years. I must also give a heartfelt thanks to my wonderful wife, Julie, who not only supports me (and tolerates my irregular hours), but also helps me by offering opinions and suggestions.

James Michael Stewart

Thanks to my boss and co-author, Ed Tittel, for including me in this book series: You have a way of asking more of me than I can give, only later to find I could I have done even more. Thanks to Dawn Rader, who trudged through countless pages of "Heilein-ish" text to extract something everyone else in the world could read and understand. To Mary Burmeister: welcome to the Peanut Gallery! To my parents, Dave and Sue, you've found a way of making living out in the sticks worthwhile—you're there. To Dave and Laura: a toast to friendship (made with a DoubleDave's pizza toll!). To Mark, I'll buy you and your wife dinner if you can ever make it back to the only city that matters: Austin! To HERbert, please stop digging your claws into the back of my neck when I'm asleep. And finally, as always, to Elvis—I've been looking high and low for a glittery white jumpsuit of my own, but it seems that Wal-Mart is always sold out!

Contents

Introduction   xxi

Chapter 1   Microsoft Certification Tests   1

The Testing Situation   2
Test Layout And Design   4
Question 1 Discussion   4
Question 2 Discussion   6
Anatomy Of A Complex Question   6
Question 3 Discussion   8
Using Microsoft's Test
   Software Effectively   8
Taking Testing Seriously   9
Question-Handling Strategies   10
Mastering The Inner Game   12
Details And Resoures   13
   Coping With Changes On The Web   14
   Third-Party Test Providers   15

Chapter 2   Domain Models   17

The Domain Concept   18
Single Domain Model   19
Master Domain Model   20
Multiple Master Domain Model   22
Complete Trust Domain Model   23
Exam Prep Questions   25
Need To Know More?   31

Chapter 3   Trust Relationships   33

Terms And Conditions Of The
Trust Relationship   34
Understanding (And Calculating)
Trust Requirements   36
Establishing And Configuring
Trust Relationships   38
Establish A Trust   38
Using Trust Relationships   40
Permissions Across Trust Relationships   40
Managing Multiple Trusts   42
Common Trust Scenarios   43
Three Domains, Interesting Relationships   43
Centralized Administrative Controls   44
Exam Prep Questions   46
Need To Know More?   57

Chapter 4   Rights, Permissions, And
User Access To Resources   59

Logon And User Identification   60
Objects   61

Access Control List   61
Checking Permissions   63
Group Memberships   **64**
Default Groups And
   Membership Assignments   **65**
NTFS Permissions   **67**
Shares And Permissions   **69**
Permission Combinations   **71**
User Rights   **71**
Exam Prep Questions   *74*
Need To Know More?   **82**

Chapter 5   Optimizing Domain Use   83
NT Server Roles   **84**
Domain Controller Synchronization   86
Synchronization Controls In The
   NT Registry   86
Server Manager Domain Controls   88
Disaster And Recovery Scenario   88
Authentication With BDCs And PDCs   89
Domain Database Info   90
User Profiles   **91**
Using A Cached Profile On Slow Connections   92
Managing NT Policies   **92**
User, Group, And Computer Policies   93
Hardware Profiles   95
Browsers   **95**

Browser Election | 96
List Maintenance | 97
Browser And The Registry | 97
Exam Prep Questions | *99*
Need To Know More? | 108

Chapter 6   NT Redundancy And Fault Tolerance | 109

Domain Controllers | 110
Directory Replication | 111
Installing Replication | 112
Additional Replication Configuration | 114
Fault Tolerance | 115
Disk Administrator | 115
Disk Structure 101 | 116
Partitions | 116
Volumes | 117
Drive Letters | 117
Master Boot Record | 118
System Security Through Fault Tolerance | 119
Disk Mirroring | 119
Disk Duplexing | 120
Disk Striping | 120
Disk Striping With Parity | 121
RAID | 123
Comparing RAID Levels | 124
Recovery | 125

Fixing Broken Mirrors And Duplexes 125
RAID Level 5: Disk Striping With Parity 126
Special Boot Considerations 127
Windows NT Backup **130**
Exam Prep Questions *131*
Need To Know More? **144**

Chapter 7   Auditing Resources And Access — 147
Auditing **148**
Enabling Auditing 148
Auditing Overhead 151
Using Audit Information 152
Account Policy **152**
Exam Prep Questions *154*
Need To Know More? **157**

Chapter 8   Network Protocols, Routing, And Relaying — 159
Built-In Windows NT Protocols **160**
NetBIOS 160
NetBEUI 161
TCP/IP 161
NWLink (IPX/SPX) 161
DLC 162
AppleTalk 162
Connectivity Issues **162**

NWLink Connectivity Issues   162
TCP/IP Connectivity Issues   164
NetBEUI Connectivity Issues   170
Protocol Bindings   170
Routing With Windows NT   **171**
Routing And IP RIP   172
Routing And IPX RIP   174
DHCP Relay Agent   175
AppleTalk Routing   175
Exam Prep Questions   *177*
Need To Know More?   **185**

Chapter 9   Windows NT Names And Name Services, Plus IIS

                                             187
NT Names And Name Services   **188**
NetBIOS Names In Windows NT   188
NetBEUI And Name Resolution   189
IPX And Name Resolution   189
IP And Name Resolution   190
Internet Information Server   **194**
Web   195
FTP   196
Gopher   196
Exam Prep Questions   *197*
Need To Know More?   **203**

Chapter 10   Windows NT Network Monitor

                                             205
**Installing And Configuring
Network Monitor**   206

Analyzing Network Monitor Data   **206**

Capture Filters   209

Capture Triggers   213

Dedicated Mode Captures   214

Addressing Security Issues   **215**

Displaying Data   **215**

Other Features   **216**

Exam Prep Questions   *218*

Need To Know More?   **223**

Chapter 11   Managing Windows NT Performance   **225**

Task Manager   **226**

Performance Monitor   **228**

Common Objects And Counters   230

Monitoring Disk Performance   231

Using The PerfMon Views   231

Baselining   233

NT Paging File   **234**

Managing Process Priorities   **236**

Optimizing Server Settings   **237**

Exam Prep Questions   *238*

Need To Know More?   **245**

Chapter 12   Advanced NetWare Topics   **247**

Protocols And Compatibility Issues   **248**

Gateway Service For NetWare   **251**

Understanding GSNW 252

Installing, Configuring, And Enabling GSNW 252

Client Service For NetWare 256

File And Print Services For NetWare 256

**Microsoft's Migration Tool
For NetWare** 257

Exam Prep Questions 259

Need To Know More? 265

Chapter 13   Advanced NT Printing 267

The Windows NT Print Lexicon 270

Printing With Windows NT Server 273

Printing Clients 274

Spooling 275

Print Priorities 275

Separate Spool Files 276

Stopping And Restarting The Spooler Service 276

Changing The Spool Location 277

Logical Printers And Printing Pools 277

Advanced Printing 278

The Print Commands And Controls 279

Printer Shares 280

Multiple Printers: Physical And Logical 281

Print Auditing 281

Ownership 282

DLC 282

TCP/IP And Unix Printers 283

Exam Prep Questions 284

Need To Know More? 290

Chapter 14   Advanced Remote
   Access Service (RAS)   291
   What Is RAS?   **292**
      RAS Clients   293
      RAS Servers   293
      Telephony API (TAPI)   295
   Installing RAS   **296**
   RAS Features   **298**
      RAS Routing, Gateway, And Firewall   298
      RAS Phonebook   299
      RAS Security   299
      The RAS Logon Process   301
      AutoDial   301
      Logging   302
      Null Modem   302
      Multiple Protocols   302
      Name Resolution   302
      DUN Monitor   303
   Exam Prep Questions   *304*
   Need To Know More?   **311**

Chapter 15   Advanced
   Troubleshooting   313
   Installation Failures   **314**
   Boot Failures   **315**
      NTLDR Error Message   315
      NTOSKRNL Missing Error Message   315
      BOOT.INI Missing Error Message   316

BOOTSECT.DOS Missing Error Message   316

NTDETECT.COM Missing Error Message   316

Repair Tools   **317**

Event Viewer   317

Last Known Good Configuration   317

The Registry   318

Emergency Repair Disk   318

Printing Solutions   **320**

Miscellaneous Troubleshooting   **321**
Issues   **321**

Permissions Problems   321

Re-creating The Setup Disks   321

Master Boot Record   321

Dr. Watson   321

BOOT.INI Switches   322

VGA Mode   323

NTDETECT Debugged   323

ESDI Hard Drives   323

Troubleshooting   **324**

Blue Screen   324

Kernel Debugger   325

Memory Dump   325

Exam Prep Questions   *326*

Need To Know More?   **332**

Chapter 16   Sample Test   **333**

Questions, Questions,
Questions   334
Picking Proper Answers   334

Decoding Ambiguity   335
Working Within The
   Framework   336
Deciding What To Memorize   336
Preparing For The Test   337
Taking The Test   337
Sample Test   336

Chapter 17   Answer Key To
  Sample Test   367

Glossary Of Terms   385

Index   411

Introduction

Welcome to the *MCSE NT Server 4 in the Enterprise Exam Cram*! This book aims to help you get ready to take—and pass—the Microsoft certification test numbered "Exam 70-068," titled "Implementing and Supporting Microsoft Windows NT Server 4 in the Enterprise." This introduction explains Microsoft's certification programs in general and talks about how the *Exam Cram* series can help you prepare for Microsoft's certification exams.

Exam Cram books help you understand and appreciate the subjects and materials you need to pass Microsoft certification exams. *Exam Cram* books are aimed strictly at test preparation and review. They do not teach you everything you need to know about a topic (such as the ins and outs of the NT Server). Instead, we (the authors) present and dissect the questions and problems that we've found that you're likely to encounter on a test. We've worked from Microsoft's own training materials, preparation guides, and tests, and from a battery of third-party test preparation tools. Our aim is to bring together as much information as possible about Microsoft certification exams.

Nevertheless, to completely prepare yourself for any Microsoft test, we recommend that you begin your studies with some classroom training, or that you pick up and read one of the many study guides available from Microsoft and third-party vendors. We also strongly recommend that you install, configure, and fool around with the software or environment that you'll be tested on, because nothing beats hands-on experience and familiarity when it comes to understanding the questions you're likely to encounter on a certification test. Book learning is essential, but hands-on experience is the best teacher of all!

The Microsoft Certified Professional (MCP) Program

The MCP Program currently includes four separate tracks, each of which boasts its own special acronym (as a would-be certificant, you need to have a high tolerance for alphabet soup of all kinds):

➤ **MCPS (Microsoft Certified Product Specialist)** This is the least prestigious of all the certification tracks from Microsoft. Attaining MCPS status requires an individual to pass at least one core operating system exam. Passing any of the major Microsoft operating system exams, including those for Windows 95, Windows NT Workstation, or Windows NT Server, qualifies an individual for MCPS credentials. Individuals can demonstrate proficiency with additional Microsoft products by passing additional certification exams.

➤ **MCSD (Microsoft Certified Solution Developer)** This track is aimed primarily at developers. This credential indicates that individuals who pass it are able to design and implement custom business solutions around particular Microsoft development tools, technologies, and operating systems. To obtain an MCSD, an individual must demonstrate the ability to analyze and interpret user requirements; select and integrate products, platforms, tools, and technologies; design and implement code and customize applications; and perform necessary software tests and quality assurance operations.

To become an MCSD, an individual must pass a total of four exams: two core topics plus two elective exams. The two core exams are the Microsoft Windows Operating Systems And Services Architecture I and II (WOSSA I and WOSSA II, numbered 70-150 and 70-151). Elective exams cover specific Microsoft applications and languages, including Visual Basic, C++, the Microsoft Foundation Classes, Access, SQL Server, Excel, and more.

➤ **MCT (Microsoft Certified Trainer)** Microsoft Certified Trainers are individuals who are deemed capable of delivering elements of the official Microsoft training curriculum, based on technical knowledge and instructional ability. Thus, it is necessary for an individual seeking MCT credentials (which are granted on a course-by-course basis) to pass the related certification exam for a course and successfully complete the official Microsoft training in the subject area, as well as demonstrate an ability to teach.

This latter criterion may be satisfied by proving that one has already attained training certification from Novell, Banyan, Lotus, the Santa Cruz Operation, or Cisco, or by taking a Microsoft-sanctioned work shop on instruction. Microsoft makes it clear that MCTs are an important cog in the Microsoft training channels. Instructors must be MCTs before Microsoft will allow them to teach in any of its official training channels, including Microsoft's affiliated Authorized Technical Education Centers (ATECs), Authorized Academic Training Programs (AATPs), and the Microsoft Online Institute (MOLI).

➤ **MCSE (Microsoft Certified Systems Engineer)** Anyone who possesses a current MCSE is warranted to possess a high level of expertise with Windows NT (either version 3.51 or 4) and other Microsoft operating systems and products. This credential is designed to prepare individuals to plan, implement, maintain, and support information systems and networks built around Microsoft Windows NT and its BackOffice family of products.

To obtain an MCSE, an individual must pass four core operating system exams, plus two elective exams. The operating system exams require individuals to demonstrate competence with desktop and server operating systems and with networking components.

At least two Windows NT-related exams must be passed to obtain an MCSE: one on Implementing and Supporting Windows NT Server (version 3.51 or 4) and the other on Implementing and Supporting Windows NT Server in the Enterprise (version 3.51 or 4). These tests are intended to indicate an individual's knowledge of Windows

NT in smaller, simpler networks and in larger, more complex, and heterogeneous networks, respectively.

Two more tests must be passed. These tests are networking and desk top operating system related. At present, the networking requirement can only be satisfied by passing the Networking Essentials test. The desktop operating system test can be satisfied by passing a Windows 3.1, Windows for Workgroups 3.11, Windows NT Workstation (the version must match whichever core curriculum is pursued), or Windows 95 test.

The two remaining exams are elective exams. The elective exams can be in any number of subject or product areas, primarily BackOffice components. These include tests on SQL Server, SNA Server, Exchange, Systems Management Server, and the like. But it is also possible to test out on electives by taking advanced networking topics like Internetworking with Microsoft TCP/IP (but here again, the version of Windows NT involved must match the version for the core requirements taken).

Whatever mix of tests is completed toward MCSE certification, individuals must pass six tests to meet the MCSE requirements. It's not ncommon for the entire process to take a year or so, and many individuals find that they must take a test more than once to pass. Our primary goal with the Exam Cram books is to make it possible, given proper study and preparation, to pass all of the MCSE tests on the first try.

Finally, certification is an ongoing activity. Once a Microsoft product becomes obsolete, MCSEs (and other MCPs) typically have 12 to 18 months to become recertified on current product versions (if individuals do not get recertified within the specified time period, their certification becomes invalid). Because technology keeps changing and new products continually supplant old ones, this should come as no surprise.

The best place to keep tabs on the MCP Program and its various certifications is on the Microsoft Web site. The current root URL for the MCP program is titled "Certification Online" at www.microsoft.com/Train_Cert/mcp/default.htm. But Microsoft's Web site changes frequently, so if this

URL doesn't work, try using the Search tool on Microsoft's site with either "MCP" or the quoted phrase "Microsoft Certified Professional Program" as the search string. This will help you find the latest and most accurate information about the company's certification programs. You can also obtain a special CD that contains a copy of the Microsoft Education And Certification Roadmap. The Roadmap covers much of the same information as the Web site, and it is updated quarterly. To obtain your copy of the CD, call Microsoft at (800) 636-7544, Monday through Friday, 6:30 a.m. through 7:30 p.m. Pacific Time.

Taking A Certification Exam

Alas, testing is not free. You'll be charged $100 for each test you take, whether you pass or fail. In the U.S. and Canada, tests are administered by Sylvan Prometric. Sylvan Prometric can be reached at (800) 755-3926 or (800) 755-EXAM, any time from 7:00 a.m. to 6:00 p.m., Central Time, Monday through Friday. If this number doesn't work, please try (612) 896-7000 or (612) 820-5707.

To schedule an exam, call at least one day in advance. To cancel or reschedule an exam, you must call at least 12 hours before the scheduled test time (or you may be charged regardless). When calling Sylvan Prometric, please have the following information ready for the telesales staffer who handles your call:

➤ Your name, organization, and mailing address.

➤ Your Microsoft Test ID. (For most U.S. citizens, this will be your social security number. Citizens of other nations can use their taxpayer IDs or make other arrangements with the order taker.)

➤ The name and number of the exam you wish to take. (For this book, the exam number is 70-068, and the exam name is "Implementing and Supporting Windows NT Server 4 in the Enterprise.")

➤ A method of payment must be arranged. (The most convenient approach is to supply a valid credit card number with sufficient available credit. Otherwise, payments by check, money order, or purchase order must be received before a test can be scheduled. If the latter methods are required, ask your order taker for more details.)

When you show up to take a test, try to arrive at least 15 minutes before the scheduled time slot. You must bring and supply two forms of identification, one of which must be a photo ID.

All exams are completely closed-book. In fact, you will not be permitted to take anything with you into the testing area, but you will be furnished with a blank sheet of paper and a pen. We suggest that you immediately write down the information about the test you're taking on the sheet of paper. In *Exam Cram* books, this information appears on The Cram Sheet. You will have some time to compose yourself, to record this information, and even to take a sample orientation exam before you must begin the real thing. We suggest you take the orientation test before taking your first exam, but because they're all more or less identical in layout, behavior, and controls, you probably won't need to do this more than once.

When you complete a Microsoft certification exam, the software will tell you whether you've passed or failed. All tests are scored on a basis of 1,000 points, and results are broken into several topical areas. Even if you fail, we suggest you ask for—and keep—the detailed report that the test administrator should print for you. You can use the report to help you prepare for another go-round, if needed. If you need to retake an exam, you'll have to call Sylvan Prometric, schedule a new test date, and pay another $100.

Tracking MCP Status

As soon as you pass any Microsoft operating system exam, you'll attain Product Specialist (MCPS) status. Microsoft also generates transcripts that indicate the exams you have passed and your corresponding test scores. You can order a transcript by email at any time by sending an email addressed to mcp@msprograms.com. You can also obtain a copy of your transcript by downloading the latest version of the MCT Guide from the Web site and consulting the section titled "Key Contacts" for a list of telephone numbers and related contacts.

Once you pass the necessary set of six exams, you'll be certified as an MCSE. Official certification normally takes anywhere from four to six weeks, so don't expect to get your credentials overnight. When the package arrives, it will include a Welcome Kit that contains a number of elements, including:

➤ An MCSE certificate, suitable for framing, along with an MCSE Professional Program Membership card and lapel pin.

➤ A license to use the MCP logo, thereby allowing you to use the logo in advertisements, promotions, and documents, and on letterhead, business cards, and so on. Along with the license comes an MCP logo sheet, which includes camera-ready artwork. (Note that before using any of the artwork, individuals must sign and return a licensing agreement that indicates they'll abide by its terms and conditions.)

➤ A one-year subscription to TechNet, a collection of CDs that includes software, documentation, service packs, databases, and more technical information than you can possibly ever read. In our minds, this is the best and most tangible benefit of attaining MCSE status.

➤ A subscription to *Microsoft Certified Professional Magazine*, which provides ongoing data about testing and certification activities, requirements, and changes to the program.

➤ A free Priority Comprehensive 10-pack with Microsoft Product Support, and a 25 percent discount on additional Priority Comprehensive 10-packs. This lets you place up to 10 free calls to Microsoft's technical support operation at a higher-than-normal priority level.

➤ A one year subscription to the Microsoft Beta Evaluation program. This subscription will get you all beta products from Microsoft for the next year. (This does not include developer products. You must join the MSDN program or become an MCSD to qualify for developer beta products.)

Many people believe that the benefits of MCSE certification go well beyond the perks that Microsoft provides to newly anointed members of this elite group. We're starting to see more job listings that request or require applicants to have an MCSE, and many individuals who complete the program can qualify for increases in pay or responsibility. As an official recognition of hard work and broad knowledge, an MCSE is indeed a badge of honor in many IT organizations.

How To Prepare For An Exam

At a minimum, preparing for a Windows NT Server-related test requires that you obtain and study the following materials:

➤ The Microsoft Windows NT Server 4 manuals (or online documentation and help files, which ship on the CD with the product and also appear on the TechNet CDs).

➤ The *Microsoft Windows NT Server Resource Kit* (for Microsoft NT Server Version 4), published by Microsoft Press, Redmond, WA, 1996. ISBN: 1-57231-344-7. Even though it costs a whopping $149.95 (list price), it's worth every penny—not just for the documentation, but also for the utilities and other software included (which add considerably to the base functionality of Windows NT Server 4).

➤ The exam prep materials, practice tests, and self-assessment exams on the Microsoft Training And Certification download page (www.microsoft.com/Train_Cert/download/downld.htm). Find the materials, download them, and use them!

In addition, you'll probably find any or all of the following materials useful in your quest for Windows NT Server expertise:

➤ **Microsoft Training Kits** While there's no training kit currently available from Microsoft Press for Windows NT Server 4, many other topics have such kits. It's worthwhile to check to see if Microsoft has come out with anything by the time you need the information.

➤ **Study Guides** Publishers like Sybex, New Riders Press, Que (in cooperation with Productivity Point, a well-known training company and Microsoft ATEC), and others all offer so-called MCSE study guides of one kind or another. We've looked at them and found the Sybex and Que titles to be fairly informative and helpful for learning the materials necessary to pass the tests.

➤ **Classroom Training** ATECs, AATPs, MOLI, and unlicensed third-party training companies (like Wave Technologies, American Research Group, Learning Tree, Data-Tech, and others) all offer classroom training on Windows NT Server 4 in the Enterprise. These companies aim to help prepare network administrators to run Windows NT installations and pass the MCSE tests. While such training runs upwards of $350 per day in class, most of the individuals lucky enough to partake (including your humble authors, who've even taught such courses)find them to be quite worthwhile.

➤ **Other Publications** You'll find direct references to other publications and resources in this text, but there's no shortage of materials available about Windows NT. To help you sift through some of the publications out there, we end each chapter with a "Need To Know More?" section that provides pointers to more complete and exhaustive resources covering the chapter's information. This should give you an idea of where we think you should look for further discussion.

➤ **The TechNet CD** TechNet is a monthly CD subscription available from Microsoft. TechNet includes all the Windows NT BackOffice Resource Kits and their product documentation. In addition, TechNet provides the contents of the Microsoft Knowledge Base and many kinds of software, white papers, training materials, and other good stuff. TechNet also contains all service packs, interim release patches, and supplemental driver software released since the last major version for most Microsoft programs and all Microsoft operating systems. A one-year subscription costs $299—worth every penny, even if only for the download time it saves.

➤ **The *Exam Cram* series** These books give you information about the material you need to know to pass the tests.

By far, this set of required and recommend materials represents a nonpareil collection of sources and resources for Windows NT Server topics and software. We anticipate that you'll find this book belongs in this company. In the section that follows, we explain how this book works, and we give you some good reasons why this book counts as a member of the required and recommended materials list.

About This Book

Each topical *Exam Cram* chapter follows a regular structure, along with graphical cues about important or useful stuff. Here's the structure of a typical chapter:

➤ **Opening Hotlists** Each chapter begins with a list of the terms, tools, and techniques that you must learn and understand before you can be fully conversant with that chapter's subject matter. We follow the hotlists with one or two introductory paragraphs to set the stage for the rest of the chapter. Here, you'll find an estimate of the number of questions related to the chapter's topic likely to appear on any given certification test.

➤ **Topical Coverage** After the opening hotlists, each chapter covers a series of at least four topics related to the chapter's subject title. Throughout this section, we highlight material likely to appear on a test using a special Exam Alert layout, like this:

 This is what an Exam Alert looks like. Normally, an Exam Alert stresses concepts, terms, software, or activities that are highly likely to appear in one or more certification test questions. For that reason, we think any information found offset in Exam Alert format is worthy of unusual attentiveness on your part. Indeed, most of the facts appearing on the inside front and back covers of this book appear as Exam Alerts within the text.

Pay close attention to material flagged as an Exam Alert, although all of the information in this book pertains to what you need to know to pass the exam, we flag certain items that are really important. That's one reason why this book is less than half the size of a typical study guide devoted to Windows NT Server 4. It's also why, as we've said before, this book alone is probably not enough to carry you through the exam process in a single try. Nevertheless, you'll find what appears in the meat of each chapter to be worth knowing, especially when preparing for a test.

Occasionally, you'll see tables called "Vital Statistics." The contents of Vital Statistics tables are worthy of an extra once-over. These tables usually contain informational tidbits that might show up in a test question, but they're not quite as serious as Exam Alerts.

In addition to the Exam Alerts and Vital Statistics tables, we have provided tips that will help build a better foundation for enterprise based knowledge. Although the information may not be on the exam, it is certainly related and will help you become a better test taker.

This is how tips are formatted. Keep your eyes open for these, and you'll become an enterprise guru in no time!

➤ **Exam Prep Questions** Although we talk about test questions and topics throughout each chapter, this section presents a series of mock test questions and explanations of both correct and incorrect answers. We also try to point out especially tricky questions by using a special icon, like this:

Ordinarily, this icon flags the presence of an especially devious question, if not an outright trick question. Trick questions are calculated to be answered incorrectly if not read more than once, and carefully, at that. Although they're not ubiquitous, such questions make regular appearances on the Microsoft exams. That's why we say exam questions are as much about reading comprehension as they are about knowing your Windows NT Server Enterprise material inside out and backwards.

➤ **Details And Resources** Every chapter ends with a "Need To Know More?" section. This section provides direct pointers to Microsoft and third-party resources offering more details on the chapter's subject. In addition, this section tries to rank or at least rate the quality and thoroughness of the topic's coverage by each resource. If you find a resource you like in this collection, use it, but don't feel compelled to use all the resources. On the other hand, we only recommend resources we use on a regular basis, so none of our recommendations will be a waste of your time or money (but purchasing them all at once probably represents an expense that many network administrators and would-be MCSEs might find hard to justify).

The bulk of the book follows this chapter structure slavishly. But, there are a few other elements that we'd like to point out. The Glossary consists of a reasonably exhaustive list of Windows NT and Microsoft terminology, and an answer key to the sample test that appears in Chapter 16. Additionally, you'll find an index that you can use to track down terms as they appear in the text. Finally, on the inside front cover of the *Exam Cram* book is The Cram Sheet, a condensed and compiled collection of facts, figures, and tips that we think you should memorize before taking the test. Because you can dump this information out of your head onto a piece of paper before answering any exam questions, you can master this information by brute force—you only need to remember it long enough to write it down when you walk into the test room. You might even want to look at it in the car or in the lobby of the testing center just before you walk in to take the test.

How To Use This Book

If you're prepping for a first-time test, we've structured the topics in this book to build on one another. Therefore, some topics in later chapters make more sense after you've read earlier chapters. That's why we suggest you read this book from front to back for your initial test preparation. If you need to brush up on a topic or you have to bone up for a second try, use the index or table of contents to go straight to the topics and questions that you need to study. Beyond the tests, we think you'll find this book useful as a tightly focused reference to some of the most important aspects of Windows NT.

Given all the book's elements and its specialized focus, we've tried to create a tool that you can use to prepare for—and pass—Microsoft Certification Exam 70-068, "Implementing and Supporting Microsoft Windows NT Server 4 in the Enterprise." Please share your feedback on the book with us, especially if you have ideas about how we can improve it for future test-takers. We'll consider everything you say carefully, and we'll respond to all suggestions. You can reach us via email at etittel@lanw.com (Ed Tittel), hudlogic@worldnet.att.net (Kurt Hudson), and michael@lanw.com (James Michael Stewart). Please remember to include the title of the book in your message; otherwise, we'll be forced to guess which book you're making a suggestion about. And we don't like to guess—we want to KNOW!

For up-to-date information on certification, online discussion forums, sample tests, content updates, and more, visit the Certification Insider Press Web site at www.examcram.com or the authors' Web site at www.lanw.com/examcram.

Microsoft
Certification Tests

1

. . . .

Terms you'll need to understand:

√ Radio button

√ Checkbox

√ Exhibit

√ Multiple-choice question formats

√ Multipart question

√ Careful reading

√ The process of elimination

Techniques you'll need to master:

√ Preparing to take a certification exam

√ Practice makes perfect

√ Making best use of the testing software

√ Budgeting your time

√ Saving the hardest questions until last

√ Guessing when you're in doubt

As experiences go, test-taking is not something that most people anticipate eagerly, no matter how well they're prepared. In most cases, familiarity helps alleviate test anxiety. In other words, you probably won't be as nervous when you take your fourth or fifth Microsoft certification exam as you will be when you take your first one.

But no matter whether it's your first or your tenth, understanding the circumstances and the testing software will help you concentrate on the material rather than the environment. Likewise, mastering a few basic test-taking skills should help you recognize—and perhaps even beat—some of the tricks and gotchas you're bound to find in some of the Microsoft test questions.

 Under no circumstances should you take the test related to this book—that is, Exam 70-068, Implementing and Supporting Microsoft Windows NT Server 4 in the Enterprise—until you've passed the basic Windows NT Server 4 exam—namely, 70-067, Implementing and Supporting Microsoft Windows NT Server 4. Taking these tests out of sequence is a complete waste of time. Plus, preparing for 70-067 will help you with 70-068.

In this chapter, we explain the testing environment and software, and describe some time-honored test-taking strategies that you should be able to use to your advantage. We've compiled this information based on the 30-plus Microsoft certification exams that we (the authors) have taken, and have drawn on the advice of our friends and colleagues, some of whom have taken more than 30 tests apiece. Please read on for what we hope is an eye-opening exposé of the testing situation....

The Testing Situation

When you arrive at the Sylvan Prometric Testing Center where you scheduled your test, you'll need to sign in with a test coordinator. He or she will ask you to produce two forms of identification, one of which must be a photo ID. Once you've signed in and your time slot arrives, you'll be asked to deposit any books, bags, or other items you brought with you. Then, you will be escorted into a closed room. Typically, the room will be furnished with anywhere from one to half a dozen computers. Each workstation is separated from the others by dividers designed to keep you from seeing what's happening on someone else's keyboard.

You'll be furnished with a pen or pencil and a blank sheet of paper, or in some cases, an erasable plastic sheet and an erasable felt-tip pen. You're allowed to write down any information you want on the paper or plastic sheet provided, and you can write stuff on both sides of the page. We suggest that you memorize as much of the material in The Cram Sheet as you find necessary, and then write that information down on the sheet provided as soon as you sit down in front of the test machine. You can refer to your information sheet any time during the test, but you'll have to surrender it when you leave the test room.

Most test rooms feature a wall with a large picture window. This is to permit the test coordinator to monitor the room, to prevent test-takers from talking to one another, and to observe anything out of the ordinary that might take place. The test coordinator will have preloaded the Microsoft certification test you've signed up for—for this book, that's Exam 70-068—and you'll be permitted to start as soon as you're seated in front of the machine.

All Microsoft certification exams give you a maximum amount of time to complete the test (the test itself will tell you, and it maintains an ongoing counter/clock on screen so you can check the time remaining at a glance any time you like). Exam 70-068 consists of between 50 and 65 questions, randomly selected from a pool of questions. You're permitted to take up to 90 minutes to complete the exam, but no longer.

All Microsoft certification exams are computer-generated and use a multiple-choice format. Although this may sound quite simple, the questions are constructed not just to check your mastery of basic facts and figures about Windows NT Server, but they also require you to evaluate one or more sets of circumstances or requirements. Often, you'll be asked to select multiple choices to answer a question. Other times, you'll be requested to select the best or most effective solution to a problem from a range of choices, all of which are technically correct. It's quite an adventure and involves real thinking, but this book shows you what to expect and how to deal with the problems, puzzles, and predicaments you're likely to find on the test.

Test Layout And Design

A typical test question is depicted here. It's a multiple-choice question, taken from Chapter 7 of this book. This question requires you to select a single correct answer. For purposes of exposition, we've reproduced the entire text of this question and its own explanation from Chapter 7, and we follow it with further explanation and discussion.

Question 1

You suspect that an Account group member is accessing a directory that the user should be prevented from reaching. This might mean that you've set up the group memberships incorrectly. You aren't sure who it is, but you do know what directory is being accessed. What feature of NT will let you track who gains access to this directory?

○   a. NTFS file activity logging

○   b. Event auditing

○   c. Event Viewer

○   d. Account lockout

The NTFS file activity logging is a fault tolerance feature used to ensure the integrity of stored data. It cannot be used to track access, so answer a is incorrect. Event auditing tracks activity around any object within Windows NT. Thus, answer b is correct. The Event Viewer is what's used to review the Security log created by the auditing system, but does not perform the actual tracking, making answer c incorrect. Finally, account lockout is used to prevent compromised accounts, or accounts thought to be under attack, from being used. Thus, answer d is incorrect as well.

Question 1 Discussion

The question appears similarly to what you'll see when taking a Microsoft certification test. If this were on screen, to select the correct answer you'd position the cursor over the radio button next to answer b and click the mouse button to select it. In this case, knowing which answer to pick depends on understanding not just what's involved in auditing events, but also knowing that the Event Viewer only provides a window to events logged by the auditing service.

Next, we'll examine a question that requires choosing multiple options to get the correct answer. This kind of question uses checkboxes to mark all appropriate selections rather than the radio buttons (which permit only one answer to be selected) used in the preceding question.

Question 2

You want to track the activity around a new high-speed color laser printer so you can use the tracking information to restrict and grant privileged and priority access. Which of the following are required steps to implement printer auditing? [Check all correct answers]

❏ a. Set the auditing switches on the printer object to track the successful print events for the Everyone group.

❏ b. Grant the Everyone group the auditing right through the User Rights policy.

❏ c. Set the Audit policy to Audit These Events through the User Manager For Domains.

❏ d. Set the audit switch named File And Object Access to Success under Audit These Events.

❏ e. Set the priority of the printer to 99 (maximum) under the Scheduling tab on the printer's Properties dialog box.

To enable printer tracking, it's necessary to set auditing switches on the printer objects to be audited. Therefore, answer a is correct. Because there is no auditing user right, answer b is incorrect. To track printer access, it is necessary to set the master auditing switch to Audit These Events. Therefore, answer c is correct. But it is also necessary to set the event type switch for File And Object Access to Success to track printer usage. Thus, answer d is also correct. Finally, setting printer priority has nothing to do with tracking access, so answer e is incorrect. The required set of answers to this question is a, c, and d.

Question 2 Discussion

For this type of question, one or more answers must be selected to answer it correctly. As far as we can tell (and Microsoft won't comment), such questions are scored incorrect unless all required selections are chosen. In other words, a partially correct answer does not result in partial credit on the test score. For Question 2, you'd have to position the cursor over the checkboxes next to items a, c, and d and check all three boxes to obtain credit for a correct answer. The key to correctly answering this particular question involves knowing that auditing any object requires auditing to be enabled, that the object itself must be audited, and that events associated with the object must also be audited (Success and/or Failure).

Although there are many forms in which these two basic types of questions can appear, they constitute the foundation for all Microsoft certification exam questions. More complex questions sometimes include so-called "exhibits," which are usually screen shots of some Windows NT utility or another. For some such questions, you'll be asked to make a selection by clicking a checkbox or radio button on the screen shot itself. For others, you'll be expected to use the information displayed therein to guide your answer to the question. In all such cases, familiarity with the underlying utility is the key to the correct answer.

Other questions for exhibits may use charts or network diagrams to help document a workplace scenario that you'll be asked to troubleshoot or configure. Paying careful attention to such exhibits is the key to success—be prepared to toggle between the picture and the question as you work. Often, both elements are complex enough that you may not be able to remember all of either one.

The most complex questions of all involve analyzing scenarios and selecting among multiple potential outcomes of a proposed solution. For that reason, the following section shows an example of such a question.

Anatomy Of A Complex Question

Following the same approach as in the preceding questions, we'll reproduce a scenario question from Chapter 2 in the book, and then we'll follow up with some discussion, including some tips and tricks to help you deal with such brainteasers.

Question 3

A company has five branch offices scattered across the globe. They are located in New York, Moscow, Paris, Mexico City, and Hong Kong. Each office has about 750 users. Your headquarters is located in San Francisco. All the branch offices are linked to headquarters via an ISDN WAN link. It is your job to implement a domain model for this company.

Required results:

- All San Francisco users must be able to access resources in Hong Kong and Moscow

- Users in New York, Paris, and Mexico City must be able to access resources in San Francisco

- Security and logon validation traffic must be minimized over the WAN links

Optional desired results:

- Centralized management of all user accounts

- Each branch office is able to manage local resources

Proposed Solution:

- Use a single domain model

- Place the PDC and all BDCs in San Francisco

Which results does the proposed solution produce?

- O a. The required results and both of the optional results

- O b. The required results and only one of the optional results

- O c. The required results but none of the optional results

- O d. The required results are not all met

Although a single domain model can support a large number of users and offers centralized management of user accounts, it cannot reduce the WAN link overhead required for user authentication. By placing a BDC in each of the branch offices, the logon traffic can be significantly reduced, but this is not part of the proposed solution. Because the required results are not met, the only possible answer to this question is d.

Question 3 Discussion

Typically, you'll see anywhere from two to six questions of this kind on the Enterprise exam. More than any of the other question types, this type of question requires careful reading and equally careful evaluation of the answers. For instance, the proposed solution in Question 3 meets the first two requirements readily, but fails to meet the third. Regardless of the optional desired results (which work for the first and fail for the second), the only possible answer to the question hinges on the solution's failure to meet the base requirements.

When faced with this kind of question, you'll want to read through it several times—once to get a feeling for the concepts and system capabilities involved, then repeatedly to check the details and ponder the relationship between the solution and the required and optional desired results. Work your way backward from d toward a. That way, you'll be able to stop cogitating as soon as you're convinced you've found the right fit between the proposal and the results.

These questions invariably follow the same format and have nearly identical answers. The real focus for your efforts must therefore be on the relationship between the proposed solution and its results. That's where you should concentrate your energy, and that's how you'll get the best response. These questions aren't always supremely difficult, but they can be confusing and should not be taken too lightly—they're also prime candidates for trick questions.

Using Microsoft's Test Software Effectively

A well-known test-taking principle is to read over the entire test from start to finish first, but to answer only those questions that you feel absolutely sure of on the first pass. On subsequent passes, you can dive into more complex questions, knowing how many such questions you have to deal with. To give you an idea of how hard the Microsoft tests can be, when using this strategy, we found that 30 to 35 questions (out of 55 or thereabouts) usually must be revisited.

Fortunately, Microsoft test software makes this approach easy to implement. At the bottom of each question, you'll find a checkbox that permits
you to mark a question for a later revisit. As you read through the exam, if
you answer questions you're sure of and check questions you want to revisit,
you can continue working through a decreasing list of open questions.

> There's at least one profound potential benefit to reading the
> test over completely before answering the trickier questions:
> Later questions may help answer earlier questions. Sometimes,
> you find information in later questions that sheds more light on
> earlier ones. Other times, information you read on later questions
> may jog your memory about Windows NT facts, figures, or be-
> havior that will help with earlier questions. Either way, you'll come
> out ahead if you choose to revisit a question when you are not
> confident in your answer.

Continue working on the exam until you are absolutely sure of all your
answers or until you know you'll run out of time. If questions remain open
and you're running out of time, you'll want to zip through them and guess.
That's because no answer guarantees no credit for a question and a guess
has at least a chance of being correct. This strategy works because Microsoft
doesn't penalize for incorrect answers (that is, Microsoft treats incorrect
and unanswered questions as equally wrong).

> At the very end of your test period, you're better off guessing than
> leaving questions blank or unanswered. A blank answer is just as
> wrong as an incorrect answer.

Taking Testing Seriously

The most important advice we can give you about taking any Microsoft
test is: Read each question carefully. Some questions are deliberately
ambiguous, some use double negatives, and others use terminology in
incredibly precise ways. We've taken numerous practice tests and real
tests ourselves, and in nearly every test, we've missed at least one question
because we didn't read closely or carefully enough.

Here's how to deal with the tendency to jump to some conclusion or another, just to get a question over with:

➤ Make sure you read every word in the question. If you find yourself jumping ahead impatiently, go back and start over.

➤ As you read, try to restate the question in your own terms. If you can do this, you should be able to pick the correct answer(s) much more easily.

➤ When returning to a question after your initial read-through, read every word again; otherwise, the mind falls quickly into a rut. Some times seeing a question afresh after turning your attention elsewhere lets you see something you missed before, but the tendency is strong to see what you've seen before. Try to avoid that tendency at all costs.

➤ If you return to a question more than twice, try to articulate to yourself what you don't understand about the question, why the answers don't appear to make sense, and what appears to be missing. If you chew on the subject for a while, your subconscious might provide some missing details, or you might notice a "trick" that will point to the answer.

Above all, deal with each question by using your knowledge of NT's utilities, characteristics, behaviors, facts, and figures. By reviewing what you know (and what you've written down on your information sheet), you will often recall or understand facts sufficiently to determine the answer to a question.

Question-Handling Strategies

Based on the tests we've taken, we've noticed a couple of interesting trends in the answers. For questions that take a single answer, it's most usually the case that two or three of the answers are obviously incorrect while two of the answers are plausible (but only one can be correct). Unless the answer leaps out at you (and if it does, reread the question to look for a trick—sometimes those are the ones you're most likely to get wrong), begin the process of answering by eliminating any obviously wrong answers.

Characteristics to look for in this category include: spurious menu choices or utility names, nonexistent software options, and terminology you've never seen before. If you've done your homework, no valid information should be completely new to you. In that case, unfamiliar or bizarre terminology probably indicates a totally bogus answer. As long as you're sure what's right, it's easy to eliminate what's wrong.

Numerous questions assume that the default behavior of a particular utility is in effect. Therefore, when dealing with matters of access and rights, it's essential to understand that the default behavior for Windows NT security is to grant Full Control rights to the local group named Everyone. The same is true for many other aspects of the system. If you know the defaults and understand what they mean, this knowledge will help you cut through many apparently Gordian knots.

Likewise, when dealing with questions that require multiple answers—such as one that asks what *must be* installed on Windows NT Server for Gateway Service For NetWare (GSNW) to work—it's vital to remember all aspects involved. In this example, you should remember that GSNW automatically installs NWLink as part of its own installation if that protocol isn't already present on the Windows NT Server in question. In English, this means that it's not necessary to install the protocol separately because GSNW does it for you if NWLink is not already available. Certainly, NWLink is absolutely required for GSNW to work, but it's not necessary for it to be installed before installing GSNW. This, too, qualifies as an example of what "careful reading" is all about.

As you work your way through the test, another counter that Microsoft thoughtfully provides will come in handy—a tally of the number of questions completed and questions outstanding. Budget your time by making sure that you've completed one-fourth of the questions one-quarter of the way through the test period (or between 13 and 17 questions in the first 22 or 23 minutes). Check again three quarters of the way through (or between 39 and 51 questions in the first 66 to 69 minutes). If you haven't answered all the questions after 85 minutes, use the last 5 minutes to guess your way through the remaining questions. Remember, guesses are potentially more valuable than blank answers, because blanks are always wrong, but a guess might turn out to be right. If you don't have a clue with any of the remaining questions, pick answers at random, or choose all a's, b's, and so on. The object is to submit a test that has an answer for each question.

Mastering The Inner Game

In the final analysis, knowledge breeds confidence, and confidence breeds success. If you study the material in this book carefully and review the "Exam Prep Questions" section at the end of each chapter, you should be aware of those areas where additional learning and study are required. Then, follow up by reading some or all of the materials recommended in the "Need To Know More?" section at the end of each chapter. The idea is to become familiar enough with the concepts and situations found in the sample questions to be able to reason your way through similar situations on a real test. If you know the material, you have every right to be confident that you can pass the test.

Once you've worked your way through the book, read the test-taking tips, and take the practice test in the final chapter. This is a reality check, and it will help you identify areas where further study is needed. Make sure you review materials related to any questions you miss before scheduling a real test. Take the real exam only after you've covered all the ground and feel comfortable with the scope of the practice test.

If you take our practice test and don't score at least 75 percent correct, you'll want to practice further. At a minimum, download the Personal Exam Prep (PEP) tests and the self-assessment tests from the Microsoft Certification And Training Web site's download page (its location appears in the "Details And Resources" section in this chapter). If you're more ambitious or better funded, you might want to purchase a practice test from a third-party vendor. We've had good luck with tests from Transcender Corporation and from Self Test Software (the vendors who supply the PEP tests). Contact information appears in the "Details And Resources" section in this chapter.

Armed with the information in this book and with the determination to augment your knowledge where missed questions indicate a need, you should be able to pass the certification exam. But if you don't work at it, you'll spend the test fee more than once before you finally pass. If you prepare seriously, the execution should go flawlessly. Good luck.

Details And Resources

By far, the best source of information about Microsoft certification tests comes from Microsoft itself. Because its products and technologies—and the tests that go with them—change frequently, the best place to go for exam and related information is online.

If you haven't already visited the Microsoft Training And Certification pages, do so right now. As of this writing, the Training And Certification home page resides at www. microsoft.com/Train_Cert/default.htm. It's depicted in Figure 1.1. However, it might not be there by the time you read this, or it might be replaced by something new and different, simply because things change regularly on the Microsoft site. Should this happen, please read the section titled "Coping With Change On The Web" that follows later in this chapter.

Careful examination of Figure 1.1 reveals several menu options in the left-hand column. The menu items point to the most important sources of information in the Training And Certification pages. Here's what to check out, at a minimum:

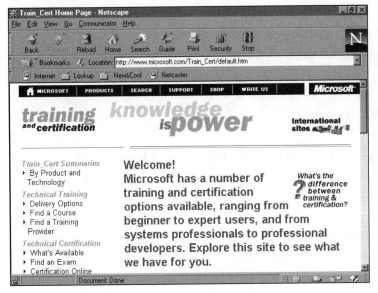

Figure 1.1   The Training And Certification home page should be your starting point for further investigation of the most current exam and preparation information.

➤ **Train_Cert Summaries/By Product and Technology** Jumps to product-based summaries of all classroom education, training materials, study guides, and other information for specific products. Under the heading of "Microsoft Windows/Windows NT Server," you'll find an entire page of information about Windows NT Server training and certification. This tells you a lot about your training and preparation options, and mentions the tests that relate to Windows NT Server.

➤ **Technical Certification/Find an Exam** Pulls up a search tool that enables you to list all Microsoft exams and locate all exams pertinent to any Microsoft certification (MCPS, MCSE, MCT, and so on) or those exams that cover a particular product. This tool is quite useful not only to examine the options, but also to obtain specific test preparation information, because each exam has its own associated preparation guide. Be sure to grab the one for 70-068, for this test!

➤ **Site Tools/Downloads** Lists the files and practice tests that Microsoft makes available to the public. These include several items worth down loading, especially the Certification Update, the Personal Exam Prep (PEP) tests, various assessment exams, and a general Exam Study Guide. Try to make time to peruse these materials before taking your first test.

Of course, these are just the high points of what's available in the Microsoft Training And Certification pages. As you browse through the pages—and we strongly recommend that you do so—you'll probably find other area that are every bit as interesting and compelling as the specific topics we mentioned here.

Coping With Change On The Web

Sooner or later, all the specifics we've shared with you about the Microsoft Training And Certification pages, and all the other Web-based resources mentioned throughout this book, will go stale or be replaced by newer information. In some cases, the URLs you find here may lead you to replacement pages. In other cases, the URLs will go nowhere, leaving you with the dreaded "404 File not found" error message.

When that happens, please don't give up. If you're willing to invest some time and energy, there is always a way to find what you want on the Web.

To begin with, most large or complex Web sites—and Microsoft's site qualifies on both counts—offer a search engine. Looking back at Figure 1.1, you can see a Search button appears on the top edge of the page. As long as you can get to the site itself (and we're pretty sure Microsoft's site will stay at www.microsoft.com for a long while yet), you can use the Search tool to help you find what you need.

The more particular, or focused, you can make a search request, the more likely your results will include usable information. For instance, you can search on the string "training and certification" to produce lots of data about the subject in general. But, if you're looking for the preparation guide for Exam 70-068, Implementing and Supporting Microsoft Windows NT Server 4 in the Enterprise, you'll be more likely to get there quickly if you use a search string like:

```
"Exam 70-068" AND "preparation guide"
```

Likewise, if you want to find the Training And Certification downloads, try a search string like:

```
"training and certification" AND "download page"
```

Finally, don't be afraid to use general search tools like www.search.com, www.altavista.com, or www.excite.com to search for related information. Even though Microsoft offers the best information about its certification exams online, there are plenty of third-party sources of information, training, and assistance in this area that do not have to follow Microsoft's party line. You may find more pointed and candid references by looking beyond the wizards in Redmond. The bottom line is: If you can't find something where the book says it lives, start looking around. If worst comes to worst, you can always email us. We just might have a clue....

Third-Party Test Providers

Transcender Corporation is located at 242 Louise Avenue, Nashville, TN 37203-1812. You can reach Transcender by phone at (615) 726-8779, by fax at (615) 320-6594, or on the Web at www.transcender.com. You can download an order form for the materials online, but the form must be mailed or faxed to Transcender for purchase. We've found these practice tests, which cost between $89 and $179 if purchased individually (with discounts available for packages containing multiple tests), to be pricey but useful.

Self Test Software is located at 4651 Woodstock Road, Suite 203-384, Roswell, GA 30075. You can reach Self Test Software by phone at (770) 641-9719 or (800) 200-6446, by fax at (770) 641-1489, or on the Web at www.stsware.com. You can even order the wares online. STS's tests are cheaper than Transcender's—$69 when purchased individually, $59 each when 2 or more are purchased simultaneously—but otherwise quite comparable, which makes them a good value.

Domain Models

Terms you'll need to understand:

√ Domain model

√ Primary Domain Controller (PDC)

√ Backup Domain Controller (BDC)

√ Trust relationships

√ Single domain model

√ Master domain model

√ Multiple master domain model

√ Complete trust domain model

√ User authentication

Techniques you'll need to master:

√ Understanding the domain model concept

√ Familiarization with each domain model

√ Knowing how to decide what domain model is best for what situation

√ Using domains to distribute user authentication loads

Microsoft uses domain models to describe and define organizational schemes for networks. In theory, the domain model can scale up to handle any size network. However, in reality, the domain model fails to offer an adequate solution for networks with over 10,000 users. But setting reality aside, you need to have a clear understanding and functional grasp of the domain models as used by Microsoft to pass the certification exam. Although there will be a few questions directly related to domains, there are numerous questions that assume familiarity with domains to decipher the question and extract the correct response. Some of these other issues include user accounts, groups, trust relationships, and domain controllers—these topics will be mentioned briefly in this chapter but will be discussed in more detail in Chapters 3 through 5.

The Domain Concept

The domain concept is the schema developed by Microsoft to organize and manage large groups of users and resources. Basically, a domain is a collection of computers that share a logical network grid for the purpose of sharing resources with a group of users. The size of a domain is usually limited by the geographic layout of the network as well as the level of hardware supporting the domain controllers.

The domain controllers—you know them as PDCs and BDCs—require significant computing power to support large, growing domains. As the number of users and resources increases, the number of relationships and security issues increases geometrically. Therefore, as the number of users grows, the demands of the domain controllers increase even faster. By monitoring simultaneous logon requests, quantity of network traffic, and performance of the domain browsers and controllers, network administrators will usually know when domain limitations have been reached. Additional domains should be created when the domain or network performance is substantially degraded.

As an afterthought, Microsoft generally recommends a maximum of 15,000 users per domain. On the other hand, there is documentation by Microsoft stating that up to 25,000 users have been supported by different configurations. Authors outside of Microsoft have agreed that 10,000 or fewer accounts is significantly more practical. (Once again, this information is not a major topic of the exam, just some helpful info.)

There are four separate models for domain administration according to Microsoft:

➤ Single domain model

➤ Master domain model

➤ Multiple master domain model

➤ Complete trust domain model

Each model is designed differently so each can accommodate organizations of various sizes and structures. It is necessary to contemplate the number of users, computers, and regions that are part of the network when you're choosing the domain model for your network. It is wise to also consider your growth potential when planning the organizational structure. The following sections briefly examine each domain model and in what situations each should be used.

Single Domain Model

The single domain model should be considered for an organization with small, single-regional networks, because it is easier than the other domain models to administer and maintain. Figure 2.1 illustrates the single domain model.

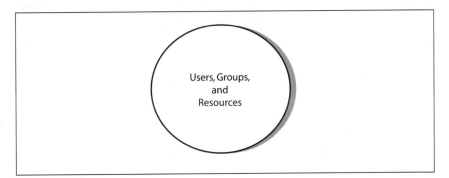

Figure 2.1   The single domain model.

The single domain model is characterized by its lack of trust relationships. No other domains are involved, so trust relationships are not necessary. The domain is regarded as a single administrative unit, in which most administrative tasks can be accomplished from a single server. There is one Primary Domain Controller (PDC) and one or more Backup Domain Controllers (BDCs) that control the security activity within the domain.

If a network experiences a significant amount of growth, the single domain model can scale into other domain models. In some cases, it may have to be split; therefore, if significant network growth is expected, you should consider using another domain model.

The advantages of the single domain model include:

➤ Works best for limited numbers of users and resources

➤ Centralized management of users and resources

➤ No trusts involved

The disadvantages of the single domain model include:

➤ Performance degradation as the domain grows

➤ Users and resources are not grouped by department

➤ Resource browsing is slowed as the number of servers increases

Master Domain Model

For growing companies or companies that already have a large user base, the master domain model is a good choice. This domain model is also useful for companies that wish to arrange the network into multiple resource domains and yet still have the benefits of centralized administration. Figure 2.2 displays the master domain model configuration.

Another name for the master domain is the accounts domain, because the user accounts for the multiple domain structure reside within it. The resource domains (all other domains) trust the master domain. In other words, all users are hosted in the top, or master, domain, and all resources are located in the lower, or subordinate, domains. With this

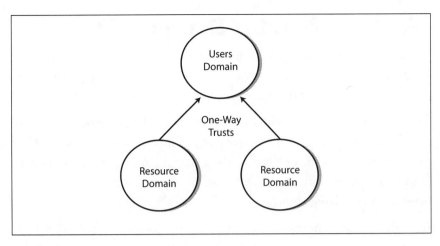

Figure 2.2   The master domain model.

model, resources can be grouped by department, geographic location, or any other organizational scheme.

The master domain model still offers centralized management, but it is split into two categories. User and group administration is performed in the top or master domain, and resource management is performed within the domain that hosts the particular resource. This gives each department control over its resources without compromising the overall security structure of the network.

The advantages of the master domain model include:

➤ A solid solution for moderately sized networks

➤ Departmental control of resources based on subordinate domains

➤ Central user account management

➤ Global groups are defined only once

The disadvantages of the master domain model include:

➤ Local groups must be defined within each resource domain

➤ Resource domains must rely on the master domain for current and secure group management

➤ Trust management is involved

Multiple Master Domain Model

The multiple master domain model can be used for companies that have a large and growing user base or that extend across multiple geographic regions. Figure 2.3 illustrates the multiple master domain model.

The master domain model and the multiple master domain model are closely related. In fact, the multiple master domain model is an extension of the master domain model. The difference is that the multiple master domain model has two or more master domains and they must trust each other via two-way trust relationships.

As with the master domain model, this model provides for centralized administration of user accounts. The other master domains you may use for this model are typically used to hold user accounts by region. For example, if a company has branches located in Asia, South America, and Europe, it may want a master domain for each location.

Implementing this domain model requires the administrator to maintain multiple trust relationships. As the number of master and resource domains increases, the number of trust relationships grows as well. The following formula will help you calculate the number of trust relationships required for a multiple master domain

```
T = M ( M - 1 ) + R M
```

where:

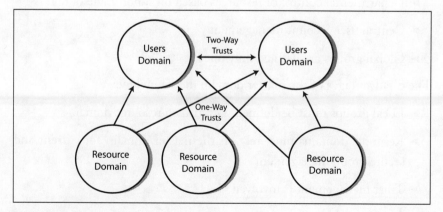

Figure 2.3   The multiple master domain model.

➤ **M** is the number of master domains in the organization.

➤ **R** is the number of resource domains in the organization.

➤ **T** is the number of trust relationships required.

The advantages of the multiple master domain model include:

➤ Good solution for very large and growing organizations

➤ Scaleable to accommodate any number of users

➤ Resources are locally and logically grouped

➤ Departmental-focused management of resources

➤ Any one of the master domains can administer all of the user accounts

The disadvantages of the multiple master domain model include:

➤ Local and global groups must be defined multiple times

➤ Large number of trust relationships to manage

➤ User accounts are spread across multiple domains

Complete Trust Domain Model

The complete trust domain model can be implemented by organizations of any size. It provides universal access to resources, while decentralizing administration of user accounts. The complete trust domain model should be considered for organizations that are spread over multiple geographic regions and do not require centralized administration. Figure 2.4 displays the complete trust domain model.

Using the complete trust domain model, users and resources can be grouped by department. With the two-way trusts, all users and all resources can be managed from any point in the network.

This model is also called a mesh. In a mesh network, every node is connected to every other node via a direct connection. As the number of nodes increases, the number of connections rapidly increases. Using Windows NT Server to establish a mesh, you must use two-way trust relationships.

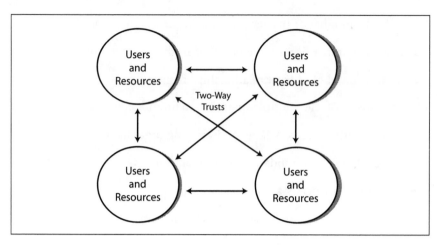

Figure 2.4 The complete trust domain model.

As you will learn in Chapter 3, a two-way trust is actually two one-way trusts created between the same two nodes. To compute the total number of trusts to create a mesh, use the following formula

```
T = N ( N - 1 )
```

where:

➤ N is the number of domains in the organization.

➤ T is the number of trust relationships required.

The advantages of the complete trust model include:

➤ Useful for organizations with no MIS department

➤ Scaleable for any number of users

➤ Each department has Full Control over it's users and resources

➤ Users and resources are located within the same domain

The disadvantages of the complete trust model include:

➤ No centralized management

➤ Many trust relationships to manage

➤ All administrators must trust each other to properly manage users, groups, and resources

Exam Prep Questions

Question 1

> Which of the following statements are true about the multiple master domain model? [Check all correct answers]
>
> ❑   a. Two-way trust relationships are used.
>
> ❑   b. One-way trust relationships are used.
>
> ❑   c. There is only one user domain.
>
> ❑   d. User management is centralized.
>
> ❑   e. Resource management is centralized.

Two-way trust relationships are used among all user domains in the multiple master domain model. Therefore, answer a is correct. One-way trust relationships are used between the resource and user domains in the multiple master domain model. Therefore, answer b is also correct. There must be more than one user domain for the multiple master domain model to exist. Therefore, answer c is incorrect. User management is centralized with the multiple master domain. Therefore, answer d is correct. Resource management is not centralized in the multiple master domain model. Each domain must control its own resources. Therefore, answer e is incorrect.

Question 2

> A small company with a few departments wants to deploy a domain model network. It requires the ability to access all servers and resources from each department and centralized management of user accounts. Which of the following domain models is best suited for this purpose?
>
> ○   a. Single domain model
>
> ○   b. Master domain model
>
> ○   c. Multiple master domain model
>
> ○   d. Complete trust domain model

The single domain model is the best solution for this situation. It offers centralized management, access to all resources, and supports small networks. Therefore, answer a is correct. The master domain model has separate domains for resources and users. This design is too much work for a small network. Therefore, answer b is incorrect. The multiple master domain model is too complicated for this size of a network Therefore, answer c is incorrect. The complete trust domain model is also an unnecessarily complex design for this situation. Therefore, answer d is incorrect.

Question 3

A company has five branch offices scattered across the globe. They are located in New York, Moscow, Paris, Mexico City, and Hong Kong. Each office has about 750 users. Your corporate office is located in San Francisco. All of the branch offices are linked to your office via an ISDN WAN link. It is your job to implement a domain model for this company.

Required results:

- All San Francisco users must be able to access resources in Hong Kong and Moscow

- Users in New York, Paris, and Mexico City must be able to access resources in San Francisco

- Security and logon validation traffic must be minimized over the WAN links

Optional desired results:

- Centralized management of all user accounts

- Each branch office is able to manage local resources

Proposed Solution:

- Use a complete trust model

- Place all users in the San Francisco domain

- All branch office domains to be used as resource domains

Which results does the proposed solution produce?

- O a. The required results and both of the optional results

- O b. The required results and only one of the optional results

- O c. The required results but none of the optional results

- O d. The required results are not all met

The correct answer is d. The complete trust model can be used as a modified master domain model with good success. However, this solution does not reduce validation traffic over the WAN links. By placing all users in the San Francisco domain, each time a branch office user logs on, he or she will connect to the corporate domain. Thus, heavy loads on the WAN links will result from this security traffic. To make this solution work, a San Francisco domain BDC should be physically placed in each of the branch offices. Each branch user would access his or her branch PDC for authentication, thereby minimizing WAN usage for that purpose.

Question 4

A company has five branch offices scattered across the globe. They are located in New York, Moscow, Paris, Mexico City, and Hong Kong. Each office has about 750 users. Your headquarters is located in San Francisco. All of the branch offices are linked to headquarters via an ISDN WAN link. It is your job to implement a domain model for this company.

Required results:

- All San Francisco users must be able to access resources in Hong Kong and Moscow

- Users in New York, Paris, and Mexico City must be able to access resources in San Francisco

- Security and logon validation traffic must be minimized over the WAN links

Optional desired results:

- Centralized management of all user accounts

- Each branch office is able to manage local resources

Proposed Solution:

- Use a single domain model

- Place the PDC and all BDCs in San Francisco

Which results does the proposed solution produce?

- ○ a. The required results and both of the optional results
- ○ b. The required results and only one of the optional results
- ○ c. The required results but none of the optional results
- ○ d. The required results are not all met

The correct answer is d. The single domain model can support a large number of users and offers centralized management of user accounts, but it does not reduce the WAN link overhead for user authentication. By placing a BDC in each of the branch offices, the logon traffic can be reduced.

Question 5

Your company is spread over multiple geographic locations within the same city. Users at each location need to access servers and resources at each of the other locations. Each office wants control over its locally hosted resources. You are solely responsible for maintaining the network at all of the locations and security is not an issue. What is the best domain model for this situation?

O a. Single domain model

O b. Master domain model

O c. Multiple master domain model

O d. Complete trust domain model

The single domain model does not offer departmentalized management of resources. Therefore, answer a is incorrect. The master domain model precludes that one domain is reserved for users for the purpose of maintaining tight security. These are not stipulations of the situation. Therefore, answer b is incorrect. The multiple master domain model is also not appropriate for this situation because it requires multiple user domains to support security. Therefore, answer c is incorrect. The complete trust model offers the ability for each office to manage resources, and you can administer the network from any server. Therefore, answer d is correct.

Question 6

Your company has 40,000 users and numerous branch offices. You want central administration of users but decentralized control of resources. Security is important. Which domain model is best suited for this situation?

○   a. Single domain model

○   b. Master domain model

○   c. Multiple master domain model

○   d. Complete trust domain model

The single domain model cannot support 40,000 users. Therefore, answer a is incorrect. The master domain model cannot support 40,000 users in its single user domain. Therefore, answer b is incorrect. The multiple master domain model can support 40,000 with its multiple user domains, and each branch office can manage its own local resources. Therefore, answer c is correct. The complete trust domain model does not offer centralized management of user accounts and does not adequately support security. Therefore, answer d is incorrect.

Question 7

What are some advantages of using a master domain model instead of a single domain model? [Check all correct answers]

❑   a. Separation of user and resource management

❑   b. Uses trust relationships

❑   c. Departmentalized resource administration

❑   d. Support for a much larger number of users

❑   e. Single definition of local groups

Separation of user and resource management is an advantage of the master domain model. Therefore, answer a is correct. The use of trust relationships is not an advantage but a liability. Therefore, answer b is incorrect. Departmentalized resource administration is a benefit of the master domain model. Therefore, answer c is also correct. Both of these domain models are able to support roughly the same number of users (give or take a modest difference), because only one user domain is present in each. Therefore, answer d is incorrect. Local groups must be defined for each of the resource domains in the master domain model. This is a disadvantage. Therefore, answer e is incorrect.

A master domain model consists of at least two user domains and one or more resource domains. What is true of the trust relationships of this domain model?

O   a. All trust relationships are two-way

O   b. A two-way trust is used to connect each user domain to every other user domain; one-way trusts are created from each resource domain to connect it with each user domain

O   c. Only one-way trusts are used

O   d. All user domains are connected to resource domains by a one-way trust; all resource domains are connected to all other resource domains with two-way trusts

---

Question 8

Answer a is incorrect. This is the trust pattern of the complete trust or mesh model. Answer b is correct. The user or master domains are connected to each other with two-way trusts, and each of the resource domains is connected with each of the user domains with a one-way trust. Answer c is incorrect. This does not describe any of the domain models. Answer d is incorrect. This does not describe any of the domain models.

Need To Know More?

 Heywood, Drew: *Inside Windows NT Server*. New Riders, Indianapolis, IN, 1995. ISBN 1-56205-472-4. Chapters 2 and 3 discuss basic domain construction and how trust relationships are used.

 Siyan, Karanjit S: *Windows NT Server 4 Professional Reference*. New Riders, Indianapolis, IN, 1996. ISBN 1-56205-731-6. Chapters 5, 6, and 7 provide extensive coverage of the Windows NT domain models.

 The Windows NT Server 4 manuals cover planning, configuration, and installation issues quite well. The *Concepts And Planning Manual* contains useful domain model issue discussions in Chapter 1.

 The *Windows NT Server Resource Kit* contains lots of useful information about Windows NT's fault tolerance. The TechNetCD (or it's online version through www.microsoft.com) can be searched using keywords like "domain model," "domains," and "centralized administration." In the *Networking Guide* volume, Chapter 2, "Network Security And Domain Planning," is an excellent resource for fully understanding and deploying Windows NT domains.

Trust
Relationships

3

Terms you'll need to understand:

√ Trust relationships

√ Trusting domain

√ Trusted domain

Techniques you'll need to master:

√ Establishing and configuring trust relationships

√ Breaking off a trust relationship

√ Setting up trusts based on domain models

√ Instituting permissions across trust relationships

√ Knowing how to manage multiple trusts

As you learned in Chapter 2, Windows NT supports domains to enable the definition of distinct collections of machines, resources, users, and groups that can be administered and secured separately and independently. But because Windows NT permits networks to include multiple domains—and indeed requires multiple domains for larger networks—managing the relationship among individual domains is important whenever multiple domains coexist. These kinds of networks are the primary focus for the Server in the Enterprise exam, so trusts appear in numerous test questions (on average, across all the Server in the Enterprise exams we took and practice tests we surveyed, 8 or 9 questions out of 55 included some mention of trusts).

Terms And Conditions Of The Trust Relationship

As is so often the case with Windows NT, a special mindset is required to appreciate and understand the terminology used to describe the trust relationships that can exist between any two domains at a time. Figure 3.1 captures most of the terminology and important nuances, which are also explained in the following series of ground rules:

➤ When Domain A trusts Domain B, A is called the trusting domain, and B is called the trusted domain.

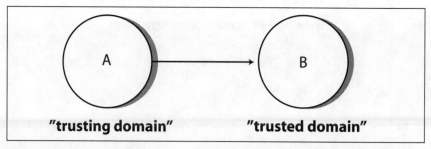

Figure 3.1 Domain A "trusts" Domain B, as indicated by the arrow that points from A to B.

➤ Although the relationship arrow points from Domain A to Domain B, it means that A may make resources available to B, not vice versa. It's essential to understand that this means only that users in B may be permitted to access resources in A. Even though the arrow points from A to B, users from B may access resources in A.

➤ All trust relationships are defined between pairs of domains. For each such relationship, there is only one trusting domain, and only one trusted domain. That's why the title of this section is "Trust Relationships Between Domains," because only two domains may participate in any single trust relationship.

➤ All trust relationships are one-way. If A trusts B, this says nothing about B's trust for A. For a two-way trust relationship to exist, it's necessary to create two separate one-way trusts, where A trusts B in one relationship, and B trusts A in the other. Even so, Microsoft uses a single two-headed arrow in its documentation and help files to indicate that two such relationships exist between a pair of domains.

➤ There is no transitivity in trust relationships, either. If A trusts B and B trusts C, this does not imply that A also trusts C. For such a relationship to exist, a third trust between A and C must be created explicitly.

➤ Creating a trust relationship simply makes it possible for an administrator in the trusting domain (A, in our example) to provide explicit access to resources for users or global groups in Domain B. By default, when a trust between two domains is created, this confers no automatic permissions for users or global groups in the trusted domain. Unless an administrator references some global group or user from Domain A in the permissions for a resource, all users and groups in B can only access resources available to the default global Domain Guests group in A.

Understanding (And Calculating) Trust Requirements

Despite these intricacies and special considerations, trust relationships are essential in large networks because they provide the foundation on which cross-domain resource access rests. In the single master domain model discussed in Chapter 2, for instance, it's necessary for all resource domains to trust the master domain. This is what makes it possible for administrators to reference global groups that belong to the master domain in local groups in any of the resource domains, thereby providing access for users from the master domain to local resources wherever they're needed. This manifold trust relationship is depicted in Figure 3.2.

Where multiple master domains exist, two-way trusts between each pair of masters are necessary to permit administrators to manage all the masters as a single logical, coherent entity. Because there are multiple master domains, it's also necessary for each resource domain to establish a trust with each individual master domain. This many-faceted trust relationship is depicted in Figure 3.5, shown later in the chapter. The number of trusts involved

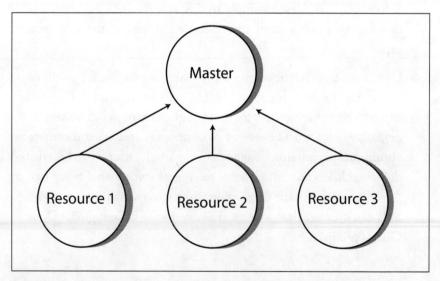

Figure 3.2   All three resource domains trust the master domain, thereby enabling global user groups from the master domain to be referenced in any resource domain.

may be calculated according to the following formula (where **m** is the number of master domains, and **n** is the number of resource domains):

```
trusts = m×(m-1) + m×n
```

In English, we can restate this as: The total number of trusts is equal to the number of trusts required among all master domains plus the number of trusts between all resource domains and every master domain. For master domains, this equals twice the number of edges in a complete mesh. (A mesh is a graph where every vertex is connected directly to all other vertices. We double this because two-way trusts are required.) This may be more simply calculated by multiplying **m** by **(m-1)**. In addition, we must also define one trust from each resource domain to each master domain (expressed mathematically as **m×n**). Because the number of master trusts grows geometrically, **m** should be kept as small as possible. For example, for 3 master domains and 10 resource domains, the value of this formula is **(3×2)+(3×10)**, or **6+30**, or **36** trust relationships.

The most complex multidomain trust model that Microsoft describes is the complete trust model. In this model, every domain maintains a two-way trust with every other domain in the network. Based on the preceding formula, this means the number of trusts is **d(d-1)**, where **d** is the number of domains. For the preceding example, with a total of **13** domains, complete trust means **13×12**, or **156** trust relationships. Microsoft no longer recommends creating complete trust among domains, even if their number remains small.

These calculations should help you understand why a single domain model is so attractive and why simple multidomain models should always be considered before using more complex models. Only organizations with large user populations should consider multiple masters. We cannot recommend the complete trust model except where nothing else works (this usually involves political considerations, not technical issues). To help you understand when multiple master domains may become necessary, please consult the section in Chapter 5 titled "Domain Database Info."

A good cutoff point for the Microsoft test is in the neighborhood of 25,000 to 26,000 users. Any less than that and a single master domain will probably suffice. Any more than 26,000 users and multiple masters become necessary.

Now that we have examined what a trust relationship is, let's move on to explore how to put these relationships to use in NT.

Establishing And Configuring Trust Relationships

Creating a trust between one domain and another is like opening a door from the trusting domain to the trusted domain. The relationship makes it possible to insert users or global groups from the trusted domain into local groups in the trusting domain. The administrative tool wherein trust relationships may be defined is the same one where you use existing trust relationships to add users or global groups from a trusted domain within a trusting one—namely, the User Manager For Domains utility.

Establish A Trust

To establish a trust, it's necessary to perform operations in both of the domains involved—that is, in both the trusted and the trusting domains. In both cases, the same menu selection in User Manager For Domains must be invoked (from Start|Programs|Administrative Tools (Common)). Beneath the Policies menu, you'll find an entry named "Trust Relationships." Selecting this entry produces the Trust Relationships dialog box shown in Figure 3.3.

In some ways, creating a trust is like a handshake (in the computing sense, rather than the human sense). That is, an administrator in Domain B must acknowledge the possibility of a trust, and an administrator in Domain A must do likewise. Both will use the User Manager For Domains utility, but A's window will show DOMAINA as the primary domain, and B's will show DOMAINB as the primary domain.

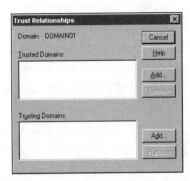

Figure 3.3   The Trust Relationships dialog shows trusts from the viewpoint of the domain in which it's opened (in this case, from DOMAIN01's perspective).

Here's the recipe for performing the handshake properly, according to Microsoft:

1. In the trusted domain (Domain B, in this example), open the Trust Relationships window in User Manager For Domains. Click the Add button next to the display area labeled "Trusting Domains." Select the name of the trusting domain (DOMAINA) from the pop-up list.

2. Specify a password for creating the trust relationship in the dialog box supplied for that purpose (this prevents the trust from unauthorized "hijack").

3. In the trusting Domain (Domain B), open the Trust Relationship window in User Manager For Domains. This time, click the Add button next to the display area labeled "Trusted Domains." Select the name of the trusted domain (DOMAINB) from the pop-up list, and supply the agreed-upon password in the ensuing dialog box.

Remember that both trusted and trusting domains must acknowledge trust relationships. Only when Step 3 is completed successfully may a trust relationship be used.

Using Trust Relationships

Once a trust relationship has been established, a domain administrator in the trusting domain will be able to view—and add—users and global groups from the trusted domain to global and local groups in that administrator's domain. To continue our ongoing saga of Domains A and B, this means that a Domain A administrator will be able to access users and global groups from Domain B when assigning permissions for resources (or, as will be more likely, when controlling membership in local groups to which resources in Domain A are attached).

This display takes the form of <domain name>\<group name> or <domain name>\<user name>. For our hypothetical example, this means that you would be able to access groups like DOMAINB\Domain Users or DOMAINB\Domain Administrators when controlling membership in local groups as an administrator for Domain A.

Remember, only users may belong to global groups, and only global groups and users may belong to local groups. You'll see many apparently correct answers to trust-related questions on Microsoft tests that assume it's okay to insert a global group from Domain B into a global group from Domain A, or even a local group from Domain B into a global group in Domain B. Don't fall for this underhanded trickery. Read the questions twice, and consider carefully the assumptions about what kinds of elements can be placed into local and global groups before answering any such questions.

Now that you know how to set up trust relationships among domains, let's explore how to assign cross-domain permissions to users.

Permissions Across Trust Relationships

Permissions across trust relationships work the same way they work within a single domain environment. Don't let the existence of multiple domains throw you off course when evaluating permissions for access to NT-based objects. You may, however, assume that when a user accesses resources across two domains that this access is remote (across the network) and not local (on the machine where the resource resides).

Given this simplifying assumption, here's how to determine permissions for an object under NTFS control (a file, folder, or application):

1. Compare all rights associated with the share, as deter-mined by the user's group memberships and individual account status. Pick the most inclusive or permissive of all such rights.

2. Compare all NTFS permissions associated with the requested object, as determined by the user's group memberships and individual account status. Again, pick the most inclusive or permissive of such rights.

3. Compare the two results, and pick the less permissive of the two. This will be the user's effective permissions to the object.

> *Note: If the object is in a FAT (File Allocation Table) volume, only the share rights apply (FAT doesn't have object-level security). Pick the most permissive right, and that's what the user can do.*

The exception that proves this rule is that any time No Access appears, it wins the selection process. If a user is assigned No Access by virtue of group membership or account status through share rights or NTFS permissions, the result is that the user has No Access to the requested object.

 Here again, it's essential to read the questions carefully. At least one or two questions will involve something like a user who belongs to Domain A logging on to Domain B. It's necessary for any user to log on to his or her home domain to obtain any rights or permissions that interdomain trust relationships may provide. If any user logs on to a domain other than his or her home domain, the user becomes a Domain Guest in the foreign domain. The trick to remember is that trusts work only when a user from a trusted domain attempts to access resources in a trusting domain. If users don't log on to a domain where they have true user accounts, they can only function as Domain Guests in the domains they do log on to.

There are a number of ways to manage user access to network resources. We have explained how trust relationships work, as well as how to define user access in a trust. Now, we move on to explain the use of multiple trust relationships in NT.

Managing Multiple Trusts

As the discussion at the end of the first section of this chapter illustrates, the number and complexity of trust relationships can quickly become mind-numbing, especially when a single or multiple master model is in use. The key to clear thinking is to remember that no matter how many trust relationships may be required to implement a particular usage scenario, such relationships can be defined and managed only between one trusted and one trusting domain at a time.

Understanding how to implement usage scenarios (covered in the next section in some depth) involves cultivating—or perhaps resuscitating—skills in reading "word problems" Microsoft will pose on the test. By inserting the right kinds of relationship arrows to match whatever trust requirements may be implied, you can find ways to understand the necessary requirements and evaluate whatever potential solutions you'll be asked to consider.

If you can remember the following basic rules and requirements, you should be able to get through even the thorniest of Microsoft's scenarios to decide what trusts are necessary to make things work or to decide if the trust arrangement described meets Microsoft's stated requirements:

➤ When users in one domain (Domain A) need access to resources in another (Domain B), this means that Domain B must trust Domain A. In other words, this requires B to be a trusting domain and A to be a trusted domain in a trust relationship. Here, you draw the arrow pointing from B to A.

➤ When users in both domains require access to resources in each other's domains, a two-way trust is required. This means two separate trusts: one where A trusts B and another where B trusts A. Here, you draw a two-headed arrow between A and B.

➤ When users in a master domain need access to resources in a resource domain, all resource domains must trust the master. Here, draw an arrow that points from each resource domain to the master domain.

➤ When multiple master domains exist, each master domain must maintain a two-way trust with each and every other master domain, to permit the entire collection of master domains to function as a logical unit.

➤ When multiple master domains exist, each resource domain must establish a one-way trust with each master domain, to permit all users in all master domains to access resources in all resource domains.

In the section that follows, we'll explore some typical question scenarios. They should help you appreciate how a simple collection of rules and requirements can produce some pretty tricky situations and circumstances that you'll be asked to interpret and understand.

Common Trust Scenarios

This will require additional effort on your part, but be prepared to sketch out the kinds of bubble diagrams you saw earlier in this chapter to match the scenarios we describe when you tackle the actual test questions. We'll provide the diagrams for the discussions that follow, however.

Three Domains, Interesting Relationships

On a hypothetical network, assume three domains exist: Sales, Marketing, and Engineering. Users in Sales and Marketing need access to each other's resources, but users in Engineering only need access to Sales and Marketing, not vice versa.

Walking through this text description, here's the translation that results:

➤ Sales and Marketing need access to each other's resources. This key phrase indicates that a two-way trust between the two domains is needed. That's why the diagram shown in Figure 3.4 depicts the trust relationship between these two domains with a two-headed arrow.

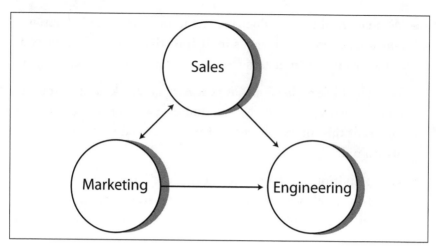

Figure 3.4 Sales and Marketing have a two-way trust between them, but it's only one-way between Sales and Engineering, and Marketing and Engineering.

> ➤ Engineering needs access to Sales and Marketing resources, but not vice versa. This means two one-way trusts are required. Because the trusting domain grants access to the trusted domain, and the arrows point from trusted to trusting, we show two arrows pointing from Sales and Marketing to Engineering, respectively.

 When the phrase "Domain X needs access to Domain Y's resources" occurs, remember that the arrow points from Y to X, not the other way around. Got it? Be prepared to map out relationships that involve three or more domains that may not involve a clear-cut use of the master or multiple master domain model, too (as in the preceding scenario).

Centralized Administrative Controls

The title of this section is something that occurs in several of the test questions we surveyed. This is often a code phrase for the kind of relationship that exists between resource domains and the master domain(s) in a master or multiple master domain model, but it can also occur when these models are not invoked by name. The key ingredients to look for, in addition to the phrases "centralized administration" and "centralized administrative controls," are multiple domains (usually three or more), where most are at the periphery of a network and where users (and more importantly, administrators) aggregate in a central or master domain.

In this case, you'll want to be sure to establish one-way trusts from all the peripheral or resource domains to the central or master domain, and to be sure that members of the Domain Administrators group in the central or master domain are added to the local Administrators group on servers in the resource or peripheral domains (this is particularly important for domain controllers). That way, the possibility of administration is not only established (through the trust relationships), but it's assured (through the inclusion of the Domain Administrator's global group from the central or master domain in local groups on individual machines in the peripheral or resource domains). Figure 3.5 shows how to set up shared resources in the master domain model.

 Why are these resource and user group shenanigans necessary? Two reasons: Creating a trust doesn't grant authority to do anything with it, and only global groups and users can belong to local groups. Don't forget the rules when reading answers to these kinds of questions. You've been warned!

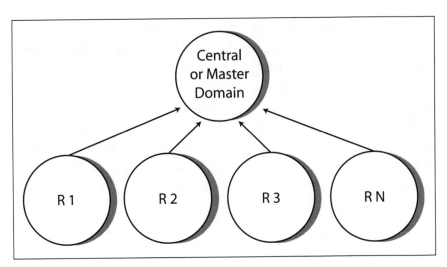

Figure 3.5   For centralized administration, all resource or peripheral domains must trust the central or master domain.

Exam Prep Questions

Question 1

Of the following assertions, which best represents the trust relationships that exist in a multiple master domain model?

○   a. Two-way trusts exist between all domains in the model.

○   b. Two-way trusts exist between all master domains, and one-way trusts exist between the master domains to all resource domains.

○   c. Two-way trusts exist between all master domains, and one-way trusts exist between each resource domain to all master domains.

○   d. One-way trusts exist between all master domains and between all resource domains; no trust relationships exist between any master and resource domains.

The short definition of the trust relationships in a multiple master domain model may be expressed as "two-way trusts between all master domains, and one-way from each resource domain to every master domain." Only answer c meets this definition and is therefore correct. Answer a fails because it asserts that all domains share two-way trusts. This defines the complete trust domain model, not the multiple master domain model. Answer b fails because it points the one-way trusts in the wrong direction. It asserts, incorrectly, that the master domains must trust the resource domains, when in fact it should be the other way around. Answer d misses the point of the master domain model completely, in that it fails to make any connection between master and resource domains at all.

Question 2

Assume two domains named "Users" and "Admin" are defined within an organization. Three members of the Users domain have been drafted to work with materials in the Admin domain, prior to their general release to the user community. To assist with prerelease testing, these three users need access to a shared NTFS folder named "\Tests" on a server named "TEST1" in the Admin domain. Admin already trusts Users. Which of the following options is the best way to grant Full Control access to the \TEST1\Tests share for those three individuals from the Users domain?

○ a. Remove the current trust relationship. Add a new trust wherein Admin trusts Users. Create a global group in the Users domain named "Utesters", and add the three individuals' accounts to that group. Create a global group named "Atesters" in the Admin domain, and add the global group Users\Utesters to Atesters. Give Atesters Full Control over the \TEST1\Tests share.

○ b. Create a global group in the Users domain named "Utesters". Assign each of the three Users domain accounts to that group. Create a global group in the Admin domain named "Atesters", and assign Users\Utesters to Atesters. Give Atesters Full Control over the \TEST1\Tests share.

○ c. Create a global group in Users called "Utesters". Add each of the three Users domain accounts to that group. Create a local group on TEST1 called "Utesters", and add the Users\Utesters global group to this local group. Grant Utesters Full Control to the \TEST1\Tests share.

○ d. Remove the current trust relationship. Add a new trust wherein Admin trusts Users. Create a global group in Users called "Utesters". Add each of the three Users domain accounts to that group. Create a local group on TEST1 called "Utesters", and add the Users\Utesters global group to this local group. Grant Utesters Full Control to the \TEST1\Tests share.

The key phrase in this question is "the best way," because two answers are actually correct. Answer d, while correct, requires removal and replacement of the existing trust from Admin to Users. This is unnecessary and may break existing trusts established for other uses. Otherwise, d is the same as c, which is correct because it:

➤ Uses an existing trust

➤ Creates a global group in the trusted domain

➤ Puts the global group into a local group on the TEST1 machine in the trusting domain

➤ Grants the local group the required access to the share

Answer a fails because it breaks an existing trust unnecessarily and because it places one global group inside another (global groups may contain only users, not other groups of any kind, whether local or global). Answer b fails for the latter reason as well, by placing one global group inside another.

Question 3

The XYZ Corporation employs a single master domain model where the name of the master domain is "XYZCorp". The Marketing domain at XYZ already trusts the XYZCorp domain. If a user belonging to the Marketing domain logs on to the XYZCorp domain, what shared resources will the user be able to access?

○ a. All folders in XYZCorp for which Marketing\Domain Users have Read access.

○ b. All folders in either XYZCorp or Marketing for which Marketing\Domain Guests have Read access.

○ c. All folders in either XYZCorp or Marketing for which XYZCorp\Domain Guests have Read access.

○ d. All folders in Marketing for which XYZCorp\Domain Users have Read access.

The key phrase to this question—and the reason it's labeled as a trick—is "logs on to the XYZCorp domain." Remember, trust relationships only confer access when a user logs on through his or her home domain. The user in this question belongs to the Marketing domain but logs on to the XYZCorp domain, so the user is automatically treated as a member of the

Domain Guests global group in the XYZCorp domain. Once this is understood, the correct answer is easy. It must be c, because the user is treated as a member of the XYZCorp\Domain Guests global group, with access to whatever resources are available to that global group in either the XYZCorp or Marketing domains. Answer a is incorrect because it attributes the login to the wrong domain (Marketing). Answer b is incorrect for the same reason. Answer d is incorrect because it omits the folders in XYZCorp where a Domain Guest might have access and because it puts the user in the Domain Users global group, not the Domain Guests user group.

 While this example may seem—and truly is—somewhat contrived, there's at least one question like this on every Enterprise test we've ever seen. Consider yourself warned.

Question 4

> Widgets, Inc. has a network that includes three domains, named "Admin", "Sales", and "Engineering". Users from Sales and Admin need access to resources from Engineering, but they also need access to resources in each other's domains. How must you set up the necessary trust relationships?
>
> ○ a. Define two-way trusts between all three domains.
>
> ○ b. Set up one-way trusts from Sales to Admin, Admin to Engineering, and Engineering to Sales.
>
> ○ c. Define a two-way trust between Sales and Admin, and another two-way trust between Engineering and Sales.
>
> ○ d. Set up two one-way trusts from Engineering to Sales and Engineering to Admin, and a two-way trust between Sales and Admin.

One good way to eliminate possibilities is to see what's missing in the question when compared to the answers. The question says nothing about Engineering requiring access to anything in Sales or Admin. This automatically knocks out answer a, because it includes two-way trusts from Sales and Admin to Engineering that are not required (and perhaps even unwanted). Likewise, this knocks out answer c because it includes a trust from Sales to Engineering, as well as the required trust from Engineering to Sales. Answer b must be eliminated because it fails to include the two-way trust between Sales and Admin implied by the key phrase "but they also need access to resources in each other's domains." Answer d is the only correct answer because it provides both the two-way trust between Sales and Admin that's required and establishes one-way trusts from Engineering to both Sales and Admin, to meet the stated requirement that "users from Sales and Admin need access to resources from Engineering." This means that Engineering must trust both domains, as the answer indicates by specifying two one-way trusts from Engineering to each of the other domains.

Question 5

The Sales, Admin, and Engineering domains include 50 user accounts apiece. All 150 users need access to files on an NT server in a fourth domain named "Resources". How must you configure the trust relationships involved?

- ○ a. Establish complete trust between all four domains.

- ○ b. Make the Resources domain the trusting domain, and Sales, Admin, and Engineering the trusted domains.

- ○ c. Make Sales, Admin, and Engineering all trusting domains, and Resources the trusted domain.

- ○ d. Establish a two-way trust between Sales and Resources, then establish trusts between Admin and Sales, and Admin and Engineering.

Here again, you can begin by eliminating answers that exceed the specifications. The question says nothing that requires two-way trusts, so you can knock answers a and d out immediately. Picking the right answer from the two remaining options requires that you understand that a trusting domain makes resources available to a trusted domain. Because the question requires that users in Sales, Admin, and Engineering obtain access to files in the Resources domain, this means that Sales, Admin, and Engineering are trusted domains, and Resources is the trusting domain. This makes b the only correct answer. Answer c reverses the correct relationship and defines the opposite of what's intended by making Sales, Admin, and Engineering make resources available to Resources.

Question 6

> If all other domains on a network trust a domain named "Admin",
> what kinds of user accounts or groups can be inserted into a glo-
> bal group in the Admin domain?
>
> ○　a. User accounts from Admin, plus any user accounts from
> 　　all trusting domains
>
> ○　b. User accounts from Admin only
>
> ○　c. User accounts and other global accounts from Admin
> 　　only
>
> ○　d. User accounts from Admin, any user accounts from all
> 　　trusting domains, plus any local groups from Admin only

The key to understanding this question is to understand what's allowed in
a global group—namely, user accounts only. This automatically disqualifies
answers c and d, which indicate that a global group in Admin can contain
global and local groups, respectively. Even where trust relationships exist,
global groups may only include users from the domain in which they're
defined. Local groups provide the mechanism for including global groups
from other domains because that's where the linkage between groups and
resources must reside in any case (in other words, this is a function of a
local group's ability to contain local or domain users and global groups, be
they from the local domain or some other domain that's trusted by the
domain in which the local group resides). This effectively disqualifies
answer a. Answer b is correct. A global group can contain only users from
the domain in which it resides. It's only because of the special default local
group Everyone that appearances to the contrary may be believed to exist.

. . . .

Question 7

Analyze the following scenario:

Your network includes two domains named "Engineering" and "Admin". Admin is a master domain, and Engineering has a one-way trust with Admin. Each domain includes a single PDC, two BDCs, three member servers, and 200 workstations, all running Windows NT Workstation 4. To ensure the availability of data on the network, you need to create a group named "TotalBack" that can back up all the machines on the network—be they domain controllers, member servers, or workstations.

Required result:

• Members of the TotalBack group must be able to back up all domain controllers, in either Engineering or Admin.

Optional desired results:

• Members of TotalBack should be able to back up all member servers in both domains.

• Members of TotalBack should be able to back up all NT workstations in both domains.

Proposed Solution:

• Create a global group called "TotalBack" in the Admin domain, and add this group to the Backup Operators local group on every domain controller, member server, and Windows NT workstation in both domains.

Which results does the proposed solution produce?

○ a. The proposed solution produces the required result, and both of the optional desired results.

○ b. The proposed solution produces the required result, but only one of the optional desired results.

○ c. The proposed solution produces the required result, but neither of the optional desired results.

○ d. The proposed solution does not produce the required result.

The answer to any "proposed solution" question on a Microsoft test is *pro forma* and nearly always follows the formula shown. The key to dealing with such a question lies in analyzing the proposed solution and deciding where it fits the matrix of possibilities. In this case, defining a global group in Admin is exactly the right thing to do because global groups in a trusted domain can be included in local groups in Admin and in any other domains that trust Admin. Engineering trusts Admin, so the global TotalBack group can be referenced in local groups in both domains. Finally, because all flavors of Windows NT mentioned—namely, domain controllers, member servers, and Windows NT Workstation machines—support the local Backup Operators group, placing a reference to Admin\TotalBack therein creates a situation where members of that group can back up all domain controllers, all member servers, and all NT workstations in either domain. Thus, the correct answer is a, because the required result and both optional desired results will be produced by the proposed solution.

Question 8

A network includes four domains named "Admin", "Engineering", "Marketing", and "Sales". Users in the Admin and Sales domains require access to a high-resolution color laser printer to produce proof prints for a sales brochure. Only Marketing and Engineering include such devices. How might you define trust relationships among these domains to grant users in Admin and Sales access to the color laser printers they need?

○   a. Define two-way trusts between all four domains.

○   b. Define two one-way trusts from Admin to Marketing and Engineering, and two more from Sales to Marketing and Engineering.

○   c. Define two one-way trusts from Engineering to Admin and Sales, and two more from Marketing to Admin and Sales.

○   d. Define a two-way trust between Admin and Sales, and another two-way trust between Engineering and Marketing.

Here again, you can begin by eliminating unnecessary relationships. So that Admin and Sales can access Engineering and Marketing resources, only one-way trusts are required (because nothing is said about Engineering and Marketing needing access to resources in either Admin or Sales). This eliminates answers a and d, both of which call for two-way trusts. Selecting the correct answer hinges on understanding how the trust relationship works. Because Admin and Sales need access to resources in

Engineering and Marketing, Engineering and Marketing must each trust Admin and Sales. This makes answer c the only correct answer, because answer b establishes the trust relationships in the wrong direction.

Question 9

Windows NT Directory Services provides trust relationships to permit secure access to occur across multiple domains. Which Windows NT Server utility provides the tools necessary to define such relationships?

○   a. Server Manager

○   b. User Manager For Domains

○   c. Control Panel, Services applet

○   d. Domain Administration

Only one utility includes mention of trust relationships. Trust relationships may only be created using the Policies|Trust Relationships menu entry in User Manager For Domains. Once defined, global groups and accounts from trusted domains may be accessed in User Manager For Domains in the trusting domain. Server Manager includes no options to create or manage trust relationships, nor does the Control Panel's Services applet. Finally, there is no utility in Windows NT Server called "Domain Administration." Therefore, answer b is the only correct answer.

Question 10

To facilitate a task group at your company, you're asked to provide temporary access to resources in your Admin domain for a group of auditors in the Auditors domain. For the same reason, you will also have to provide temporary access to the same group of users in other domains in the coming months. There is already a trust relationship where Admin trusts Auditors. Which of the following represents the best way to supply temporary access to Admin for this group of auditors?

○   a. Create a global group in the Admin domain that includes the auditors' user accounts. Add this group to the Guests local group on all servers in the Admin domain.

○   b. Create a global group in the Auditors domain that includes the auditors' user accounts. Add this group to the local group on the server (or servers) in the Admin domain that contain(s) the needed resources.

○   c. Create a local group in the Admin domain that includes the auditors' user accounts on each server where the needed resources reside.

○   d. Create a local group in the Auditors domain that includes the auditors' user accounts. Add this group to the local group on the server (or servers) in the Admin domain that contain(s) the needed resources.

There are two legitimate ways to meet the stated requirements. One of them simply entails adding the users from the Auditors domain into the local group (or groups) in the Admin domain where the needed resources reside. The other puts a global group in-between, by defining a global group in Auditors that may then be placed into global groups in Admin. Both options are legal, because Admin trusts Auditors. This makes answers b and c potentially correct. But because the question mentions a need to put the same group elsewhere in the future, creating a global group will ultimately be less work. That's because when the current temporary situation expires, the reference to the Auditors' global group need only be expunged from the local group (or groups) in Admin. To add this same group into another domain, the global group only needs to be added to the local groups in that domain (provided, of course, that the necessary trust relationship from the new domain to the Auditors domain exists). Thus, answer b represents the best way to meet all requirements. Answer a fails because it assumes that Guests will be able to access the necessary resources, without indicating whether this is true. Answer d fails because it puts one local group within another (only global groups and users may occur within local groups).

Need To Know More?

 Heywood, Drew: *Inside Windows NT Server*. New Riders, Indianapolis, IN, 1995. ISBN 1-56205-472-4. Pages 83 through 85 cover trust relationships and include some interesting details on the subject.

 Siyan, Karanjit S: *Windows NT Server 4 Professional Reference*. New Riders, Indianapolis, IN, 1996. ISBN 1-56205-731-6. Pages 196 through 204 cover trust relationships. As usual, Siyan offers the most detailed and thorough coverage of this subject.

 The Windows NT Server 4 manuals cover trust relationships only in passing. The *Concepts And Planning Manual* includes the most information on this subject. However, Lesson 10 in the Windows NT 4 Upgrade Training CD-ROM, Microsoft Press, Redmond, WA, 1996, covers this subject in great detail. ISBN 1-57231-528-8.

 The *Windows NT Server Resource Kit* contains scattered bits of information about trust relationships and related domain issues. You can search the TechNet CD (or its online version through www.microsoft.com), using keywords like "trust relationships" and "interdomain trusts."

Rights, Permissions, And User Access To Resources

4

Terms you'll need to understand:

√ Authentication

√ User rights

√ Permissions

√ Security Accounts
   Manager (SAM)

√ Access token

√ Objects

√ Attributes

√ Services

√ Access control list (ACL)

√ Groups

√ Read

√ Write

√ Execute

√ Delete

√ Change

√ Take Ownership

√ Full Control

√ No Access

√ List

Techniques you'll need to master:

√ Understanding how users are granted access to resources

√ Assigning permissions

√ Implementing groups and group access

√ Knowing NT's built-in groups and the default users of those groups

√ Understanding the difference between local and global groups, and
   when to use each

√ Establishing share permissions

√ Understanding the effects of combining permissions

59

The Server Enterprise exam demands a solid working understanding of rights, permissions, and user access. Hopefully, you've already mastered these topics for the Server test. In this chapter, we review these topics and introduce you to the added difficulty of an enterprise-level network. This chapter assumes you've already read and comprehended the previous two chapters on domains and trust relationships.

Logon And User Identification

The first step in understanding NT security must start where every user starts—at logon. By pressing Ctrl+Alt+Del at the initial NT splash screen, you initiate the WinLogon utility. This utility displays the logon dialog box and sends the supplied data to the security manager. The security manager (part of the executive services in the kernel) verifies the name and password, creates an access token, and launches the user's shell (usually NT Explorer). The verification process is the act of comparing the user name and password with the data stored in the Security Accounts Manager (SAM). This database also contains the list of access privileges for each user. The access token is built from this list. Once this process is complete, the user is able to access network resources.

The access token created by the security manager is a collection of identifiers and permissions unique to each individual. It is this access token that the network operating system (NOS) uses to verify authority to access and manipulate every object and resource. The access token is built by combining the individual settings of a user with those of each group to which they belong.

 The access token is created when a user logs on, and it is not changed until the user logs off and logs on again. This means that any access changes to a user or a group to which that user belongs will not affect those currently logged on. The changes will only affect them the next time they log on.

If you want to force a user to log off and back on, you can do this through Server Manager. In Server Manager, double-click the computer name where the user is currently logged on. This pulls up the Properties dialog. In the Properties dialog box, click on the Users button. Highlight the user's name, and click Disconnect. This forces the user off the network.

The access token not only defines what objects and resources with which a user can interact, but it is also attached to every process launched by that user. WinLogon uses the access token it creates to launch the shell for a user. The shell inherits the same access privileges as the user based on the access token. Every process launched by the user or a process initiated by the user can only have the level of access authority granted by the user's access token or less. (In fact, every single process has an access token assigned to it, based on the spawning heritage.) Under NT, it is not possible for a user to launch a process or access an object (directly or through a spawned process) that requires a higher level of access than that defined by his or her current access token.

The ultimate purpose of security is to control who has access to what. The WinLogon process determines the "who," and objects are the "what."

Objects

Within the world of Windows NT, everything is an object. An object has a type, a collection of services, and a set of attributes.

The type of an object defines what services and attributes are valid. Object types within NT include files, directories, symbolic links, printers, processes, threads, ports, devices, and even windows.

The services of an object are the activities that can be performed on, with, or by an object. For example, a directory object has services of List, Read, Change, Delete, and so on, but a printer object has services of Print, Manage, Delete, and so forth.

The attributes of an object include the name of the object, the actual data, and the access control list. Figure 4.1 illustrates a Windows NT object.

Each object has an access control list (ACL). An access control list is the attribute of each object that defines which users and groups have what level of services for an object.

Access Control List

An ACL comprises a list of services (Read, Write, Delete) and the associated users and groups who can perform each action (Mary, Bob, Sales group,

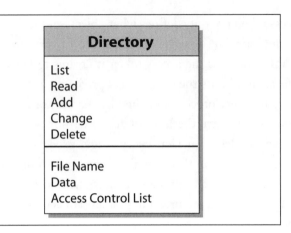

Figure 4.1 A Windows NT object.

Marketing group). Figure 4.2 illustrates an object's access control list along with a user's access token.

 When a user attempts to use an object, the user's access token is compared to the ACL of the object. You can think of the access token as a key ring with multiple keys, each related to a group membership or specific permission setting for that user. You can also think of the ACL as a linked group of padlocks for each object. Each lock will open only for a specific user or group key and only allow the specified level of access.

You should remember from the NT Server test that you can set the ACLs on an object in two ways. First, you can use the GUI dialog boxes and your mouse to point and click to make any and all ACL changes you desire. Go check it out for yourself. Right-click on an object, select Properties, click on the Securities tab, then click on the Permissions button. The second method is to use the **CACLS** command. This command can display or modify the ACL of files. Here's the syntax:

```
cacls filename [/t] [/e] [/c] [/g user:r|c|f] [/r user [...]]
[/p user:n|r|c|f [...]] [/d user [...]]
```

The parameters are as follows:

➤ **filename** Displays ACLs of specified file(s).

➤ **/t** Changes ACLs of specified files in the current directory and all subdirectories.

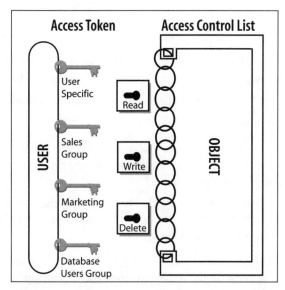

Figure 4.2 A visualization of a user's access token and an object's access control list.

➤ **/e** Edits the ACL instead of replacing it.

➤ **/c** Continues changing ACLs, ignoring errors.

➤ **/g user:r|c|f** Grants specified user access rights of Read, Change, or Full Control.

➤ **/r user** Revokes specified user's access rights.

➤ **/p user:n|r|c|f** Replaces specified user's access rights of none, read, change, or full control.

Now that we have defined these parameters, let's continue the discussion with how to ensure that users are assigned the proper access permissions.

Checking Permissions

When a user attempts to access an object, the security system performs a permissions check to determine if the user has proper authority to access the object and with which services he or she can interact. Using the key and lock analogy, the security system tries the keys on the user's key ring (access token) in each of the object's locks (ACL). If a match is found, the user can proceed with the intended activity.

This analogy doesn't quite explain every aspect of the permissions check, but it does give you a good mental image of what takes place. One important facet regarding permissions that the lock and key analogy fails to communicate is the No Access setting. Any user or group can be assigned No Access privileges for an object. If such an assignment is made, then a user cannot gain any access whatsoever.

Putting the lock and key imagery aside, when a user requests access to an object's service, the security system performs the following authority check:

1. Checks for any specified No Access for the user or any groups the user belongs to. If No Access is found, the user is denied access.

2. Checks for any specific granting of access based on the service requested for the user and any groups. If access is found, the user is granted access.

3. If neither a specific No Access nor service permission is found, the default of No Access is used. Therefore, the user is denied access.

As you can see, a specific No Access is like a trump card. It overrides any other settings, including specific granting of access. Plus, if no specific permission is given (i.e., no key is present in the access token), the user cannot gain entry.

Note that No Access under NT prevents a user from using any of the six file operations, but a user is still able to see the name of the object as stored in the Master Browser object list. Now that we have discussed individual user settings, let's examine how group memberships affect permissions for users.

Group Memberships

The use of groups can greatly simplify the feat of assigning access permissions to numerous individuals. As you learned when studying for the Server test, groups are a significant part of the security configuration of NT.I

A user can belong to many groups. When a user does belong to multiple groups, the access privileges for that user is a combination of the privileges granted by each group. You can think of group permissions as additive or cumulative. For example, if Sales has read access to an object, Marketing has write access to the same object, and you are a member of both groups, you have read and write access to that object.

The only exception to this addition rule is when any one group has No Access specified for the object. Once again, No Access means *no access* even if every other group offers full access privileges.

Because of the No Access trump, it is important to carefully plan the membership and access patterns of your users. It is common to mistakenly give a user too much access or no access at all through poor planning of group memberships.

Default Groups And Membership Assignments

There are a host of default groups, two default users, and a handful of important membership assignments you need to know about. These are the same as those you memorized for the Server test. Table 4.1 describes the groups.

Table 4.1	Default groups and their descriptions.	
Group	**Type**	**Description**
Account Operators	Local	Administration of domain user and group accounts
Administrators	Local	Full administrative privileges to a domain and the server
Backup Operators	Local	Bypass security restrictions to archive files from network storage devices
Domain Admins	Global	Administration of user and computer accounts within a domain
Domain Guests	Global	Guest access to domain resources

(continued)

Table 4.1   Default groups and their descriptions *(continued)*.

Group	Type	Description
Domain Users	Global	All users in a domain are part of this group
Everyone	Global	Contains all users in a domain and trusted domains
Guests	Local	Guest access to domain resources
Print Operators	Local	Administration of domain printers
Replicator	Local	Special group for replication
Server Operators	Local	Administration of servers
Users	Local	Server users

 You should remember that global groups can be used across a network on any machine within a domain or a trusted domain. Global groups can also be thought of as network groups. Local groups only apply to a single computer. By Microsoft's recommendation, global groups should contain users and local groups should contain resources. Then, global user groups should be placed into the local resource groups to allow users to access these resources.

The two default user accounts of Windows NT Server are:

➤ **Administrator** This account has unrestricted access to every object and resource within a domain. This account can be renamed but not deleted or disabled.

➤ **Guest** This account has limited access to domain resources for a temporary user. This account can be renamed and disabled but not deleted. This account has a blank password by default. Thus, any remote user can log on unless you set a password. This account does not save user preferences or configuration changes. This account is disabled by default.

It is highly recommended to rename the Administrator and Guest accounts immediately after installing NT. This will improve the security of your network by removing a "known" user account, thereby thwarting many would-be hackers. It is also a good idea to create separate Administrator accounts for each administrator within your MIS department. This allows the actions of each person to be tracked individually. Table 4.2 defines the default memberships of the default and new user accounts for NT's built-in groups.

If you add users to these groups, be aware of how the group settings affect that user's access rights. In addition to these rights, there are some settings that are specific to NTFS partitions, which we examine next.

NTFS Permissions

The NTFS file system has a standard set of access permissions for files and directories. Through these permissions, every file and directory within the file system name space can be controlled through the use of access tokens and ACLs. There are six specific operations that can occur on a file or directory:

➤ R Read. The object's data contents can be accessed.

➤ W Write. The object's data contents can be changed.

Table 4.2   NT's default members of built-in groups.

Group	Default Members
Account Operators	None
Administrators	Domain Users (global group), Administrator
Backup Operators	None
Domain Admins	Administrator
Domain Guests	Guest
Domain Users	Administrator
Everyone	Every account in a domain and trusted domains
Guests	Domain Guests (global group), Guest
Print Operators	None
Replicator	None
Server Operators	None
Users	Domain Users (global group), Administrator

➤ X Execute. The object can be executed (in relation to directories, this means the directory can be opened).

➤ D Delete. The object can be deleted.

➤ P Change Permissions. The object's access permissions can be altered.

➤ O Take Ownership. The ownership of the object can be changed.

These six operations are combined into the standard permissions sets for files and directories. The standard permissions for files are:

➤ **Read (RX)** Allows file to be read and/or execute.

➤ **Change (RWXD)** Includes read (RX), plus modify and delete.

➤ **Full Control (RWXDPO)** Includes change (RWXD), plus change permissions and take ownership.

➤ **No Access ()** Allows absolutely no access.

The standard permissions for directories are (the first parentheses refer to the directory itself, the second refer to the contents of the directory but not the contents in any subdirectories):

➤ **List (RX)(not specified)** Users can view the names of the contents of this directory. No content-specific settings are specified.

➤ **Read (RX)(RX)** Users can read and traverse the directory, as well as read and execute the contents.

➤ **Add (WX)(not specified)** Users can add files to the directory, but they cannot read or change the contents of the directory.

➤ **Add And Read (RWX)(RX)** Users can add files to and read files from the directory, but they cannot change them.

➤ **Change (RWXD)(RWXD)** Users can add, read, execute, modify, and delete the directory and its contents.

➤ **Full Control (RWXDPO)(RWXDPO)** Users have full control over the directory and its contents.

➤ **No Access ()()** Users have absolutely no access to the directory and its contents.

In addition to these sets of standard file and directory permissions, special access can be defined on a directory or file basis. Special access consists of one or more of the six file/directory object operations (RWXDPO).

Other object types have their own unique set of operations and permissions. For example, print objects have a print operator but do not have a read operator. For each object type, the NTFS permissions may be slightly different to accommodate the functionality of that object. For the printers permission discussion, please see Chapter 13.

NT uses two types of permission settings to control object access: local and remote. Local access is the NTFS permissions we just discussed. Remote access is controlled by shares.

Shares And Permissions

A share is a network resource that allows remote users to gain access to an object. The share is an object in itself that points to the resource object. The share knows how to translate data from the user (or, more specifically, an application employed by the user) to interact with the resource over the network. Shares enable a local resource to be used anywhere on the network.

Shares have their own set of permission levels:

➤ **No Access** Absolutely no access.

➤ **Read (RX)** Read and execute.

➤ **Change (RWXD)** Read, execute, modify, and delete.

➤ **Full Control (RWXDPO)** Full control.

Share permissions grant or restrict a user's interaction with the share itself. If a user has access, the NTFS permissions on the object itself determine what services the user can access. When a share is used to access a resource, the combination of the share restrictions and NTFS restrictions results in granting only the most restrictive permissions common to both the share and the object.

You can think of a share as a door and the services of an object as boxes. The share will only allow object services to pass through its gateway if they are the same as or less restrictive than the permissions on the share itself. As you can see in Figure 4.3, the "boxes" of NTFS permissions will only fit through the "doors" of a share if the boxes are smaller than the opening.

Permissions on a share only apply to users attempting to access a resource through that share (i.e., over the network). Local users are not affected by the share restrictions because they have direct access to the resource. Thus, local users are only restricted by the NTFS permissions on an object while remote or network users are restricted by both the share permissions and the NTFS object permissions.

Here's an extremely important item to remember about shares: *The initial default settings of all newly created shares is Full Control to the Everyone group.* You'll need to remember this for the test, plus this can cause some interesting problems if you don't reduce the access range for premium shares.

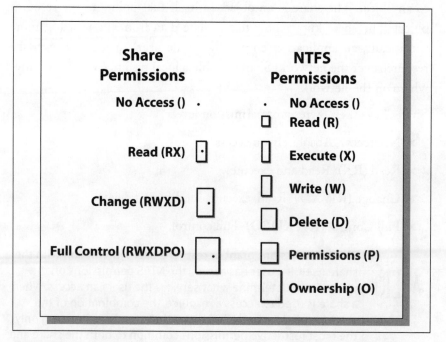

Figure 4.3   A visualization of share permissions in relation to NTFS object permissions.

Permission Combinations

Each time a user attempts to access an object, there are many hurdles that the user's security settings must pass to reach the object. The specified settings of the user account and each group membership must be examined for both the share and the object. Here are some items to keep in mind when deciphering permission combinations:

➤ No Access on the share or the object prevents all access, even if Full Control is granted by another group membership.

➤ The permissions from all groups of which a user is a member are cumulative. This applies both to shares and objects.

➤ The most restrictive set of common permissions between a share and an object are used.

In addition to access tokens and ACLs to control user abilities to access object and resources, NT also provides a set of user rights, which we'll look at in the next section.

User Rights

User rights restrict or grant specific computer-based abilities to a user or group. User rights are assigned through the Policies menu of the User Manager For Domains.

There are 11 basic user rights and an additional 16 advanced rights. Through the User Rights Policy dialog box, you can view any of these rights, in addition to the users and groups to which each right is currently granted. Note that to view the advanced rights, you must check the Show Advanced User Rights option at the bottom of the dialog box.

The basic user rights, their purpose, and their members (in parentheses) are as follows:

➤ **Access computer from network** Logon or connect to this computer from a client on the network (Administrators).

➤ **Add workstations to domain** Add computers to the domain database in Server Manager (none).

➤ **Back up files and directories** Back up files or directories on this server and bypass file permissions (Administrators, Backup Operators).

➤ **Change system time** Change the time on the server (Administrators, Backup Operators).

➤ **Force remote shutdown** Issue a shutdown command remotely (Administrators, Server Operators).

➤ **Load/unload device drivers** Load device drivers on this server (Administrators).

➤ **Log on locally** Direct physical logon to this server (Administrators, Server Operators, Backup Operators, Account Operators, Print Operators).

➤ **Manage audit and logs** Manage audit details and work with log files (Administrators).

➤ **Restore files/directories** Restore files or directories from server backups (Administrators, Server Operators, Backup Operators).

➤ **Shut down the system** Shut down the system from the system console (Administrators, Server Operators, Backup Operators, Account Operators, Print Operators).

➤ **Take ownership of files or objects** Take ownership of files, directories, or objects (Administrators).

The advanced rights are not required knowledge for the Enterprise exam because they are used for programming and development instead of standard network administration. However, it is a good idea to at least be familiar with the names of these rights:

➤ Act as part of an operating system

➤ Bypass traverse checking

➤ Create a pagefile

➤ Create a token object

➤ Create permanent shared objects

➤ Debug programs

➤ Generate security audits

➤ Increase quotas

➤ Increase scheduling priority

➤ Lock pages in memory

➤ Log on as a batch job

➤ Log on as a service

➤ Modify firmware environment values

➤ Profile single process

➤ Profile system performance

➤ Replace process-level tokens

Exam Prep Questions

Question 1

> You need to gain access to a file named "VENDORS.TXT" in the newly created \\Sales\Documents shared folder in the Sales domain. You are a member of the Sales domain. There is a trust relationship established so that the Sales domain trusts the Marketing domain. What additional settings must be made to offer you access to the VENDORS.TXT file?
>
> ○ a. Set the Read permission on the Documents folder to your user account.
>
> ○ b. Your user account must be added to the Everyone group in the Sales domain.
>
> ○ c. None, Full Control to all trusted users is the default on all new shares.
>
> ○ d. A new Sales domain-based user account must be created.

Assigning specific permissions for the object to your user account is not required because your account is a default member of the Everyone group and a new share offers Full Control to this group by default. Therefore, answer a is incorrect. Your user account automatically becomes a member of the Everyone group when your domain is trusted. Therefore, answer b is incorrect. No action is required because your account becomes a member of the Sales domain Everyone group, which has Full Control to new shares by default. Therefore, answer c is correct. You do not need a new account in the Sales domain to access the file. Therefore, answer d is incorrect.

Question 2

There are two domains within an organization: Sales and Research. New beta software has been deployed on the Research domain for testing, but four members of the Sales domain need to gain access to the beta software to aid in the test process. The beta software resides in an NTFS-based share named "WEBKIT2" on the BETA server in the Research domain. If the Research domain trusts the Sales domain, what additional steps are required to give the four Sales users access to the beta software?

○ a. Create a global group in the Sales domain called "Sales_Beta" and add the four Sales users to this group. Create a local group called "Soft_Beta" on server BETA with Full Control over the WEBKIT2 share. Add the Sales_Beta global group to the Soft_Test local group.

○ b. Create new accounts for the Sales users in the Research domain.

○ c. Remove the existing trust. Establish a new trust where the Sales domain trusts the Research domain. Create a global group in the Sales domain called "Sales_Beta" and add the four Sales users to this group. Create a local group called "Soft_Test" on server BETA with Full Control over the WEBKIT2 share. Add the Sales_Beta global group to the Soft_Test local group.

○ d. Create a global group in the Sales domain called "Sales_Beta" and add the four Sales users to this group. Create a global group called "Soft_Test" on server BETA with Full Control over the WEBKIT2 share. Add the Sales_Beta global group to the Soft_Test global group.

Answer a is the proper sequence of steps required to give the Sales users access to the beta software. Therefore, answer a is correct. Adding new accounts to the Research domain is insecure and will result in twice the administration to maintain two accounts for each user. Therefore, answer b is incorrect. The existing trust will allow Sales users to use Research resources. Reversing the trust will prevent access and destroy other possible links currently relying on the trust. Therefore, answer c is incorrect. It is not possible to add a global group to another global group. Plus, Microsoft recommends using local groups to manage resource permissions. Therefore, answer d is incorrect.

Question 3

> Your network uses the single master domain model where the CORP domain is the master. One of the resource domains, SALES, trusts the CORP domain. When a user logs on to the CORP domain using a computer attached to the SALES domain, what objects will that user be able to view?
>
> ○ a. All objects in both the SALES and CORP domains for which the CORP\Domain Users group has been granted Read access
>
> ○ b. All objects in both the SALES and CORP domains for which the SALES\Domain Users group has been granted Read access
>
> ○ c. All objects in the SALES domain for which the SALES\Domain Guests group has been granted Read access
>
> ○ d. All objects in both the SALES and CORP domains for which the CORP\Domain Guests group has been granted Read access

The use of the master domain model implies that all user accounts are present in the CORP domain. Thus, all user accounts are members of the CORP\Domain Users group. Because CORP is trusted by the SALES domain, every user who logs on through a SALES domain workstation will be able to view all objects to which permissions have been granted to the CORP\Domain Users group in either domain. Thus, answer a is correct. The SALES\DomainUsers group is a null set because all users are in the CORP domain. Therefore, answer b is incorrect. The SALES\Domain Guests and CORP\Domain Guests groups do not have standard users as members. Therefore, answers c and d are both incorrect.

Question 4

> Which of the following is not a directory or file standard permission?
>
> O   a. Read
>
> O   b. List
>
> O   c. Create Directory
>
> O   d. Change
>
> O   e. Add

Read is both a directory and a file permission. Therefore, answer a is incorrect. List is a directory permission. Therefore, answer b is incorrect. Create Directory is not a permission. Therefore, answer c is correct. Change is both a directory and file permission. Therefore, answer d is incorrect. Add is a directory permission. Therefore, answer e is incorrect.

Question 5

> You attempt to add new information into a document stored on a remote server. Using the Documents share, you are able to locate and open the document into your word processor. You have Full Control of the object. You are a member of the Sales group. The Sales group has Read access to the Documents share. You are unable to save your changes to the file, why?
>
> O   a. You cannot edit documents over a network.
>
> O   b. Your resultant permissions for the file object are just Read.
>
> O   c. The Sales group has the save privilege revoked.
>
> O   d. Only administrators can Save files over the network.

It is possible to edit documents over a network. The only stipulation is that you must have the proper access level to modify remote objects. Therefore, answer a is incorrect. Accessing objects through shares results in the most restrictive shared permissions. Therefore, answer b is correct. There is no Save privilege in the NT environment. The Sales group merely has Read access to the share. Therefore, answer c is incorrect. The ability to save documents (i.e., modify objects) is not limited to administrators. Therefore, answer d is incorrect.

Question 6

> What are the recommended actions to increase security for the Administrator account? [Check all correct answers]
>
> ❑ a. Rename the Administrator account.
>
> ❑ b. Disable the Administrator account.
>
> ❑ c. Create user accounts for each system administrator and add them to the Administrators group.
>
> ❑ d. Use a blank password for the Administrator account.
>
> ❑ e. Use a difficult password for the Administrator account.

Renaming the account is an improvement in security. Therefore, answer a is correct. It is not possible to disable this account. Therefore, answer b is incorrect. Creating individual administrator accounts for each system admin is a good way to protect your network. Therefore, answer c is correct. Using a blank password for the Administrator account is inviting trouble. Therefore, answer d is incorrect. Using a difficult password is a good security measure. Therefore, answer e is correct. Thus, answers a, c, and e are correct.

Question 7

> Which of the following are attributes of an object? [Check all correct answers]
>
> ❑ a. Data
>
> ❑ b. ACL
>
> ❑ c. Services
>
> ❑ d. Name

The data associated with an object is an attribute. Therefore, answer a is correct. The ACL of an object is an attribute. Therefore, answer b is correct.

The services of an object are services, not attributes. Therefore, answer c is incorrect. The name of an object is an attribute. Therefore, answer d is correct. Thus, answers a, b, and d are correct.

Question 8

> You attempt to access a file in the NTFS directory share \UserGuide. Sales has Change access to the share. Marketing has Read access to the share. Accounting has No Access to the share. You have Full Control of the object. You are a member of all three groups. What are your resultant access privileges?
>
> O   a. No Access
>
> O   b. Read
>
> O   c. Change
>
> O   d. Full Control

No Access results if any group of which you are a member has No Access. Therefore, answer a is correct. Read is the access for the Marketing group, but you are also a member of the Accounting group, which has No Access. Therefore, answer b is incorrect. Change is the access for the Sales group, but you are also a member of the Accounting group, which has No Access. Therefore, answer c is incorrect. You have Full Control of the object only when accessing it directly. By using a share, you are restricted by your group settings that result in No Access. Therefore, answer d is incorrect.

Question 9

> The Administrator account is a default member of what groups? [Check all correct answers]
>
> ❑   a. Domain Guests
>
> ❑   b. Domain Users
>
> ❑   c. Users
>
> ❑   d. Power Users
>
> ❑   e. Everyone

The Domain Guests group contains only the Guest account by default. Therefore, answer a is incorrect. The Domain Users group contains the Administrator account by default. Therefore, answer b is correct. The Users group contains the Administrator account by default. Therefore, answer c is correct. Power Users is a group from Windows NT Workstation, and it is not present by default in NT Server. Therefore, answer d is incorrect. The Everyone group includes the administrator account. Therefore, answer e is correct. Thus, answers b, c, and e are correct.

Question 10

A network is comprised of two domains: SALES and CORP. The master domain is CORP, and SALES is the resource domain. SALES trusts CORP. Both domains have numerous servers and workstations. You want to create a group called "NetBack" that can perform backup operations on all computers throughout the network. Which of the following are required steps to accomplishing this goal? [Check all correct answers]

❏ a. Create a NetBack global group in the SALES domain.

❏ b. Create a NetBack global group in the CORP domain.

❏ c. Add the NetBack global group to the Backup Operators local group on each machine in both domains.

❏ d. Add the NetBack global group to the CORP\Domain Users group.

❏ e. Assign Read access to the NetBack global group for every file object on every machine in the network.

A global group in the resource domain cannot be granted any permissions from the master domain due to the nature of the one-way trust. Therefore, answer a is incorrect. Creating the global group in the master domain is one of the correct steps. Therefore, answer b is correct. Adding the NetBack group to the local Backup Operators group is a required step. Therefore, answer c is correct. The NetBack group should not be added to the Domain Users group, nor can it be, because both are global groups. Therefore, answer d is incorrect. Assigning Read permissions across the network is an unnecessary and worthless task. The act of adding the NetBack group to the Backup Operators group on each machine in effect performs this activity without compromising security. Therefore, answer e is incorrect. Thus, only answers b and c are correct.

Question 11

If no configuration changes have been made to a server, what prevents a standard user from logging on to a server by walking up to the local console?

- ○   a. There is no restriction to prevent users from logging in.
- ○   b. Servers don't allow anyone to log on to them.
- ○   c. Log on locally user right is not assigned to standard users.
- ○   d. The user has No Access permission set for the server object.

There is a default restriction to prevent general users from logging in locally to a server. It is the log on locally right, and it is not assigned to users by default. Therefore, answer a is incorrect. Servers allow members of the Administrators, Server Operators, Backup Operators, Account Operators, and Print Operators groups to log on to them. Therefore, answer b is incorrect. The log on locally right is not assigned to standard users specifically to prevent them from gaining easy access to the server. Therefore, answer c is correct. There is no server object to which No Access permissions apply. Therefore, answer d is incorrect.

Need To Know More?

 Heywood, Drew: *Inside Windows NT Server*. New Riders, Indianapolis, IN, 1995. ISBN 1-56205-472-4. Chapters 2, 4, and 5 discuss rights, permission, and gaining access to resources.

 Siyan, Karanjit S: *Windows NT Server 4 Professional Reference*. New Riders, Indianapolis, IN, 1996. ISBN 1-56205-731-6. Chapters 7 and 9 have extensive coverage of the Windows NT domain accounts and security system.

 The Windows NT Server 4 manuals cover planning, configuration, and installation issues quite well. The *Concepts And Planning Manual* Chapters 1, 2, and 4 contain lots of basic and background information on rights, permissions, and shared resources.

 The *Windows NT Server Resource Kit* contains lots of useful information about Windows NT's fault tolerance. The TechNet CD or *Resource Kit* CD can be searched using keywords like "user rights," "permissions," and "share." In the *Networking Guide* volume, Chapter 2, "Network Security And Domain Planning," is a great place to learn more about configuring users and groups for solid security and controlled access.

Optimizing Domain Use

5

Terms you'll need to understand:

- √ Primary Domain Controller (PDC)
- √ Backup Domain Controller (BDC)
- √ Member server
- √ Stand-Alone server
- √ Authentication
- √ User profiles
- √ System policies
- √ Domain browsers

Techniques you'll need to master:

- √ Establishing server roles
- √ Easing the user authentication load
- √ Setting up user profiles
- √ Managing user, group, and computer policies
- √ Administering the SAM database
- √ Maintaining domain controller synchronization

In Chapter 2, we discussed domain concepts. In this chapter, we continue the domain discussion with information on domain controllers, authentication, user profiles, system policies, and browsers. In keeping with the format of the series, we cover the details you need to know to pass the Server in the Enterprise exam and point you to additional resources for further discussion on these topics.

NT Server Roles

Windows NT Server can be one of three types of servers within a client/ server network. The three server types are Primary Domain Controller (PDC), Backup Domain Controller (BDC), and member server. There is actually a fourth server classification, Stand-Alone server, but this is only used in relation to workgroup networks, and it is the same type of setup as a member server. In fact, the installation screen for NT offers a choice of PDC, BDC, or Stand-Alone server. Thus, you should almost consider the terms "member server" and "Stand-Alone server" interchangeable.

PDCs and BDCs have additional server components installed that a member server does not have. These extra components enable the domain controllers to store and maintain the Security Accounts Manager (SAM) security database, plus handle account administration. A member server is a system that serves network resources to clients, such as files, printers, and applications. Other than the management of the SAM database, there is no difference between domain controllers and member servers.

You select which type of server to configure during installation. Once a server is installed as a domain controller, it cannot be changed to a member server, nor can a member server be changed to a domain controller without reinstalling the Network Operating System (NOS). This is due to the way the Registry is constructed for domain controllers. The entire system has to be reinitiated for the domain controller structure to be created or removed. However, PDCs and BDCs can switch roles without any significant hassle. A single domain can have only one PDC and any number of BDCs or member servers.

Just as every user account has a SID (Security ID), so does every server. Once a domain controller has been installed on a domain, it cannot change domains without being reinstalled. The domain itself can be renamed (a significant hassle in itself), but the domain controllers cannot be moved from one domain to another. This is because the SIDs of each domain controller are associated with a specific domain.

The PDC is the central storage and management server for the SAM database. This database maintains all security information for a domain. The SAM database on a PDC can be modified when needed, such as adding new accounts or changing group memberships. At regular intervals, the modifications to the SAM database are pushed out to the BDCs within the domain.

A BDC is a redundant system to protect the integrity and availability of the SAM database. BDCs are not able to make any changes or modifications, but they can use the database to authenticate users. Another benefit of BDCs is load balancing. A BDC shares the burden of authenticating users at logon. The domain controller closest to the machine being booted handles user authentication. If your network is large and uses WAN (Wide Area Network) links, BDCs can be placed in the remote locations to handle local authentication without requiring the logon procedure to tie up the WAN link to communicate with the PDC. If your WAN link goes down, users can still log on through a BDC and access local resources. Having at least one BDC is recommended for redundancy and fault tolerance, even if you do not have a large network or WAN links.

A PDC must be fully installed to establish a network. Once the PDC is fully booted and operational, BDCs can be installed. You should always have a functioning network connection to a PDC when installing a BDC. The BDC must communicate with the PDC to establish a domain-based SID, create a computer account for the BDC computer, gain authority to interact with the SAM database, and make its first copy of the database.

If a PDC is not available, installation of the BDC will fail. Once you've installed one or more BDCs, then adding member servers and clients can occur. You can add additional BDCs at any time as long as a connection can be established to the PDC.

Domain Controller Synchronization

After the domain controllers have been installed, the PDC will regularly send out updates to the BDCs so their copy of the SAM database is current. Because any domain controller can authenticate users, it is important for the database stored on each domain controller to be current and accurate. The process of maintaining accurate copies of the accounts database on the BDCs is called "synchronization."

There are two types of synchronization: partial and full. Partial is just the modifications made to the database since the last update. This is the fastest and most common form of synchronization. Full is when the PDC sends out the entire SAM database. This occurs when a new BDC is brought online or at other times. The BDC maintains a change log that lists the changes made to its copy of the database. When the log reaches 64 K (its maximum size)—about 2,000 changes—it requests a full synchronization from the PDC. Full synch can also occur when a BDC's database copy is found to be incomplete or when an administrator forces a full synch. In the following section, we continue our discussion of synchronization, with an eye toward synch management from the Windows NT Registry.

Synchronization Controls In The NT Registry

Depending on the layout, size, and composition of your domain, altering the default settings for synchronization may improve the operation and reliability of your security system. The parameters for the synchronization process are stored in the NetLogon section of the NT Registry.

Using either of the Windows NT Registry Editors—REGEDT32.EXE, or REGEDIT.EXE—open the following key:

```
HKEY_LOCAL_MACHINE\System\CurrentControlSet\Services\Netlogon\Parameters
```

Within this key, you can add or modify the following parameters to change the behavior of synchronization:

➤ **Pulse (60 through 3,600 seconds)** Defines the typical pulse frequency. All SAM database changes since the last pulse are collected and sent to each BDC when the pulse time has expired. No pulse is sent to up-to-date BDCs. Default=300.

➤**PulseConcurrency (1 through 500)** Defines the maximum number of BDCs that the PDC pulses simultaneously. By increasing the setting, you increase the load on the PDC. By decreasing the PulseConcurrency setting, you increase the time it takes to update the BDCs within the domain. Default=20.

➤**PulseMaximum (60 through 86,400 seconds)** Sends every BDC a pulse at this interval, whether or not a BCD's SAM database is up-to-date. Default=7,200.

➤**PulseTimeout1 (1 through 120 seconds)** Defines the amount of time a PDC will wait for a BDC to respond to a pulse. If the BDC does not respond within the specified time, it is considered nonresponsive. A domain with many nonresponsive BDCs takes longer to finish the synchronization process if the PulseTimeout setting is too high. On the other hand, if the setting is too low, the BDCs may be misjudged as unresponsive. A partial synchronization is received when the BDCs do respond. Default=5.

➤**PulseTimeout2 (60 through 3,600 seconds)** Defines how long the PDC waits for a BDC to complete partial synchronization. It is necessary for the BDC to continue to make progress during the process of receiving a database synchronization. The BDC will be thought of as unresponsive if the BDC stops calling the PDC during a synchronization. If the number is too high, the BDC will be slow and take up one of the PulseConcurrency slots, which keeps the PDC from notifying another BDC at that time. If the number is too low, the load on the PDC will be increased if there many BDCs performing partial synchronization. Default=300.

➤**Randomize (0 through 120 seconds)** Defines a back-off period for the BDCs. When the BDCs get a pulse from the PDC, they wait the "randomize" number of seconds before they call the PDC. Randomize should always be less than the PulseTimeout1 setting. Default=1.

➤**ReplicationGovernor (0 through 100 percent)** Defines the packet size used in the synch process. Synchronization may take up more bandwidth than you are willing to use if it's running over a slow WAN. To alter the amount of bandwidth consumed by synchronization, the Replication- Governor can be used to reduce the packet size used in the synch process to a percentage of the 128 K standard package. Too low a setting prevents synchronization from ever completing. A setting of zero prevents all synchronization from occurring. Default=100.

That's it for synchronization, you should be familiar with the preceding materials to be able to accurately respond to the Enterprise exam questions. To further discuss domain optimization issues, we now turn our attention toward one of the most often used tools in NT management, the Server Manager.

Server Manager Domain Controls

Through the Server Manager tool, you can perform numerous operations on domain controllers that you might find invaluable to the reliability of your network. These operations include controller promotion, synchronization, and adding computer accounts. As you learned for the Server exam, the Computer menu from the Server Manager is where all of this takes place. First, highlight the server you wish to modify, then choose the appropriate command from the Computer pull-down menu.

 Domain controller promotion is used to recover from a PDC failure. In the event of a PDC malfunction, the BDC continues to authenticate users, but it cannot make changes to the SAM database. A BDC can be promoted to a PDC to take over the responsibility of the failed system if the PDC cannot be brought back online quickly. The promoted machine functions as if it were the PDC all along. Once the failed PDC is repaired, it can be brought back online. This may result in two PDCs within a single domain. In such a case, one of the PDCs can be demoted using the Demote To BDC command. Take note that this command only appears in the Computer menu when two PDCs are present in a domain.

The original PDC can resume its control over the network if its SID was not changed. Depending on the failure, you may need to completely reinstall NT. In such a case, the old PDC should be installed as a BDC, then promoted back to a PDC once installation is complete. To help make this clearer, review the following section, "Disaster And Recovery Scenario."

Disaster And Recovery Scenario

A domain has SRVR-A as its PDC and SRVR-B as a BDC. The hard drive fails on SRVR-A, and a replacement is not readily available. The administrator promotes SRVR-B to a PDC. Later, SRVR-A is repaired, but the original NOS is destroyed. The administrator attaches SRVR-A to the network and performs a new installation of NT, making SRVR-A a BDC. This new installation causes a new SID to be generated for SRVR-A. After the installation is complete, the administrator forces a synchronization from the PDC SRVR-B. Then, the administrator promotes SRVR-A to a PDC. This restores the roles of the servers to their original state, but the SID of SRVR-A is now different.

Each time NT is reinstalled, the server is assigned a new SID. Even if nothing else about the computer changed (meaning the previous configuration was duplicated), the domain considers it a completely different computer. The only time a new SID is not assigned is when an upgrade installation is performed.

Synchronization can be forced. There are two variations to this command: synchronize entire domain or synchronize with the PDC. When you select a PDC and execute the synch command, the PDC sends out update information to every BDC in the domain. When you select a BDC, the BDC requests an update from the PDC, and no other BDCs are affected.

Creating computer accounts enables new systems to easily join the domain. The Add To Domain command can be used to create accounts for NT workstations, NT Server member servers, or NT Server BDCs. Every NT Workstation- or NT Server-based computer must have a computer account in a domain to participate as a member of the network. Using Server Manager to add a computer to the domain bypasses the need for the administrator's name and password during the installation of NT on the new computer.

Now that we've covered the details of how PDCs and BDCs work, we continue the discussion with how these domain controllers authenticate users on the network.

Authentication With BDCs And PDCs

To take advantage of distributed authentication, you must duplicate all scripts, profiles, and policies from the PDC to each BDC. This is accomplished using the replication service. For details on configuring this service, see Chapter 6.

Logon scripts must be stored in the \%winntroot%\System32\ Repl\Export\Scripts directory. Then, as part of configuring replication, make sure you replicate (import) to your export server. This places the scripts in the \%winntroot%\System32\ Repl\Import\Scripts directory, which is shared by the system as NetLogon. Thus, as described in the next section, a user's profile can point to NetLogon\MYSCRIPT.BAT, and the user will always load script from the NetLogon share from the authenticating domain controller.

A User profile must be translated into a roaming profile and stored in a publicly accessible share to be useful for a roaming user. By taking advantage of the existing NetLogon share, roaming profiles can be stored in a subdirectory of \%winntroot%\System32\Repl\Export, such as \Profiles, and referenced with NetLogon\Profiles\%username%\.

System policies should also be stored in the \%winntroot%\ System32\Repl\Export\Scripts directory. Thus, they can be referenced by the NetLogon share and are present in the import directory of all BDCs (at least those configured to replicate).

 The Replication Service included on the original Windows NT 4 CD is broken and does not work properly. Install SP3 (or higher) to fix its problems.

Continuing our discussions of how users are authenticated and retain important settings, let's move on to what Microsoft says regarding this important system information.

Domain Database Info

Microsoft recommends that the domain database maintained by the PDCs and BDCs not exceed 40 MB. Each domain database stores three types of information: user accounts, computer accounts, and group accounts. Each user account requires 1 K, each computer account requires 0.5 K, and each group account requires 4 K. Therefore, a 40 MB domain database can maintain 26,000 user accounts (26 MB), 26,000 computer accounts (13 MB), and 250 group accounts (1 MB). (Unfortunately, the only way to determine the size of the SAM or domain database is to calculate it manually.)

With these domain settings in mind, we move forward to explore how to set up access rights and system settings through the use of user profiles.

User Profiles

A user profile is simply the configuration and environmental settings for a user's desktop, menus, network connections, color scheme, and personal applications. User profiles enable a number of people to use a workstation, while retaining each person's customized settings. By default, all user profiles are local, meaning they only apply to a single machine. But user profiles can be configured so they roam with the user to any workstation attached to the domain.

User profiles are either mandatory or customizable. A mandatory profile does not save any changes made by a user, whereas a customizable profile does save the changes (hence the name). Mandatory profiles lend themselves well to group usage, because everyone sees the same setup and no user can make changes. Customizable profiles should only be assigned to a single user, so users can't change each other's settings.

A new customizable profile is created when a user logs on for the first time, or a mandatory profile can be assigned by the administrator during the account creation process. All profiles are created by logging in as a user and making whatever changes are desired. During logoff, all changes are saved. If the NTUSER.DAT file is renamed to "NTUSER.MAN", then a customizable profile becomes a mandatory profile. Thus, an administrator can create a user, log in as that user, modify the environment, log off, log back in as administrator, rename the DAT file to ".MAN," then assign the new mandatory profile, as needed.

By default, all user profiles are stored in the \%winntroot%\ Profiles directory. A subdirectory with the same name as the user is created, and the profile information is stored within the subdirectory. One of the files stored in a profile is theNTUSER.DAT file. If the workstation is a Windows 95 machine, this file is named "USER.DAT". The profiles stored by Windows 95 and Windows NT are not compatible, but by changing USER.DAT to USER.MAN, you get a mandatory Win 95 user profile.

Once a profile is created, it can be turned into a roaming profile using the System application located in the Control Panel. The User Profiles tab offers you the ability to copy a profile to an

> alternate location, such as the \%winntroot%\System32\Repl\
> Export directory. Once copied, you can set the copied profile to
> be a roaming profile.
>
> Once a roaming profile has been created, you can assign that
> profile to a user (or users, if it is a mandatory profile). This is done
> through the User Manager For Domains. Open the properties for
> a user, click the Profile button, then type in the UNC name in the
> User Profile Path text box, such as \\PDC1\NetLogon\
> %username%.

Let's move on with our discussion of profiles. In the following section, we explain what happens when a user is unable to download the most recent copy of his or her profile.

Using A Cached Profile On Slow Connections

Roaming user profiles are helpful for maintaining a consistent desktop. However, when users log on to a domain via a slow connection, download-ing the user profiles might cause a needless delay (this is especially true if the profiles are the same as they were during their last logon).

Users might want to use a locally cached profile rather than a centrally located profile if the logon process is taking an unusually long time. In the System Properties dialog box, under the User Profiles tab, there is a checkbox for this purpose.

In addition to user profiles, you can also maintain user settings through the use of a system policy, which we discuss next.

Managing NT Policies

An NT system policy is a configuration file that presets the system con-figuration for a user, group, or computer. System policies actually edit the Registry of the local computer to reflect the changes prescribed by the administrator-defined policy. System policies are created and modified through the System Policy Editor.

Initially, no restrictions are enabled in the default policies. They must be created and implemented by an administrator. This gives you the greatest breadth of freedom with the operation and configuration of your user's network environment. As a general rule, it is unwise to ever initiate a Default User or Default Computer policy. Default policies apply to everyone, including the administrator. It is not too difficult to create a policy that restricts a user and a computer so much that nothing can be done—so much so that you could not even correct your mistake without reinstalling NT.

In addition to the default and system policies, you can also create policies for individual users, computers, and groups, as we explain in the following section.

User, Group, And Computer Policies

User and group policies modify the HKEY_CURRENT_USER section of the Registry, while computer policies alter the HKEY_LOCAL_MACHINE section. Once again, policies overwrite existing Registry settings on the local machine to enforce the settings defined in that policy. User policies can apply to a specific user or to all users (called "Default User"). Likewise, computer policies can apply to a specific computer or to all computers (called "Default Computer"). Group policies can only apply to a specific group.

User and group policies can be used to set, alter, or control access to:

- ➤ Screen saver

- ➤ Appearance

- ➤ Wallpaper

- ➤ Color scheme

- ➤ Shell restrictions (shut down, save on exit, network neighborhood, hiding drives)

- ➤ Registry editing

- ➤ Windows application restrictions

➤ Custom folders

➤ Explorer access

Computer profiles can be used to set, alter, or control access to:

➤ Network updates

➤ Simple Network Management Protocol (SNMP) configuration info

➤ Startup applications

➤ Hidden drive shares

➤ Printer settings

➤ RAS callback settings

➤ Custom shell settings

➤ Logon policies

➤ User profile handling

User, group, and computer policies are automatically applied based on their name. When a new policy is created, you must assign it a name. A user policy should be given a user's name, a group policy a group's name, and a computer policy a computer's name. It is recommended to create the user, group, or computer before creating the policy that applies to it.

The logon system looks for system policies in the NetLogon share. All policies are stored in a single file called "NTCONFIG.POL." This should be saved in the \%winntroot%\System32\Repl \Export\Scripts directory so it can be accessible throughout the domain.

When more than one policy can apply to a user, the following priority order is used:

1. If a user has a user profile, it takes priority over all group-related policies.

2. If a user does not have a user profile, then all group-related policies are merged (see the following).

3. If a user has no specified profiles, the default user profile applies.

> When more than one group applies to a single user, the pre-defined group priority settings are used. This is defined through the System Policy Editor's Options|Group Priorities command. Settings in a priority group (i.e., higher in the list) apply to a user instead of the settings on the same parameters from other groups.
>
> *Note:* Only a single policy is used on a user except in the case of group policies, where all applicable policies are merged based on priority.

Hardware Profiles

Hardware profiles are useful for notebook computers with PC Card (previously called PCMCIA) slots and/or docking stations. Multiple hardware profiles can be defined so only the drivers needed for a particular hardware configuration are loaded and system errors are avoided. Hardware profiles are controlled through the Hardware Profiles tab of the System application, which is located in the Control Panel. The main settings indicate whether the current configuration is docked and if network access is present.

Now that we have discussed how to manage access by users to network resources, let's examine how NT makes those resources available, starting with the Windows NT Browser service.

Browsers

The NT Browser service maintains a list of all network resources within a domain and provides lists of these domains, servers, and resource objects to any Explorer-type interface that requests it (e.g., browse lists).

Each computer within a domain participates in the Browser service. Each time a computer is brought up within the domain, it announces itself and the resources it has to share (if any). This is the most common level of participation for computers within a domain. The most important role within the Browser service is that of the Master Browser. The Master Browser maintains the main list of all available resources within a domain (including links to external domains).

Note: On some TCP/IP networks, another role—the Domain Master Browser (DMB)—is used to enable resource lists to be communicated across subnets within the same domain. By default, the DMB is the PDC. Plus, a Master Browser is present within each subnet.

Two other important roles are the Backup Browser and the Potential Browser. The Backup Browser maintains a duplicate list of the resources and acts in a similar way within the Browser Service as does the BDC within domain control. The Backup Browser can serve lists of resources to clients. A Potential Browser is any machine capable of becoming a Backup or Master Browser. As needed, the Browser service changes the role of a machine from Potential Browser to Backup Browser. Within any domain, the Browser service attempts to maintain the maximum of three Backup Browsers, but any number of Potential Browsers can exist.

Only the following computer setups can serve as Potential Browsers:

➤ NT Server 3.5 or higher

➤ NT Advanced Server 3.1

➤ NT Workstation 3.1 or higher

➤ Windows 95

➤ Windows for Workgroups 3.11

Any of these computer setups can also be set to be non-browsers so they will not participate in supporting the browser lists, except to announce themselves upon boot-up.

In the next few sections, we continue our discussion of the Browser service. This includes how networks are chosen (elected), in addition to how the browse list is maintained and how it can be managed through the Windows NT Registry.

Browser Election

When a Master Browser goes offline, or when another machine that has the ability to claim the role of Master Browser comes online, an election occurs. The results of the election determine which machine becomes the active Master Browser. An election packet is transmitted by the new computer or by a Backup once the Master is no longer detected. This packet travels to each potential browser within the domain. The winner of the election is determined by the following hierarchy of criteria (presented in order of priority):

➤ **Operating System** NT Servers, NT Workstations, Windows 95, WFW

➤ **Operating System Version** NT 4.0, 3.51, 3.5, Windows 95, 3.11, 3.1

➤ **Current Browser Role** Master Browser, Backup Browser, Potential Browser

➤ **Alphabetical** Further election is resolved through the alphabetical order of the computer names

List Maintenance

When a computer comes online, it announces itself. Initially, it announces itself once a minute, with the interval decreasing to once every 12 minutes. This repeated announcement is used by the Master Browser to determine if a resource is still available. The Master Browser maintains the list of resources for any machine for three missed announcements, to accommodate performance dips and communication bottlenecks. Thus, after a machine has been up and running for a reasonable time, then goes offline, its resources can remain in the Master Browser's list for up to 36 minutes.

Backup Browsers poll the Master Browser every 15 minutes to request an updated version of the browse list. Therefore, a failed resource can remain in the Backup Browser's list for up to 51 minutes. If a Backup Browser requests an update from the Master and receives no response, it initiates an election.

Browser And The Registry

The status of any Potential Browser can be altered through two Registry parameters. The parameters are located in HKEY_LOCAL_MACHINE \SYSTEM\CurrentControlSet\Services\Browser\Parameters. The first value, **MaintainServerList**, determines whether a machine can be a potential browser. It can have a value of **No, Yes,** or **Auto**. **No** sets the machine to be a non-browser. **Yes** forces the machine to be a Master or Backup Browser. And, **Auto** allows the Browser Service to determine the role as needed. The second value, **IsDomainMaster**, sets the machine to be the Master Browser. It can have the values of **True** or **False**.

Exam Prep Questions

Question 1

You are the administrator of domain SALES1. There are no BDCs within SALES1. A power outage destroys some system files on the PDC. You attempt to correct the problem by reinstalling a new version of NT onto the PDC machine. After the installation, no workstations are able to connect to SALES1. What could be the problem?

○   a. The PDC was disconnected from the network.

○   b. A member server was automatically promoted to PDC status, and it is in conflict with the reinstalled PDC.

○   c. The new installation of NT created a new SID for the PDC.

○   d. A BDC in a trusting domain promoted itself to act as the PDC in SALES1. The reinstalled PDC has caused a control conflict.

The PDC was not disconnected from the network, instead the new SID of the PDC is the culprit. Therefore, answer a is incorrect. Member servers can never be domain controllers. Therefore, answer b is incorrect. The SID of the PDC is the defining element of a domain, not its name. Thus, the new SID created a new domain in which none of the workstations is a member. Therefore, answer c is correct. BDCs in trusting domains cannot authenticate users nor can they act as PDCs for the trusted domain. Therefore, answer d is incorrect.

Question 2

You want to establish a standard desktop configuration for the entire Sales group. Which of the following tactics will provide you with this result?

O   a. Create a computer policy, and restrict access to change the desktop environment.

O   b. Establish a user profile with the desktop configuration you wish to use, rename the NTUSER.DAT file to "NTUSER.MAN", and set this user profile for each member of the Sales group.

O   c. Create a group policy restricting access to the desktop configuration controls.

O   d. Establish a user profile, and set this profile for each member of the Sales group.

A computer policy restricts a machine from accessing certain applications to prevent changes or alterations to the environment. A computer policy would prevent users from changing any settings, but it does not establish a common desktop configuration. Therefore, answer a is incorrect. Creating a mandatory user profile is the correct method to establish a standard desktop configuration for a group. Therefore, answer b is correct. A group policy acts the same as a computer policy, but it restricts members of a group. No matter what machine they are using, group policies do not set a configuration but can be used to prevent change to a configuration. Therefore, answer c is incorrect. A customizable profile, the type created by default, can be altered by users. Thus, it would not create a standard configuration. Therefore, answer d is incorrect.

Question 3

Your network consists of five domains in a single domain model configuration. Where should you place the logon scripts to make administration simplest?

○   a. On the PDC in the trusted domain

○   b. In the PDC's \%winntroot%\System32\Repl\ Export\Scripts directory within each trusting domain

○   c. Within the NetLogon share of each domain

○   d. On the local workstations

The PDC of the trusted domain, i.e., the user domain, is the best place for administration control of user scripts. Therefore, answer a is correct. The PDCs within the trusting domains, i.e., the resource domains, are not used to authenticate users. Plus, there are many of these machines, thereby increasing the administration difficulty. Therefore, answer b is incorrect. The NetLogon share within each domain is the same problem presented in answer b—multiple administration sites within non-authenticating domains. Therefore, answer c is incorrect. A local workstation is not the correct place to store logon scripts, especially for easy administration. Therefore, answer d is incorrect.

Question 4

> Bob received a promotion that includes a new office with a great view. The new office has a better computer than he was using before, so he decides to use it instead of dragging his old one in. Previously, Bob had only used one machine and never moved about the organization. But when Bob logs on using his new computer, which runs the same OS as his old computer, he is surprised to find that his wallpaper, Start menu items, drive mappings, and color scheme are different. What could account for this?
>
> ○ a. Bob has been reassigned a mandatory user profile.
>
> ○ b. Bob mistakenly logs in with the Load Default Profile option selected in the WinLogon box.
>
> ○ c. Bob's new computer is not compatible with his previous desktop settings.
>
> ○ d. Bob's user profile is not roaming.

A profile assignment would remove Bob's previous settings from appearing, but this situation does not lean toward this as a solution, because most promotions improve one's computer access and control instead of reduce it. Therefore, answer a is incorrect. There is no such Load Default Profile option anywhere within NT. Therefore, answer b is incorrect. User profiles are not dependent on the computer hardware to function, but rather the OS. Because both machines Bob used supported the same OS, compatibility is not an issue. Therefore, answer c is incorrect. Bob never moved around the organization previously, so the administrator probably never bothered to set his profile to roaming. Therefore, answer d is correct.

Question 5

> A system administrator installs NT onto a new server. She wants to restrict everyone's ability to use the new server other than herself. She attempts to impose such a restriction by editing the default user policy and restricting all possible options. The next time she logs onto this server, she discovers that she is unable to do anything with the machine. What has happened?
>
> ○ a. The new computer hardware has a system fault.
>
> ○ b. The default user policy affects the Administrator.
>
> ○ c. The system administrator failed to log on using the Administrator account.
>
> ○ d. The PAGEFILE.SYS file has been deleted.

If the system is able to boot and log a user in, then it is not a hardware-related fault. The system is operational on the current hardware. Therefore, answer a is incorrect. The default user policy affects even the Administrator, so by restricting everything, the computer is worthless. NT will have to be reinstalled to correct the problem. Therefore, answer b is correct. Even if the system administrator failed to log in with the Administrator account, every user attempting to use this computer will be so restricted. Therefore, answer c is incorrect. The PAGEFILE.SYS file is not associated with this problem, but if it was deleted, the system would rebuild it during bootup. Therefore, answer d is incorrect.

Question 6

> Users complain that network performance is poor during the early part of the day and right after lunch—the times when users are authenticated by the domain controllers. Currently, there is one PDC and two BDCs within the domain. You inspect the performance levels of the domain controllers and determine that they are operating at acceptable levels. What is the best way to improve network performance?
>
> ○   a. Add additional BDCs.
>
> ○   b. Increase the RAM on all servers.
>
> ○   c. Decrease the Pulse Registry setting on the PDC.
>
> ○   d. Install an additional PDC in the domain.

Adding additional BDCs will improve network performance by distributing the user authentication. Therefore, answer a is correct. Adding RAM to the servers will not improve the network performance because the performance levels are acceptable. Therefore, answer b is incorrect. The Pulse Registry setting would have a negative effect on performance by increasing background network traffic. Therefore, answer c is incorrect. Only one PDC can exist within a domain. Therefore, answer d is incorrect.

Question 7

> Which of the following computer systems can act as a Potential Browser? [Check all correct answers]
>
> ❑   a. NT Server 4
>
> ❑   b. Windows 3.1
>
> ❑   c. NT Server 3.1
>
> ❑   d. Windows for Workgroups 3.11
>
> ❑   e. NT Workstation 3.5
>
> ❑   f. OS/2 Warp

NT Server 4, Windows 3.1, WFW 3.11, and NT Workstation 3.5 are all valid system types that can be Potential Browsers. Therefore, answers a, b, d, and e are correct. NT Server 3.1 and OS/2 Warp are invalid system types for Potential Browsers. Therefore, answers c and f are incorrect.

Question 8

What is the minimum number of user domains you must have in a multiple master domain model to support 40,000 users, 40,000 computers, and 300 groups?

- ○ a. 1
- ○ b. 2
- ○ c. 3
- ○ d. 4

One user domain can only sustain 26,000 user accounts, 26,000 computer accounts, and 250 groups. Therefore, answer a is incorrect. Two user domains would adequately support this level of users, computers, and groups, and it is the least number of domains that would be able to do so. Therefore, answer b is correct. Both three and four user domains can support this number of users, computers, and groups, but only two are required. Therefore, answers c and d are incorrect.

Question 9

> Your domain consists of two groups of computers connected by a long-distance WAN link. There are multiple BDCs located in each group. The available bandwidth of the WAN link must be maximized. Which of the following changes to the domain controller synchronization will reduce the load placed on the link by the PDC and the BDCs? [Check all correct answers]
>
> ❏ a. Set Pulse to 60
>
> ❏ b. Set PulseConcurrency to 1
>
> ❏ c. Set PulseMaximum to 60
>
> ❏ d. Set MaintainServerList to Auto
>
> ❏ e. Set ReplicationGovernor to 50

Setting Pulse low (60) causes updates to take place too frequently and place extra traffic on the WAN link. Therefore, answer a is incorrect. Setting PulseConcurrency low (1) updates a fewer number of BDCs on each Pulse interval, thus reducing WAN traffic. Therefore, answer b is correct. Setting PulseMaximum low (60) forces a full update more often. Therefore, answer c is incorrect. MaintainServerList is a browser setting, not a domain controller synchronization setting. Therefore, answer d is incorrect. Setting the ReplicationGovernor to 50 percent will reduce the packet size transmitted over the WAN. More packets will be required, but each one uses less bandwidth. Therefore, answer e is correct. Thus, only answers b and e are correct.

Question 10

Your network has a single BDC to protect the PDC. During a storm, your PDC's motherboard and hard drives are destroyed. You do not have equipment on hand to replace the PDC. Which of the following activities can help you restore your network to proper working order? [Check all correct answers]

- ❏ a. Promote the BDC to a PDC.

- ❏ b. Restore the data saved to a backup tape from the failed PDC to the current BDC.

- ❏ c. Repair the failed machine, and reinstall NT as a BDC on this machine.

- ❏ d. Repair the failed machine, and reinstall NT as a PDC on this machine.

- ❏ e. Perform a new version installation of NT on the operating BDC to transform it into a PDC.

Promoting the BDC to a PDC allows the network to authenticate users and make changes to the SAM database. Any resources on the failed machine will no longer be available, but the promoted PDC will support the network. Therefore, answer a is correct. Restoring backed-up data to the BDC will probably cause problems because the hardware configurations and system settings are different between two machines. This is not a step in restoring normalcy. Therefore, answer b is incorrect. Reinstalling NT on the repaired machine to be a BDC is the second step, after promoting the current BDC to a PDC. Once the failed server is operating as a BDC, it can be promoted to its previous role as a PDC without problem. Therefore, answer c is correct. Reinstalling NT on the repaired machine to be a PDC will cause a new SID to be created and will not allow the server to participate in the existing network. Therefore, answer d is incorrect. Reinstalling NT onto the working BDC to make it a PDC will not only destroy the only working copy of the SAM database, but it will change the SID of the machine and destroy the domain as well. Therefore, answer e is incorrect. Thus, only answers a and c are correct.

Need To Know More?

 Donald, Lisa and James Chellis: *MSCE: NT Server 4 In The Enterprise Study Guide*. Sybex Network Press, San Francisco, CA, 1997. ISBN 0-7821-1970-0. Chapter 1 contains information on domain controllers and server roles. Chapter 7 runs the gamut on domain management. User profiles and system policies are covered in Chapter 5. The Browser service is examined in Chapter 7.

 Heywood, Drew: *Inside Windows NT Server*. New Riders, Indianapolis, IN, 1995. ISBN 1-56205-472-4. Chapter 2 discusses domain controllers and synchronization. Chapter 8 discusses user profiles and system policies. Brief information about browsers is contained in Chapter 13 on pages 576 through 577.

 Siyan, Karanjit S: *Windows NT Server 4 Professional Reference*. New Riders, Indianapolis, IN, 1996. ISBN 1-56205-731-6. Chapters 5 and 6 contain detailed information about domain synchronization, promotion, and other domain issues. Chapter 8 delves into user profiles and system policies. The Browser service is examined in Chapter 19.

 The Windows NT Server 4 manuals cover planning, configuration, and installation issues quite well. The *Concepts And Planning Manual* contains domain controller, server role, synchronization, user profiles, system policies, and Browser service issue discussions.

 The *Windows NT Server Resource Kit* contains lots of useful information about Windows NT's fault tolerance. The TechNet CD (or its online version at www.microsoft.com) can be searched using keywords like "domain controller," "synchronization," "user profiles," "system policies," and "browser service." In the *Networking Guide*, Chapter 2, "Network Security And Domain Planning," contains information on domain controllers and synchronization. Plus, Chapter 3, "Windows NT Browser Service," focuses on the Browser service.

NT Redundancy And Fault Tolerance

6

Terms you'll need to understand:

√ Fault tolerance

√ Directory Replication service

√ Import server

√ Export server

√ Partitions

√ Primary partition

√ Extended partition

√ Redundant Array of Inexpensive Disks (RAID)

√ Volume set

Techniques you'll need to master:

√ Understanding and implementing fault tolerance

√ Installing and configuring NT's Directory Replication service

√ Familiarization with Disk Administrator

√ Restoring data through fault tolerance

√ Implementing and configuring backup

The Windows NT operating system is designed to provide reliable network services. The reliability of NT rests upon many specialized features, including domain synchronization, directory replication, fault tolerance, and backup. In this chapter, we cover the topics you need to know regarding domain controllers, replication, and fault tolerance so you can successfully complete these portions of the Microsoft Certification exam.

Domain Controllers

The broad and complex topic of domain controllers is discussed in detail in the previous chapter, but we include it here, as well, to emphasize its role in NT's system reliability.

The Microsoft domain concept prescribes that each domain should have at least one Backup Domain Controller (BDC) to mirror and support the Primary Domain Controller (PDC). Because the PDC is the central control point for the entire Security Accounts Manager (SAM) security database, it is an important component of your network. A BDC is the only reliable method for maintaining a realtime duplicate of the SAM database. If the PDC goes offline for any reason, a BDC will continue to support user authentication in its stead. However, a BDC cannot record new security information, so you need to restore your PDC as quickly as possible or upgrade the BDC to a PDC.

 One of the benefits of BDCs when the PDC is still active is that BDCs can still authenticate users. In fact, if a BDC is electronically closer to the user than a PDC, it will most likely handle the authentication and serving of user profiles, logon scripts, and system policies. This results in load balancing that improves the overall performance of the network. However, for this process to really work, you'll need to use the Directory Replication service, as described in the next section.

Note: Please refer to Chapter 5 for complete details on the PDC and BDC relationship, synchronization, and disaster recovery for domain controllers.

Directory Replication

Another aspect of NT redundancy is Directory Replication. This service is designed to disseminate often-used and regularly updated data (such as user profiles, logon scripts, and system policies) to multiple computers to speed file access and improve reliability. Some early Microsoft documentation also claimed this service was useful for distributing large directory trees, but this suggestion has recently been repealed. The level of traffic caused by the replication service would bring any network to its knees if more than 2 MB of data was replicated.

For the Enterprise exam, you need to assume that the Directory Replication service actually works. In the real world, NT's replication fails 9 times out of 10, straight out of the box. According to Microsoft, the service has been repaired through Service Pack 3.

Replication is a simple idea in concept, but it's a bit tricky to implement. The replication service is not enabled or even set up by default. Microsoft left that wonderful task up to you. We'll briefly list all the steps you'll need to know, but other than the 10,000-foot view, the test doesn't focus on the initial setup of replication.

Replication is the process of duplicating a directory and its contents from an export server to any number of import servers. Any NT server can act as an export server, but both NT Server and Workstation machines, plus LAN Manager servers, can be import servers.

 All data placed in an export server's export directory will be duplicated to all import servers' import directories. By default, the export directory is:

`\%winntroot%\System32\Repl\Export\`

And the default import directory is:

`\%winntroot%\System32\Repl\Import\`

All files and directories beneath these two directories are under the control of the replication service. Any files added to the export directory will eventually appear in the import directory. Any files deleted from the export directory will be removed from

> the import directory. In other words, the service performs
> whatever actions are necessary to ensure that the import
> directory exactly matches the export directory.

Beneath these directories is a default standard directory named "Scripts". This is where logon scripts are usually placed. Plus, the NETLOGON share points to the \Import\Scripts directory. This makes defining user profiles easy by allowing the general share name to proceed the script name, such as "NETLOGON\BOB.BAT." Thus, when a BDC or PDC authenticates that user, it knows to grab the file from the closest NETLOGON share.

Now that we have covered the basics of what directory replication is and what it does, let's move on to discuss how to get it up and running.

Installing Replication

The steps for initiating replication are as follows:

1. Create a replication user account with the following data:

   ➤ User name: ReplUser

   ➤ Password: (Any will do. The service will change it once it is activated, but you'll need one to get it started.)

   ➤ Deselect: User Must Change Password At Next Logon

   ➤ Select: Password Never Expires

   ➤ Group Membership: Replicator

2. Configure the Directory Replicator service in the Services application in Control Panel using the Startup button:

   ➤ Startup Type: Automatic

   ➤ Logon As: ReplUser

   ➤ Password: (As entered for the account.)

3. Configure Directory Replication through the Server Manager, open the Properties dialog box for the export or import server (by double-clicking the computer name), and click the Replication button.

➤ If Export: Select the Export Directories radio button. The default directory will appear in the From Path field.

➤ If Import: Select the Import Directories radio button. The default directory will appear in the To Path field.

➤ Click Add under Export or Import, and select the computer to export to or import from.

4. Place material in the Export directory.

5. Reboot all export and import servers.

A few important items regarding replication:

➤ Replication will not work if any application is accessing or viewing the export or import directories. This causes the file system to lock and prevents replication. The service treats this as if changes are being made to files, and it is designed to wait until files and directories are inactive before replicating

➤ The Manage button found in the Directory Replication on COMPUTERNAME dialog box of the Properties window of a server in Server Manager offers some information about the status of replication:

  ➤ **OK** Replication was successful.

  ➤ **No Master** The import server is not receiving updates from the export server, or the replication service may not be running.

  ➤ **No Sync** This means there was an incomplete replication (e.g., communication errors, locked files, and so forth).

  ➤ **[blank]** No replication has been attempted.

  ➤ The Application log of the Event Viewer displays error messages from the replication service. The error codes can be deciphered using the following command prompt command:

  NET HELPMSG <error message number>

➤ The export directory must be on an NTFS partition.

> ➤ Replication will only occur between computers with system clocks that are set within 59 minutes of each other. Thus, servers in different time zones will not replicate.

> ➤ All applications should point (or pull) from an import directory only.

> ➤ Use the replication service only for small and important security data. For large or noncritical data, use the **AT** command with an xcopy batch file (or one of the great copy programs from the Resource Kit).

> ➤ Always export to the import directory on your export server.

Additional Replication Configuration

Replication from the export server to the import servers will occur every five minutes. This default setting can be changed by editing the following Registry key:

```
HKEY_LOCAL_MACHINE\SYSTEM\CurrentControlSet\Services\Replicator\Parameters
```

The value **Interval** controls how often broadcasts are sent from the export server. **Interval** can have a value of 1 through 60 minutes (it is of data type **REG_DWORD**).

Another important entry in this key is **GuardTime**. This is the number of minutes the export server will wait after a directory becomes stable before attempting to replicate. The default value is two minutes, but it can be set from zero to one-half of **Interval** (it is also of data type **REG_DWORD**).

These are the only two replication items related to the Registry that you need to be aware of. There are additional keys and values referenced in the *Resource Kit* that you should examine if you plan on using this service.

Now that we have covered directory replication, let's move on to discuss keeping your data safe through the use of Windows NT's built-in fault tolerance features.

Fault Tolerance

The issues around hard drive storage fault tolerance are the same for the Enterprise exam as they were for the Server exam. If you mastered this material for Server, then you've already got a head start on the Enterprise exam.

The specific topics that fall under the heading of fault tolerance for Windows NT Server include: disk mirroring, disk duplexing, and disk striping (both with and without parity). Other relevant fault tolerance topics include disaster recovery, using NT's built-in Disk Administrator utility, and several general storage, controller, and bootup matters.

All the fault tolerant features of NT are focused on, or at least related to, the Disk Administrator utility. This makes it imperative to examine this tool thoroughly so you understand Microsoft's implementation of fault tolerance for Windows NT Server.

Disk Administrator

The better your knowledge of the Disk Administrator's tools and menus (see Figure 6.1), the more likely it is that you will understand the numerous

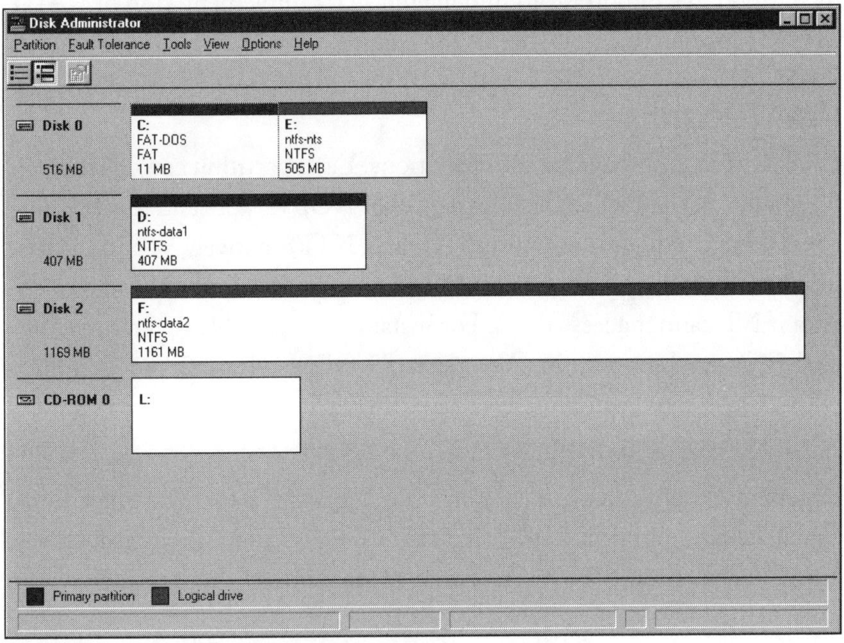

Figure 6.1 The Disk Administrator utility.

fault tolerance questions that appear on the exam. The Enterprise exam does not focus as much on the organization of the menus of Disk Administrator, but familiarity with them can only improve your score. Remember, Disk Administrator appears beneath the Start Menu, in the Programs| Administrative Tools (Common) menu.

 One important command is the Commit Changes Now option in the Partition menu. This command instructs Windows NT to make your requested changes to the affected storage devices. In other words, partitions and drives will not be created or changed in Disk Administrator until this menu option is chosen.

We have examined the basics of NT's fault tolerance, but let's step back a moment and examine the specifics of setting up a secure disk structure.

Disk Structure 101

Hopefully, you are already familiar with storage devices and the terminology used to describe their configuration and operation. But just to be sure you're equipped with the bare minimum of such information, here's a short refresher on partitions, volumes, drive letters, and the Master Boot Record. In addition, it's important to understand NT's implementation of RAID, which is covered in detail later in the chapter.

Partitions

Hard drives are subdivided into partitions. Each partition can contain one file system, each of which enables an OS or NOS to store and retrieve files. Even though NT only supports FAT and NTFS natively, partitions that support other file systems can reside on a machine that runs Windows NT, even if NT cannot access them. For instance, it's possible that a drive on a dual-boot machine running Windows 95 OEM release 2 and Windows NT Server 4 could contain a FAT32 partition. In that case, only Windows 95 could access that partition.

In general, a hard drive can contain from 1 through 32 separate partitions. Thus, a single physical hard drive can appear as multiple logical drives. Hard drives should be partitioned to maximize their usage by the underlying NOS and its applications. If you attempt to change a partition, any information stored in that disk space will be destroyed. If there is free unpartitioned space on a drive, you may create new partitions without damaging existing partitions. Likewise, deleting any one partition does not affect other partitions on a drive.

The NTFS file system supports a variety of partition schemes. A single drive may contain up to four primary partitions, or one through three primary partitions and a single extended partition. An extended partition can be further subdivided into multiple logical drives. But the total number of primary partitions, plus logical drives, cannot exceed 32 on any one physical hard drive under NT's control.

Volumes

A volume is an organizational structure imposed on one or more partitions that support file storage. If you select one or more partitions on a physical drive and format them with a specific file system, the resulting disk structure is a volume. Under Windows NT, volumes can even span multiple partitions on one or more physical drives.

A volume set is a volume comprised of 2 through 32 partitions. A volume set may be extended at any time by adding another partition to the set without damaging existing data stored therein. However, a volume set and its data must be destroyed to reduce the size of a volume. All the partitions in a volume set must use the same file system, and the entire volume set is assigned a single drive letter. A volume provides no fault tolerance for its data. If any one of the partitions or drives within a volume set fails, all of the volume's data is lost.

The best way to remember the impact of losing a volume set element is the following phrase: You lose one, you lose them all. This also means that the only way to recover data in a damaged volume set is to restore the data from a backup.

Drive Letters

Nearly every volume on a Windows NT machine has an associated drive letter. In fact, Windows NT cannot access a volume unless it has an associated drive letter. Drive letters simplify the identification of an exact physical drive, partition, and volume for any referenced folder or file. NT can assign drive letters to storage devices using the letters C through Z (A and B are reserved for floppy drives). Because this only covers 24 potential drives, and Windows NT supports as many as 32, the assumption is that some volumes will span multiple physical drives (which all share a single drive letter). There is one exception to the floppy drive letter rule. If you do not have a drive B, you can assign a network mapped drive to that letter (but this isn't on the exam).

 NT automatically assigns the next available drive letter to each new volume that's created. But you can dynamically reassign or shuffle drive letters using the Assign Drive Letter option on the Tools menu in Disk Administrator.

Another exception to the association of volumes with drive letters applies to volumes formatted with file systems not supported by Windows NT. These volumes are generally not assigned drive letters because NT cannot access them anyway.

Master Boot Record

The Master Boot Record (MBR) is a BIOS bootstrap routine used by low-level, hardware-based system code stored in Read-Only Memory (ROM) to initiate the boot sequence on a PC. This in turn calls a bootstrap loader, which then commences loading the machine's designated operating system. The MBR directs the hardware to a so-called "active partition" from whence the designated operating system may be loaded (for more information on this topic, look at Chapter 13).

 To be active, a partition must be a primary partition. A primary partition can be made active by using the Mark Active command on the Disk Administrator's Partition menu. The boot partition is that partition where the MBR and boot loader reside. For Windows NT, the system partition is the partition where the Windows NT system files reside.

Now that we have cleared up where NT looks for boot files, let's continue our discussion of NT's fault tolerance features.

System Security Through Fault Tolerance

Fault tolerance describes the resilience of a system in the presence of errors, mistakes, or disasters without causing damage or loss to its data. Windows NT's fault tolerance features vary from disk partition organization, to high-level file system operations, to backup techniques. When these are combined, they make NT a reliable and solid network operating system.

The NTFS file system supports internal and automatic fault tolerance. Using a method called "hot fixing," every storage device write is monitored and written sectors checked for integrity. If any verification fails, the questionable sectors are flagged, and the data is rewritten to another working location on disk. This is performed automatically by the file system and does not report error messages to any applications. NTFS also logs all changes to the file system so that changes may be undone or reapplied if a discrepancy is found or if damage is caused by a system failure or power loss.

Windows NT 4 Server supports three types of fault tolerant disk structures: disk mirroring, disk duplexing, and disk striping with parity. These structures may be implemented using the Fault Tolerance menu in the Disk Administrator utility. But as you'll soon learn, only disk striping with parity qualifies as fault tolerant. Disk striping without parity does not qualify, even though it's another legal way to aggregate multiple partitions in Disk Administrator.

Disk Mirroring

Disk mirroring creates an exact duplicate of one physical and logical storage device on a separate physical storage device. Both the original drive and the "backup," or mirrored drive, are attached to the same hard drive controller. If the original disk fails, there is no loss of data because everything written to the original disk is also written to the mirror. Barring other physical component problems, when the original drive fails, the system automatically switches to the mirrored drive to continue operation.

Drawbacks to disk mirroring include:

➤ **Slow performance** The act of writing the same data twice takes longer than writing it once.

➤ **Increased cost** Every mirror must be a separate physical device. Thus, you must purchase twice the storage capacity.

➤ **No protection from controller failure** If the disk controller fails, the mirrored drive is just as inaccessible as the original drive.

 The boot and system partitions can be the original disk in a disk mirror set. But if the original fails, it will be necessary to hand-edit the BOOT.INI FILE on the boot drive to point to the ARC (Advanced RISC Computing) name for the mirror, instead (ARC names and BOOT.INI editing are covered in Chapter 13.)

Disk Duplexing

Disk duplexing is similar to disk mirroring, but more robust. Like mirroring, disk duplexing uses a duplicate physical and logical drive on a separate hard disk. Unlike mirroring, however, the drive is connected to the system via a separate controller. If the original drive or controller fails, the system continues to operate using the duplexed drive. Duplexing causes no system performance degradation because writing the same data twice through two disk controllers requires no additional time and both writes occur simultaneously.

One significant drawback to disk duplexing is the cost—it requires double the storage space and a second disk controller.

 As with mirroring, the boot and system partitions can be the original disk in a disk duplexing set. But again, if the original fails, you must edit the BOOT.INI file by hand to point to the ARC name for the duplexed drive.

Disk Striping

Disk striping stores data across multiple physical storage devices. In a stripe set, multiple partitions of equal size on separate devices are combined into a single logical device. When data is stored to a stripe set, it is written in 64 K chunks across all partitions in the set. An example of a stripe set is depicted in Figure 6.2. Here, data is written in "stripes" across the drives,

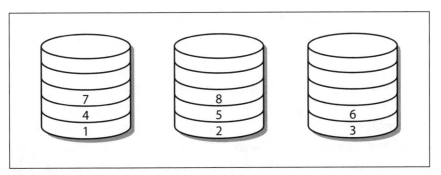

Figure 6.2   A stripe set using three physical disks.

starting at the drive on the left with data block 1, then on the middle drive with data block 2, and so on.

Disk striping is fast, especially when the individual storage devices are attached to separate disk controllers. Disk striping does not have the same cost drawbacks as mirroring and duplexing, because all or most of the storage space you purchase is fully available to you. You only need two devices to create a stripe set without parity, and such a stripe set can include as many as 32 devices. Disk striping can be implemented using either FAT or NTFS.

Disk striping without parity, however, provides no fault tolerance whatsoever. Should any one of the drives in a stripe set without parity fail, all data on all disks is lost. (Once again: If you lose one, you lose them all.) If any of the drive controllers fails, none of the data is accessible until that drive controller is repaired.

The boot and system partitions cannot be part of a disk stripe set without parity (or otherwise, in fact, as you'll see in the next section). Warning! If the test says anything about a stripe set but does not mention "parity" (with or without), you must assume that this means a stripe set without parity, and answer accordingly.

Disk Striping With Parity

Disk striping with parity offers most of the benefits of parity-free disk striping without the same risk of data loss. Parity defines a storage method where the data that's written across the stripes is recorded so that data stored on any one drive is duplicated across all the other devices in the stripe set. The duplicate data is called "parity information." If any one of the drives in a parity stripe set fails, that data can be rebuilt from the parity information on the remaining devices without loss.

To record parity information within a stripe set, additional space is required. Unfortunately, this means that the total amount of storage capacity is smaller than the sum of the partitions on each member of the stripe set. To calculate the total capacity (**T**) of a stripe set with parity, use the following formula (where **P** is the size of any single partition, and **n** is the number of partitions in the set):

```
T = P * (n - 1)
```

When you create a stripe set using the Create Stripe Set With Parity option on the Disk Administrator's Fault Tolerance menu, you will be presented with a dialog box that displays the total size of the set. This number is **P * n**, which equals the size of the smallest partition multiplied by the total number of partitions. This number does not reflect the amount of actual usable storage space of a stripe set with parity. (That number is determined by the preceding formula, which takes the space requirements for parity information into account.)

Here are a few important items to remember about disk striping with parity:

➤ All partitions within a stripe set must be of equal size (or nearly so).

➤ Each partition must be on a separate physical disk.

➤ NTFS must be used as the file system on a stripe set with parity.

➤ A minimum of 3 devices is required to build a stripe set with parity, and the maximum number of devices is 32.

➤ Writing performance is slightly slower than disk striping without parity, but faster than disk mirroring.

➤ If one drive in a set fails, the data set can be rebuilt from the remaining devices.

➤ Neither the boot nor system partitions can reside in a disk stripe set, even with parity.

In continuing our coverage of fault tolerance, it's important to detail the various levels of RAID security, which we cover in the following section.

RAID

The four partition organizations we've described for Windows NT represent software implementations of RAID (which stands for Redundant Array of Inexpensive—or Individual—Disks). In other words, RAID is a storage method that uses numerous devices in combination to store large amounts of data.

 RAID also addresses various levels of fault tolerance and recoverability for specific configurations and storage techniques. There are six distinct levels recognized in RAID subsystems, starting with level 0 and ending with level 5. Windows NT Server supports RAID levels 0, 1, and 5. Here's an explanation of these levels:

➤ **RAID 0** Disk striping without parity. This level provides no fault tolerance, but it is the fastest method. RAID 0 includes non-striped volume sets as well as disk striping without parity.

➤ **RAID 1** Disk mirroring. This level provides a reasonable level of data protection, but it has some performance consequences. Disk duplexing is also sometimes categorized as RAID 1, because it provides the same level of data protection with improved performance. Both mirroring and duplexing require twice as much physical storage as the data to be stored (because there are two identical copies of everything).

➤ **RAID 5** Disk striping with parity. This level provides the highest level of data protection with only a minor dip in performance and modest overhead storage requirements for parity information.

Remember, NT's software implementation of RAID requires additional system overhead, especially when large numbers of devices are involved. Software RAID is convenient and inexpensive because it is included with NT, but hardware RAID is faster and offers more options and reliability (like hot-swappable drives and controllers).

Comparing RAID Levels

On the Enterprise exam, you'll encounter questions that ask you to designate a level of fault tolerance for a particular system or configuration. Remember, disk striping without parity (RAID 0) offers no fault tolerance whatsoever. In addition to the RAID levels and fault tolerance features of the various partition organizations, remain aware of expense and hardware requirements.

Here's a list of things to consider when comparing disk mirroring (or duplexing) to disk striping with parity:

➤ Two physical disks per mirror set are required for disk mirroring.

➤ No less than 3 and no more than 32 physical disks may be used with disk striping with parity.

➤ You mirror (or duplex) the volumes where system and boot files for Windows NT are stored (these are the Windows NT system and boot partitions, respectively).

➤ You cannot use disk striping (with or without parity) for Windows NT system and boot partitions.

➤ Because it relies on simple duplication, disk mirroring requires half the disk space for copies that might otherwise be used for data storage. The same is true for disk duplexing.

➤ Disk striping with parity uses **1/n** of the total disk space available to store parity information (where **n** is the number of partitions in the stripe set).

➤ If a disk stripe set with parity or a mirror set loses more than one physical drive, the entire set's data will be lost. If that happens, the set must be repaired, rebuilt, and the data restored from backup.

It's one thing to make sure that you have backed up your data for later recovery if warranted. The following section explains how to recover stored data.

Recovery

As long as the physical disk(s) that contain the system and boot partitions do not fail, recovery from disk failure is relatively simple. However, recovery without resort to a backup is only possible with a disk mirror, disk duplex, or stripe set with parity. All other partition structures offer no "live recovery" for the data they store. In addition, if the partition that contains Windows NT's system files fails, there are some special boot considerations that you need to address.

Fixing Broken Mirrors And Duplexes

When the original member of a disk mirror (or duplex) set fails, NT automatically uses the other member of the set to continue operation. But whenever a member of a mirror or duplex set fails, you must replace the failed member and reestablish the mirror. Otherwise, you will no longer benefit from the data protection. In fact, the NT Server will be unable to reboot at all if the original set member fails, because the BOOT.INI file points to that member (that's why it's necessary to hand-edit the ARC name in the boot file to point to the other member of the set to restart the system).

The first step in repairing a mirrored set is to break the mirror. This is accomplished in the Disk Administrator utility, using the Break Mirror option in the Fault Tolerance drop-down menu. Once the mirror is broken, you must assign the drive letter previously assigned to the set to the remaining member of the now broken mirror set. For example, if Drives 1 and 2 are mirrored and assigned drive letter D, and Drive 1 fails, you must break the mirrored set, and then assign drive letter D to Drive 2.

The second step is to replace the failed drive and create a partition on the new drive equal in size to the drive to be mirrored. Then, you must re-create the mirror by using the Establish Mirror option from the Fault Tolerance drop-down menu. (Note that his effectively switches the roles of the previous original and mirrored drives.) Once NT reboots, the mirror set will be rebuilt using the new member, but the original drive will now be Drive 2, based on the example in the preceding paragraph.

If the mirror set includes a boot partition and the drive that failed was the original member of the set, you must boot with a floppy to regain access to the system to run the Disk Administrator utility to repair the set. You must create an up-to-date boot floppy for the system so this process can work. That boot floppy should contain the following files:

➤ **BOOT.INI**

➤ **NTLDR**

➤ **NTDETECT.COM**

➤ **NTBOOTTDD.SYS** (only if you are using a SCSI controller with BIOS translation disabled or missing)

➤ **BOOTSECT.DOS** (only if you need to boot into MS-DOS or another operating system present on your system)

You may need to edit the BOOT.INI FILE to match new parameters and the new location of boot and system partitions. For further information, read the section titled "Special Boot Considerations" later in this chapter.

RAID Level 5: Disk Striping With Parity

Recovering from a device failure with disk striping with parity is easy. Once the device fails, the system is able to rebuild data on the fly from parity information stored on the still-operational devices. But because regeneration is CPU-intensive, performance slows dramatically. Even so, the system continues to operate, even with a failed set member.

 Once a set member fails, it's important to replace it quickly to restore fault tolerance and system performance levels to normal. First, fix the hardware by replacing or repairing the failed drive. Next, using Disk Administrator, create a new partition equal in size to the one that failed (skip this step if the original disk is brought back online without losing its partition structure). Select the stripe set and the partition that replaces the failed member (which could be the original partition if it wasn't destroyed). Then, select the Regenerate command from the Fault Tolerance drop-down menu. After NT reboots, the stripe set will be rebuilt by copying parity information to re-create the new member.

Special Boot Considerations

If the partition that contains Windows NT's system files fails, you will find where those mirrored system files are mapped in BOOT.INI, which uses ARC name syntax to map a path to the system files. This path designation starts by identifying the hard disk controller and finishes with the name of the folder that contains the Windows NT system files.

Here are a couple of examples of BOOT.INI entries:

```
multi(1)disk(0)rdisk(1)partition(2)\WINNT="Windows NT Server
Version 4.00"

scsi(0)disk(0)rdisk(0)partition(1)\WINNT="Windows NT Server
Version 4.00"
```

Should a boot or system partition fail, these entries may need to be changed, especially if the order, number, or configuration of your drives and partitions change, or if the Windows NT system files must be accessed from an alternate location (like the other member of a mirror or duplex set).

If the original drive in a mirror set fails and that drive was the boot partition, BOOT.INI on the mirror drive (which must now function as the boot partition) must be edited to reflect the new, correct location of these files. You might also edit the BOOT.INI file on a boot floppy to perform the same function, especially if you plan to restore the original drive quickly and return the system to its previous state.

BOOT.INI lives in the boot partition on your Windows NT machine, usually on the C drive. BOOT.INI is a text file that you can edit with any text editor. But BOOT.INI attributes are set as a system and read-only file. Therefore, you must turn off these attribute settings before you can edit the file. Then, you need to reset those attributes once your changes are complete. Here's an example of a BOOT.INI file:

```
[boot loader]
timeout=10
default=scsi(0)disk(0)rdisk(0)partition(1)\WINNT
[operating systems]
scsi(0)disk(0)rdisk(0)partition(1)\WINNT="Windows NT Server
Version 4.00"
```

```
scsi(0)disk(0)rdisk(0)partition(1)\WINNT="Windows NT Server Version
4.00 [VGA mode]" /basevideo /sos
C:\="MS-DOS 6.22"
```

To edit the BOOT.INI file properly, here are several things you must know about ARC names:

➤ To change the BOOT.INI file to point to the proper location, you must edit both the **default=** line and the main NOS line (which is **scsi(0)disk(0)rdisk(0)partition(1)\WINNT ="Windows NT Server Version 4.00"** in the preceding example). Both ARC names must match exactly.

➤ The first four elements of an ARC name are always lowercase in the BOOT.INI file.

➤ The first element in an ARC name is the controller type. This will be either **scsi** or **multi**. **scsi** indicates that a SCSI disk controller is being used that does not support BIOS translation. If **scsi** appears, it also means that a driver file named "NTBOOTDD.SYS" must appear in the system partition to handle BIOS translation for the controller. **multi** indicates any other controller type support BIOS translation, including IDE and SCSI, among others.

➤ The number immediately following **scsi** or **multi** identifies the position of the controller within the system, defined with ordinal numbers. Thus, the first controller is numbered zero, the second is one, and the third is two.

➤ The second element in an ARC name, **disk**, designates the device number for a SCSI controller with no BIOS translation abilities. But if **scsi** is the first element in the name, then the number that follows **disk** identifies the storage device, again, with ordinal numbers. Thus, the first device is also numbered zero, the second is one, and so on. If **multi** appears first in an ARC name, **disk** is ignored and will always be set to zero.

➤ The third element, **rdisk**, designates the device number for a BIOS translating SCSI controller, or for any other controller. **rdisk** always appears in any ARC name. But only if **multi** is its first element does the number following **rdisk** identify the storage device, numbered ordinally. Again, the first device is numbered zero, the second device is one, and so on. If **scsi** appears first in an ARC name, **rdisk** is ignored and is always set to zero.

➤ The fourth element in an ARC name identifies a disk partition. **partition** indicates the partition where system files
reside, numbered cardinally. Unlike the other terms, the first
partition is one, the second is two, the third is three, and so on.

➤ The fifth element in an ARC name is the name of the folder
where the system files reside. **\winnt** indicates that the
folder (or directory) on the specified partition named
"WINNT" is where system information can be found. Whatever the directory is named, this element must reflect the
exact name.

➤ The data following the folder name provides the information
that appears in the Windows NT Boot menu. The equal sign
and the quotes that enclose the text string must follow the
folder name without any additional spaces outside the
quotes.

➤ After the Boot menu name, additional command line
parameter switches may be added to control how Windows
NT boots. These switches include **/sos** and **/basevideo**. **/sos**
causes Windows NT to print the names of drivers to the
screen as they load during system boot. **/basevideo** puts
Windows NT into VGA Mode, which is useful when trouble
shooting video configuration problems.

One important item to remember for the exam is that Microsoft
reversed what you might expect the terms "boot partition" and
"system partition" to mean. As it happens, boot files are stored on
the system partition, where the default WINNT directory resides.
System files are stored on the boot partition—that is, the active
partition where BOOT.INI and NTLDR reside. When a question
requests the ARC name of a partition that contains boot files,
remember that these files reside on the system partition. We can
only guess at Microsoft's thinking—namely, that system files are
for low-level hardware initiation of the boot process, and thus
reside on the boot partition, and boot files supply bootup
intelligence for Windows NT itself, and therefore reside on the
system partition.

Just remember that it's the opposite of common sense, and you'll
do just fine.

Let's continue our discussion of securing data by taking a look at the backup
elements that are covered on the exam.

Windows NT Backup

The Server Enterprise exam does not focus on actually using the NT Backup utility. Rather, most backup-related questions pertain to maintaining data, protecting an entire network, and restoring damaged systems. If you are familiar with the NT Backup interface and the utility's capabilities, you'll be able to decipher the exam without a hitch.

> Using a backup to protect data is an additional fault tolerant feature of NT. Backups should be used in addition to BDCs and disk striping (or disk mirror/duplexing). Microsoft suggests that no less than three copies of critical data be maintained, with one copy being kept off-site. These copies can be two sets of backup tapes plus a drive duplication (or stripe set).
>
> Although NT Backup is included with NT Server and it has the ability to back up files over a network, it should not be used in a production environment. But for the test, it's all you've got to work with.

NT Backup can access data stored on both local and remote (networked) drives. Plus, it can copy the local system Registry. However, it cannot back up open files and remote Registries, and it cannot be scheduled.

If you'd like more information about NT Backup, you can consult the *Windows NT Resource Kit*, Microsoft TechNet, or the Administering Microsoft Windows NT 4 course material. Otherwise, you can scan the material in the Server Exam Cram if you are feeling rusty, but we doubt you'll need it.

Exam Prep Questions

Question 1

> Using free, unpartitioned space on a SCSI drive, you create a new partition. You highlight the free space, select Create from the Partition menu, specify the size of the partition, and click OK. Now, the new drive appears in the Disk Administrator display. What should you do next in your endeavor to create a new place to store data?
>
> ○ a. Assign a drive letter
>
> ○ b. Select Configuration|Save
>
> ○ c. Format
>
> ○ d. Use the Commit Changes Now command

It is not possible to assign a drive letter to a partition unless it is formatted. Therefore, answer a is incorrect. The Configuration|Save command stores the current configuration status as stored in the Registry to an Emergency Repair Disk. This is not a step toward creating a usable volume, so answer b is also incorrect. Formatting a partition to create a volume is required, but this cannot occur until partition creation changes are committed, making answer c incorrect as well. You must use the Commit Changes Now command to save the partition creation changes as your next step. Then, you can proceed to format the partition and assign it a drive letter. Therefore, answer d is correct.

Question 2

You have two IDE hard drives on a single drive controller in your Windows NT Server computer. There is only one partition on each of the two drives. The first drive's partition is formatted with FAT, and the second drive's partition is formatted with NTFS. The boot files are located on the second drive. What is the ARC name for the system partition?

- ○ a. multi(0)disk(1)rdisk(0)partition(1)
- ○ b. multi(0)disk(0)rdisk(1)partition(1)
- ○ c. multi(1)disk(0)rdisk(1)partition(1)
- ○ d. multi(0)disk(0)rdisk(1)partition(0)
- ○ e. multi(1)disk(0)rdisk(0)partition(1)

Answer a displays an improperly composed ARC name—when **multi** is used, the **disk(n)** number must be set to zero. Therefore, answer a is incorrect. Answer b indicates the first partition of the second hard drive on the first **multi** type drive controller. Because this is indeed the location of the system partition for this configuration, answer b is correct. Answer c points to a second drive controller that doesn't exist in this example. Consequently, answer c is incorrect. Answer d supplies an incorrect number for the partition element—namely, partitions are numbered cardinally, so a partition number can never be zero. Because the first partition is numbered one, answer d is incorrect. Answer e names a second, nonexistent drive controller, and points to the first drive on that controller. Because the system partition for this question is attached to the first (and only) disk controller on the second hard drive, answer e is incorrect.

Question 3

Your network is a single domain, but it connects four remote locations with the central office. What is the best plan of action to maintain reliable performance and user authentication? [Check all correct answers]

❏ a. Install a BDC at each location.

❏ b. Install four BDCs at the central office.

❏ c. Configure disk striping on the PDC machine to protect the SAM database.

❏ d. Initiate disk duplexing on the PDC to protect the SAM database.

❏ e. Perform regular backups of the PDC.

Installing a BDC at each location will improve performance and maintain a local copy of the SAM database. Therefore, answer a is correct. Installing four BDCs at the central office will protect the SAM, but it will not improve performance of the network because all authentication will still have to travel over the lengthy communication links. Therefore, answer b is incorrect. Disk striping will not provide fault tolerance, plus the SAM database is stored on the boot partition of the server and cannot be a member of a stripe set. Therefore, answer c is incorrect. Disk duplexing will create a duplicate of the SAM database and will not degrade performance. Therefore, answer d is correct. Performing regular backups will protect all data on the network. Therefore, answer e is correct. Thus, the correct answers are a, d, and e.

Question 4

> What is the best method for implementing fault tolerance on a Windows NT Server computer with two high-speed SCSI drives, each on a separate controller card?
>
> ○　a. Disk duplexing
>
> ○　b. Disk striping without parity
>
> ○　c. Disk mirroring
>
> ○　d. Create a volume set across both drives

Disk duplexing is the fault tolerance method that utilizes two drives, each on separate controllers. Therefore, answer a is correct. Disk striping without parity offers no fault tolerance, making answer b incorrect. Disk mirroring utilizes two drives on the same controller, making answer c incorrect as well. Finally, a volume set offers no fault tolerance, making answer d incorrect.

Question 5

> Which items below describe disk striping with parity? [Check all correct answers]
>
> ❑　a. Requires three physical drives.
>
> ❑　b. Can be implemented with FAT.
>
> ❑　c. Provides fault tolerance.
>
> ❑　d. Has faster read-write performance than disk mirroring.
>
> ❑　e. Data cannot be recovered if a single drive within the set fails.

Disk striping with parity requires a minimum of three physical drives, so answer a is correct. Disk striping with parity requires NTFS, not FAT, so answer b is incorrect. Because disk striping with parity is indeed a fault-tolerant storage method, answer c is also correct. Disk striping with parity offers better performance than disk mirroring because it spreads the load across more drives. Thus, answer d is correct as well. Disk striping with parity can recover from a single drive failure. Therefore, answer e is incorrect. This means the correct answers are a, c, and d.

Question 6

Which of the following ARC names indicates the third partition of the fourth SCSI drive on the second controller that has its BIOS disabled?

○ a. multi(1)disk(3)rdisk(0)partition(3)

○ b. multi(1)disk(0)rdisk(3)partition(3)

○ c. scsi(1)disk(3)rdisk(0)partition(3)

○ d. scsi(1)disk(3)rdisk(0)partition(4)

Answer a indicates a BIOS-enabled controller. Therefore, answer a is incorrect. Answer b indicates the same condition and is equally incorrect. Answer c indicates the third partition on the fourth drive on a non-BIOS SCSI controller, which means it's correct. Answer d is close, but indicates the fourth partition and is therefore incorrect.

Question 7

Which type of data should not be distributed via the replication service?

○ a. Logon scripts

○ b. User profiles

○ c. Relational database files

○ d. System policies

Logon scripts, user profiles, and system policies are the only files that should be distributed by the replication service. Therefore, answers a, b, and d are incorrect. Relational database files are often very large and would cause severe performance degradation to the network if their distribution was handled by the replication service. Therefore, answer c is correct.

Question 8

You want to implement fault tolerance on your Windows NT Server computer so your data will be protected in the event of a power failure or hardware malfunction. Which of the following techniques will provide you some type of fault tolerance? [Check all correct answers]

❑   a. RAID 1

❑   b. Disk duplexing

❑   c. Volume set

❑   d. Disk striping without parity

❑   e. RAID 5

RAID 1 indicates disk mirroring, which provides some fault tolerance. Therefore, answer a is correct. Disk duplexing is another fault tolerant storage method, so answer b is also correct. A volume set is not fault tolerant, making answer c incorrect. Likewise, disk striping without parity is not fault tolerant, so answer d is incorrect. RAID 5 is the same thing as disk striping with parity. Because this scheme provides fault tolerance, answer e is also correct. The complete set of correct answers to this question is a, b, and e.

Question 9

Your Windows NT Server computer has two physical disks. What forms of storage can be implemented with only two drives? [Check all correct answers]

❑   a. Disk striping with parity

❑   b. Disk mirroring

❑   c. Disk duplexing

❑   d. Volume set

❑   e. Disk striping without parity

Disk striping with parity requires a minimum of three drives, which makes answer a incorrect. Disk mirroring uses only two drives, but they must be on the same controller, so answer b is correct. Disk duplexing uses only two drives, but they must be on different controllers. Therefore, answer c is also correct. A volume set can consist of up to 32 partitions on any number of drives. Therefore, answer d is also correct. Disk striping without parity requires a minimum of two drives. Therefore, answer e is also correct.

Question 10

Where does the replication service place distributed files by default?

O a. \%winntroot%\System32\repl\Export of an import server

O b. \Program Files\Replication of an export server

O c. \%winntroot%\System32\repl\Import of an import server

O d. \%winntroot%\System32\repl\Export of an export server

The directory listed in answer a is not the default destination server on an import server. Therefore, answer a is incorrect. The directory listed in answer b is not the standard import directory on an import server. Therefore, answer b is incorrect. The directory list in answer c is the correct default destination directory on an import server. Therefore, answer c is correct. The directory listed in answer d is the export directory on an export server. This is where files are accessed for distribution. Therefore, answer d is incorrect.

Question 11

Which of the following drive sets supported by Windows NT Server can contain the system and/or boot partitions? [Check all correct answers]

❏ a. Disk mirroring

❏ b. Disk striping without parity

❏ c. Volume set

❏ d. Disk duplexing

Disk mirroring can contain system or boot partitions, or both, on the original disk. Therefore, answer a is correct. No kind of stripe set can contain either system or boot partitions, so disk striping without parity cannot contain the system or boot partitions. Of course, this means that answer b is incorrect. A volume set cannot contain either system or boot partitions, making answer c incorrect. Finally, disk duplexing can accommodate either the system or boot partitions, or both, on the original disk, so answer d is also correct. The complete set of correct answers to this question is a and d.

Question 12

What files should be placed on a boot disk in order to boot to the duplicate drive of a disk duplex from a floppy in the event of a failure of the original drive? Assume the drive controller is SCSI that does not support BIOS translation. [Check all correct answers]

❑   a. NTDETECT.COM

❑   b. BOOT.INI

❑   c. NTLDR

❑   d. WINA20.386

❑   e. NTBOOTDD.SYS

NTDETECT.COM is required on the boot floppy. Therefore, answer a is correct. BOOT.INI is required on the boot floppy, making answer b correct. NTLDR is required on the boot floppy. Therefore, answer c is also correct. WINA20.386 is a Windows device driver that is not needed on the boot floppy, so answer d is incorrect. NTBOOTDD.SYS is the driver for SCSI translation required for non-BIOS controllers, making answer e correct as well. The full set of correct answers to this question is a, b, c, and e.

Question 13

> Which of the following are valid steps in the process for implementing the replication service? [Check all correct answers]
>
> ❏ a. Watching the import directory to see files as they are deposited.
>
> ❏ b. Create a replication user account.
>
> ❏ c. Change the startup parameters of the replication service.
>
> ❏ d. Define export and import servers.
>
> ❏ e. Load the drivers for replication through Services tab of the Network application in Control Panel.

Answer a is not a step in the implementation process, plus it will prevent replication from occurring by locking the directory. Therefore, answer a is incorrect. Creating a replication user account is a required step for implementing replication. Therefore, answer b is correct. Modifying the startup parameters of the replication service through the Services application of Control Panel is a required step for implementing replication. Therefore, answer c is correct. Defining the servers and destinations for replication is a required step for implementing replication. Therefore, answer d is correct. The Network application is not involved with the implementation of the replication service. Therefore, answer e is incorrect. Thus, the correct answers are b, c, and d.

Question 14

The original disk of a disk mirror fails. The mirror did not contain the system or boot partitions. What are the steps required to restore the mirror set?

- ○ a. Replace the failed disk, reformat both drives, re-create a mirror set, and restore the data from a backup tape.
- ○ b. Replace the failed disk. Windows NT Server will automatically restore the mirror set.
- ○ c. Replace the failed disk, break the mirror set, and re-create the mirror set.
- ○ d. Replace the failed disk, select the mirror set and the replaced drive, and select Regenerate from the Fault Tolerance menu.

The steps in answer a cause you to perform many long and unnecessary steps—neither formatting the two drives nor restoring from tape backup is required. Therefore, answer a is incorrect. Windows NT will not automatically restore a mirror set, so answer b is also incorrect. The steps in answer c will properly restore a mirror set, with the roles of the drives reversed, making answer c correct. The steps in answer d are used to repair a stripe set with parity, so answer d is incorrect.

Question 15

You have a Windows NT Server where the system partition is the original drive of a disk duplex set. If your system partition fails, what modification should you make to a boot floppy to boot to the mirrored partition?

- ○ a. Add the **/MIRROR** switch to the default line of the BOOT.INI file.
- ○ b. Edit the ARC name in the BOOT.INI file to reflect the location of the mirrored partition.
- ○ c. A boot floppy is not needed.
- ○ d. Change the **PATH** statement in the AUTOEXEC.BAT.

The /**MIRROR** switch is not a valid command parameter, so answer a is incorrect. Editing the ARC name enables you to boot the mirrored partition. Thus, answer b is correct. A boot floppy is indeed required, so answer c is incorrect. There is no AUTOEXEC.BAT file on an NT boot floppy, making answer d incorrect.

Question 16

You add four new drives to your Windows NT Server computer of sizes 800, 600, 500, and 300 MB. You wish to establish a disk stripe set with parity. What is the total size of the largest set you can create using any or all of these drives?

○   a. 1,200 MB

○   b. 1,000 MB

○   c. 800 MB

○   d. 1,500 MB

1,200 MB would be the size of the set if you used all 4 drives with 300 MB on each one. Because this is not the largest possible sum using this set of drives, answer a is incorrect. 1,000 MB is indeed the amount of data that could be stored on the largest set created from these drives, but the question requested the total size of the set, making answer b incorrect. Likewise, although 800 MB represents the size of the largest individual drive, you must use three drives to create a disk stripe set with parity. Therefore, answer c is incorrect. As it happens, 1,500 MB is the total size of the largest set that may be created from these drives, using only the 800, 600, and 500 MB drives, making answer d the correct reply.

Question 17

Windows NT Server is a fault tolerant network operating system.
Which of the following are features of NT that support fault tolerance and data redundancy? [Check all correct answers]

❑   a. Disk striping

❑   b. Software RAID

❑   c. Symmetric multiprocessing

❑   d. NTFS hot-fixing

❑   e. NT Backup

❑   f. TCP/IP protocol

❑   g. BDCs

Disk striping is not a fault tolerant disk structure. Therefore, answer a is
incorrect. Software RAID provides fault tolerance and data redundancy; however, only for RAID 1 and 5. Therefore, answer b is correct. Symmetric multiprocessing is a feature of NT, but it is not related to fault tolerance. Therefore, answer c is incorrect. NTFS hot-fixing is a realtime automatic fault
tolerant feature of the file system that is hidden from applications. Therefore,
answer d is correct. NT Backup, although not useful for large networks, is a
fault tolerant feature of NT. Therefore, answer e is correct. The TCP/IP
protocol enables NT to support almost every computer platform in existence
as a client, but it is not related to fault tolerance. Therefore, answer f is incorrect. BDCs protect the SAM database by duplicating the PDC. Therefore,
answer g is correct. Thus, the correct answers are b, d, e, and g.

Question 18

If you do not care about fault tolerance, what is the best method
to maximize your data storage space on your Windows NT Server
computer?

○   a. Disk mirroring

○   b. Disk striping with parity

○   c. Volume set

○   d. Disk stacking

Disk mirroring cuts storage capacity in half to implement fault tolerance, making answer a incorrect. Disk striping with parity reduces storage capacity by one full partition to implement fault tolerance, making answer b incorrect. A volume set maximizes storage capacity and allows you to add additional space as needed, making answer c correct. Disk stacking is not a valid Windows NT storage technology, so d is incorrect.

Need To Know More?

 Donald, Lisa and James Chellis: *MSCE: NT Server 4 In The Enterprise Study Guide*. Sybex Network Press, San Francisco, CA, 1997. ISBN 0-7821-1970-0. Chapter 1 discusses domain controllers. Chapter 7 looks into directory replication through the Server Manager. Chapter 17 breezes through the disk fault tolerant features of NT.

 Heywood, Drew: *Inside Windows NT Server*. New Riders, Indianapolis, IN, 1995. ISBN 1-56205-472-4. Chapter 10 discusses fault tolerance issues, implementation tips, and troubleshooting techniques for storage under Windows NT Server. Chapters 2 and 3 discuss PDC and BDC issues. Chapter 11 looks at the backup utility of NT. And Chapter 15 examines directory replication.

 Siyan, Karanjit S: *Windows NT Server 4 Professional Reference*. New Riders, Indianapolis, IN, 1996. ISBN 1-56205-731-6. Chapter 9 has extensive coverage of NT's storage capabilities and fault tolerant features. Chapters 5 and 6 look into domain controllers and the directory replication service. Chapter 20 looks into NT Backup and the other data protection schemes of NT.

 The Windows NT Server 4 manuals cover planning, configuration, and installation issues quite well. The *Concepts And Planning Manual* contains useful fault tolerance, domain controller, directory replication, and backup issue discussions.

 The Windows NT Server Resource Kit contains a lot of useful information about Windows NT's fault tolerance. The TechNet CD (or its online version through www.microsoft .com) can be searched using keywords like "fault tolerance," "replication," "domain controller," and "backup." In the *Resource Guide* volume, Chapter 3, "Disk Management Basics," Chapter 4, "Planning A Reliable Configuration," and Chapter 5, "Preparing For And Performing Recovery," contain

useful background, implementation, and reference information on NT's fault tolerance features. The *Networking Guide*
Chapter 5, "Network Services—Enterprise Level," contains
a great discussion of the replication service, and Chapter 2,
"Network Security And Domain Planning," contains information about domain controllers.

Auditing Resources And Access

Terms you'll need to understand:

√   Auditing

√   Account policies

√   User rights

Techniques you'll need to master:

√   Enabling auditing through User Manager For Domains

√   Using audit information

√   Establishing policies through User Manager For Domains

√   Managing user rights through policies

The auditing capabilities of Windows NT Server are part of the overall security system. Auditing, account (and password) policies, and user rights, are all part of the security policies of NT. In this chapter, we take a look at auditing. Account policies are covered in more detail for the Server exam, but they are briefly repeated at the end of this chapter. User rights are discussed in Chapter 4 of this book.

Auditing

On a computer running Windows NT, the administrator has the option to audit access to resources such as directories, printers, and shares. The audit will inform the administrator if someone attempts to access secured resources or just how often a particular resource is accessed. The information gathered by NT's auditing system can be brought to bear against performance problems, security risks, and expansion planning.

Enabling Auditing

The auditing system is designed to watch every event occurrence on your entire network. To simplify the act of fine-tuning the areas you wish to audit, there are three levels of switches with which you'll need to work. The master switch is the Audit These Events radio button located on the Audit Policy dialog box (see Figure 7.1). This dialog box is accessed through the User Manager For Domains' Policies pull-down menu.

This master switch turns on or off NT's entire audit system. By default, this switch is set to Do Not Audit.

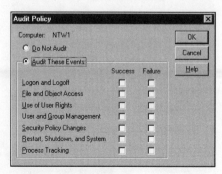

Figure 7.1   The Audit Policy dialog box.

The second level of switches becomes available when you set the master switch. There are seven event types listed in the Audit Policy dialog box. Each of these event types can be audited by tracking its success and/or failure. Here are the seven event types and descriptions of the events they control:

➤ **Logon And Logoff** Tracks logons, logoffs, and network connections.

➤ **File And Object Access** Tracks access to files, directories, and other NTFS objects. This includes printers.

➤ **Use Of User Rights** Tracks when users make use of user rights.

➤ **User And Group Management** Tracks changes in the accounts of users and groups (password changes, account deletions, group memberships, renaming, and so forth).

➤ **Security Policy Changes** Tracks changes of user rights, audit policies, and trusts.

➤ **Restart, Shutdown, And System** Tracks server shutdown and restarts, also logs events affecting system security.

➤ **Process Tracking** Tracks program activation, program termination, and other object/process access.

The third level of audit switches is on the object level. This level of control only applies to File And Object Access events. These switches reside within the properties of each NTFS-based object, such as files, directories, and printers. Figures 7.2 through 7.4 show the Audit switch screens for file, directory, and print access. Note the differences in the tracking events among the object types. Both the file and directory have Read, Write, Execute, Delete, Change Permissions, and Take Ownership. But the printer object has Print, Full Control, Delete, Change Permissions, and Take Ownership.

A second, important difference to notice is on the directory object. The directory object allows you to change the files and/or subdirectories within the current directory to the same audit settings. Although this is convenient, you should use it with caution, because any current audit settings on these objects will be cleared and replaced with the new settings.

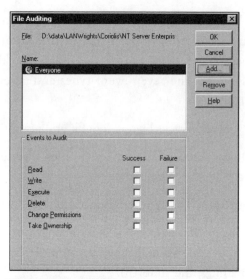

Figure 7.2   The File Auditing dialog box.

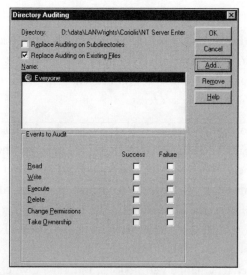

Figure 7.3   The Directory Auditing dialog box.

To get to these dialog boxes, right-click over the object, select Properties from the pop-up menu, select the Security tab, then click the Auditing button. Remember, object auditing is only available to NTFS objects, not FAT objects.

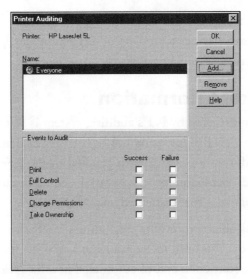

Figure 7.4   The Printer Auditing dialog box.

Note: By default, the object level audit switches are all blank with no users or groups present in the Name field. We added the Everyone group before taking these images so the Events list at the bottom of these dialog boxes would become readable instead of their default near-invisible gray.

The object level audit dialog boxes allow you to set the same success/failure event tracking for all users and groups listed in the Name field. You cannot track success for one group and failure for another.

Let's repeat the steps required to audit:

1. Turn on the master Audit These Events switch.

2. Select one or more of the event types to track success or failure.

3. If you choose the File And Object Access option, you must also edit the auditing settings for each NTFS object.

Auditing Overhead

The activity of auditing system events demands large amounts of computing overhead, especially if the event monitored occurs often, such as file access. It is not recommended to audit any event or object more than is absolutely necessary to track a problem or test equipment. Otherwise, your system will experience overall performance degradation.

Using Audit Information

The information gathered by NT's auditing system is stored in the Security log. You can view this log using the Event Viewer. The Event Viewer lists detailed information about each tracked event. Some of the data recorded includes user logon identification, the computer used, time, date, and the action or event that instigated an audit.

When numerous objects or events are audited, the Security log can grow large quite quickly. You need to monitor the size of this log and possibly implement a size restriction and/or automated new file creation to prevent data loss and maximize the usefulness of the gathered data.

This concludes our discussion of auditing in Windows NT. Let's now discuss how to control access through the use of Policies.

Account Policy

You really don't need to know a whole lot about the account policies for the Enterprise exam, but you do need to be familiar with what is possible with this feature. If you need more details than what we include here, please consult the NT Server manuals, the *Resource Kit*, or the Server *Exam Cram* book.

The account policy is set through the Policy menu of the User Manager For Domains. The Account Policy dialog box (see Figure 7.5) is divided into two main sections: Password Restrictions and Account Lockout.

You can use the Account Policy dialog box to set the following parameters:

➤ Maximum and minimum password age

➤ Password length

➤ Password uniqueness

➤ Account lockout after specified failed attempts

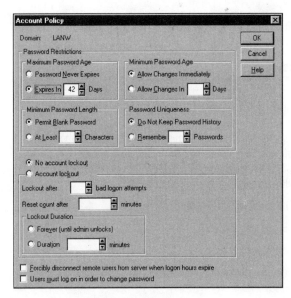

Figure 7.5   The Account Policy dialog box.

➤ Failed counter reset

➤ Lockout duration

➤ Force users off when hours expire

➤ Require logon before password change

That's all you need to know regarding account policies for this exam.

Exam Prep Questions

Question 1

You suspect that an Account group member is accessing a directory that the user should be prevented from reaching. This might mean that you've set up the group memberships incorrectly. You aren't sure who it is, but you do know what directory is being accessed. What feature of NT will let you track who gains access to this directory?

○   a. NTFS file activity logging

○   b. Event auditing

○   c. Event Viewer

○   d. Account lockout

The NTFS file activity logging is a fault tolerance feature used to ensure the integrity of stored data. It cannot be used to track access. Therefore, answer a is incorrect. Event auditing will track the activity around any object within NT. Therefore, answer b is correct. The Event Viewer is used to review the Security log created by the auditing system, but it is not the feature that does the actual tracking. Therefore, answer c is incorrect. Account lockout is the feature used to prevent compromised accounts from being used. Therefore, answer d is incorrect.

Question 2

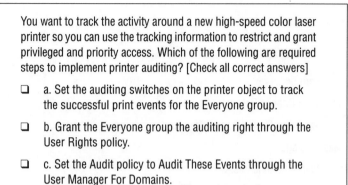

You want to track the activity around a new high-speed color laser printer so you can use the tracking information to restrict and grant privileged and priority access. Which of the following are required steps to implement printer auditing? [Check all correct answers]

❏   a. Set the auditing switches on the printer object to track the successful print events for the Everyone group.

❏   b. Grant the Everyone group the auditing right through the User Rights policy.

❏   c. Set the Audit policy to Audit These Events through the User Manager For Domains.

❏   d. Set the audit switch of File And Object Access to Success under Audit These Events.

❏   e. Set the priority of the printer to 99 (maximum) under the Scheduling tab on the printer's Properties dialog box.

Setting the auditing switches on the object is required to enable printer tracking. Therefore, answer a is correct. There is not an auditing right for users. Therefore, answer b is incorrect. Setting the master auditing switch to Audit These Events is required to track printer access. Therefore, answer c is correct. Setting the event type switch of File And Object Access to Success is required to track printer usage. Therefore, answer d is correct. Setting a printer's priority has nothing to do with tracking access. Therefore, answer e is incorrect.

Question 3

> Which of the following settings cannot be managed through the account policy? [Check all correct answers]
>
> ❑   a. Password length
>
> ❑   b. Password history
>
> ❑   c. User Must Change Password At Next Logon
>
> ❑   d. User Must Log On To Change Password
>
> ❑   e. Password age
>
> ❑   f. User Cannot Change Password

Password length, history, age, and User Must Log On To Change Password are all set by using the account policy. Thus, answers a, b, d, and e are incorrect. User Must Change Password At Next Logon and User Cannot Change Password are settings of the user account through the Properties dialog box of each account. Therefore, answers c and f are correct.

Question 4

> An important new custom application is conflicting with an existing utility. The conflict seems to cause both programs to terminate prematurely. Which audit event type should be tracked to record some information about the conflict and which programs are affected?
>
> ○   a. File And Object Access
>
> ○   b. Security Policy Changes
>
> ○   c. Restart, Shutdown, And System
>
> ○   d. Process Tracking
>
> ○   e. Application Activity

File And Object Access is for tracking NTFS objects, such as files and printers. Therefore, answer a is incorrect. Security Policy Changes tracks modifications to security and policies. Therefore, answer b is incorrect. Restart, Shutdown, And System tracks system restarts. Therefore, answer c is incorrect. Process Tracking tracks threads and process (e.g., applications). Therefore, answer d is correct. Application Activity is not a valid selection. Therefore, answer e is incorrect.

Need To Know More?

 Donald, Lisa and James Chellis: *MSCE: NT Server 4 In The Enterprise Study Guide*. Sybex Network Press, San Francisco, CA, 1997. ISBN 0-7821-1970-0. Brief file auditing information is listed on pages 129 through 132 of Chapter 4, and print auditing is on page 226 of Chapter 8. The account policy is discussed in Chapter 3 on pages 91 through 95.

 Heywood, Drew: *Inside Windows NT Server*. New Riders, Indianapolis, IN, 1995. ISBN 1-56205-472-4. Chapter 12 contains information on the auditing features of NT. Chapter 4 also has a discussion of the Account policy.

 Siyan, Karanjit S: *Windows NT Server 4 Professional Reference*. New Riders, Indianapolis, IN, 1996. ISBN 1-56205-731-6. Chapter 9 covers auditing as part of the NT security system. Pages 273 through 275 list the account policy features.

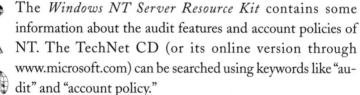 The *Windows NT Server Resource Kit* contains some information about the audit features and account policies of NT. The TechNet CD (or its online version through www.microsoft.com) can be searched using keywords like "audit" and "account policy."

Network Protocols, Routing, And Relaying

8

Terms you'll need to understand:

√ Protocols

√ Network Basic Input/Output System (NetBIOS)

√ NetBIOS Extended User Interface (NetBEUI)

√ Transmission Control Protocol/ Internet Protocol (TCP/IP)

√ Simple Network Management Protocol (SNMP)

√ Dynamic Host Configuration Protocol (DHCP)

√ Windows Internet Name Service (WINS)

√ Domain Name Service (DNS)

√ Serial Line Internet Protocol (SLIP)

√ Point-To-Point Protocol (PPP)

√ Point-To-Point Tunneling Protocol (PPTP)

√ File Transfer Protocol (FTP)

√ Hypertext Transfer Protocol (HTTP)

√ NWLink Internetwork Packet Exchange/Sequenced Packet Exchange (IPX/SPX)

√ Client Service For NetWare (CSNW)

√ Gateway Service For NetWare (GSNW)

√ File And Print Services For NetWare (FPNW)

√ Frame types

√ Data Link Control (DLC)

√ AppleTalk

√ Protocol bindings

√ Multiprotocol Router (MPR)

√ RIP (Routing Information Protocol)

√ BOOTP Relay Agent

√ DHCP Relay Agent

Techniques you'll need to master:

√ Installing and configuring network protocols

√ Familiarization with services associated with certain protocols

√ Establishing a protocol binding order

√ Manually adjusting the Ethernet frame type

To enable communications on a computer network, you must tell NT how it's supposed to "talk" to other computers and peripheral devices. In the networking world, this is established through the use of protocols. Basically, a protocol is an agreed upon set of standards that defines how computers communicate. In this chapter, we explain the protocols available with Windows NT Server, when to use which protocol, and the properties of each protocol. We also discuss the connectivity and routing features of NT, including RIP and the DHCP Relay Agent. In keeping with the tone of this book, we only cover the details of what you need to know to pass the networking portion of the Enterprise exam. We do, however, provide pointers to additional resources for this topic.

Built-In Windows NT Protocols

Windows NT Server comes with a number of protocols. The following list presents the available protocols:

- ➤ Network Basic Input/Output System (NetBIOS)
- ➤ NetBIOS Extended User Interface (NetBEUI)
- ➤ Transmission Control Protocol/Internet Protocol (TCP/IP)
- ➤ NWLink Internetwork Packet Exchange/Sequenced Packet Exchange (IPX/SPX)
- ➤ Data Link Control (DLC)
- ➤ AppleTalk

In the upcoming sections, we'll define and explain these protocols and their uses.

NetBIOS

NetBIOS was originally developed by IBM in the 1980s, and it provides the underlying communication mechanism for some basic NT functions, such as browsing and interprocess communications between network servers. NetBIOS is an extremely fast protocol that requires very little communications overhead, which is why it's used by NT for basic operations. Unfortunately, it is not a routable protocol; therefore, it cannot be used as the primary protocol for networks that need routing capabilities.

NetBEUI

NetBEUI is a simple network layer transport protocol that was developed to support NetBIOS networks. Like NetBIOS, NetBEUI is not routable, so it really has no place on an enterprise network. NetBEUI is the fastest transport protocol available to NT. It's great for fast transmission, but it is not usable across routed networks. Benefits of NetBEUI include its speed, good error protection, easy implementation, and small memory overhead. Disadvantages include the fact that it is not routable, has very little support for cross-platform applications, and has very few troubleshooting tools available.

NetBEUI should be selected only when your network is small. NetBEUI is not a useful choice for networks that require routing or involve WAN links.

TCP/IP

TCP/IP is the most widely used protocol in networking today. This is due in part to the vast growth of the global Internet. TCP/IP is the most flexible of the transport protocols and is able to span wide areas. In addition, it has excellent cross-platform support, routing capabilities, and support for the Simple Network Management Protocol (SNMP), Dynamic Host Configuration Protocol (DHCP), Windows Internet Name Service (WINS), Domain Name Service (DNS), and a host of other useful protocols (which we discuss later in this chapter, in the section titled "TCP/IP Connectivity Issues").

TCP/IP can be used in any networking situation; however, it is not recommended for small networks due to its overhead. It can support large heterogeneous networks, but it requires a significant amount of configuration.

NWLink (IPX/SPX)

NWLink is Microsoft's "clean room" implementation of Novell's IPX/SPX protocol suite for NetWare networks. This protocol is included with NT to enable communication with NetWare servers. With NWLink enabled, NT clients can access resources located on a NetWare server, and vice versa.

Put simply, Windows NT server requires NWLink to be installed to enable communications with NetWare clients and servers. In addition, the File And Print Service For NetWare is also required for NetWare clients and servers to access NT files and printers. The Client Service For NetWare (CSNW) is designed for Windows NT workstations that require a direct link to NetWare servers. The Gateway Service For NetWare (GSNW) lets Windows NT servers map a drive to a NetWare server, which provides access to NetWare server resources for Windows NT workstations (via a gateway). We cover additional details for NWLink later in this chapter, in the section titled "NWLink Connectivity Issues."

NWLink should be used on networks that require NetWare connectivity or on networks that need routing capabilities but can't support the overhead of TCP/IP.

DLC

Windows NT uses the Data Link Control (DLC) protocol primarily for connectivity to SNA (Systems Network Architecture) gateways, and, more importantly, for connecting to network-attached printers, such as JetDirect cards by Hewlett-Packard. This is detailed more in Chapter 13, "Advanced Printing Topics."

AppleTalk

It should come as no surprise that the AppleTalk protocol is used for communication with Macintosh computers. By enabling AppleTalk, you allow Mac clients to store and access files located on an NT Server, print to NT printers, and vice versa. An item of note: You must first install the NT Services For Macintosh before you can install AppleTalk. Also, Mac support is only available from NTFS partitions.

Connectivity Issues

There are a couple of protocols—namely, IPX/SPX and TCP/IP—that must have special settings changed for them to work properly. The following sections detail these issues, with an eye toward the Enterprise exam.

NWLink Connectivity Issues

As mentioned earlier in this chapter, NWLink is IPX for Windows NT— IPX is the protocol, and NWLink is the networking component that provides the protocol. NWLink is provided for connectivity to NetWare networks to allow NetWare clients to access NT servers, as well as to allow NT clients to access NetWare servers. It is important to note, however, that NWLink by itself does not enable this type of communication. You must first install the Client Service For NetWare and the Gateway Service For NetWare. Basically, CSNW is a redirector, whereas GSNW is what makes file and print sharing on NetWare servers available to Microsoft clients.

IPX has a number of benefits: It supports routing between networks, it's faster than TCP/IP, and it's easy to install and maintain. Unfortunately, IPX doesn't have a sufficient central addressing scheme to prohibit multiple networks from making use of identical addresses, and it doesn't support the Simple Network Management Protocol (SNMP).

Installing NWLink

Installing the NWLink protocol is much like installing other protocols in Windows NT. There are, however, some special issues that must be dealt with. To install NWLink, perform the following steps:

1. Open the Control Panel (Start|Settings|Control Panel).

2. Double-click the Network icon.

3. Click on the Protocols tab in the Network dialog box.

4. Click the Add button.

5. Select NWLink IPX/SPX Compatible Transport from the list of available protocols.

6. Enter the path to the Windows NT Server installation CD in the Path field of the setup dialog box, then click Continue. If you have installed NT's Remote Access Service (RAS), NT will ask if you want to bind NWLink to RAS. Either click OK to enable binding or click Cancel to not enable binding.

7. Click the Close button, then click Yes when NT asks whether to restart computer.

In most cases, it's fine to leave the default frame type (auto) as is; however, some Ethernet adapters don't work well with this setting. For new installations, it's recommended that you set this to the Ethernet 802.2 setting.

Changing The Ethernet Setting

To change the Ethernet frame type and IPX network number, perform the following steps:

1. Open the Control Panel (Start|Settings|Control Panel).

2. Double-click the Network icon.

3. Click the Protocols tab in the Network dialog box.

4. Double-click NWLink IPX/SPX Compatible Transport from the list of available protocols.

5. Click the Manual Frame Type Detection button.

6. Click the Add button.

7. Select your preferred frame type.

8. Enter the IPX network number for the adapter in the Network Number field.

9. Click the Add button.

10. Repeat Steps 7 through 9 for each frame type.

11. Click OK, then click the Close button.

12. Click Yes when asked to restart the computer.

There are more issues to consider when establishing communications between NT and NetWare networks. These details are covered in Chapter 12, "Advanced NetWare Topics."

TCP/IP Connectivity Issues

As previously mentioned, TCP/IP is currently the most-used networking protocol as well as the standard protocol of the Internet. The beauty of the TCP/IP protocol suite lies in its ability to link many disparate kinds of computers and peripheral devices. Using this protocol stack, you enable most TCP/IP clients to access NT-based resources, and vice versa.

Windows NT provides for a number of useful TCP/IP services. Included are the following:

➤ **Dynamic Host Configuration Protocol (DHCP)** This service enables the assignment of dynamic TCP/IP network addresses, based on a specified pool of available addresses. When a network client configured for DHCP logs on to the network, the DHCP service assigns the next available TCP/IP address for that network session. This really simplifies address administration.

➤ **Windows Internet Name Service (WINS)** This service enables the resolution of network names to IP addresses (similar to the Unix DNS). This way, you don't have to remember the IP address of the client with which you are trying to communicate. You can enter the network name, and NT does the rest. Also, if a TCP/IP-based network does not have a WINS server, then each time one computer tries to access another, it must send a b-node broadcast, which creates a lot of unnecessary network traffic and can bring a busy network to a crawl. WINS servers provide computer-name-to-IP address resolution, thereby reducing broadcast messages and improving network performance.

➤ **Serial Line Internet Protocol (SLIP)** SLIP was originally developed for the Unix environment and is still widely used among Internet providers. Although SLIP provides good performance with little systemoverhead requirements, it does not support error checking, flow control, or security features. SLIP is good for connecting to Unix hosts or Internet providers. While this protocol has its uses, it is quickly being replaced by PPP.

➤ **Point-To-Point Protocol (PPP)** PPP addresses many of the insufficiencies of SLIP, such as providing the ability to encrypt logons and supporting additional transport protocols, error checking, and recovery. In addition, PPP is optimized for low-bandwidth connections and, in general, is a more efficient protocol than SLIP.

➤ **Point-To-Point Tunneling Protocol (PPTP)** PPTP is a protocol that creates secure connections between private networks over the Internet. Benefits of PPTP include lower administrative, transmission, and hardware costs than other solutions for this type of connectivity. By taking advantage of the Internet, PPTP drastically reduces costs in these areas.

➤ **World Wide Web (WWW)** This service comes as a part of NT Server 4 and has the ability to publish Web pages, whether for an Internet based Web site or an intranet.

➤ **File Transfer Protocol (FTP)** This protocol is great for the fast transfers of files to and from a local hard drive to an FTP server located elsewhere on another TCP/IP-based network (such as the Internet).

➤ **Gopher** This service serves text and links to other Gopher sites. Gopher predates HTTP (the Web protocol) but has become obsolete (because of HTTP).

➤ **Hypertext Transfer Protocol (HTTP)** This is the World Wide Web protocol that allows for the transfer of HTML documents over the Internet or intranets, which responds to actions like a user clicking on hypertext links.

Installing TCP/IP

There are a few items you need to have on hand when you install TCP/IP. The following list describes these items:

➤ **Your server's (Class C) IP address** This is the unique address that identifies your computer on a TCP/IP network. This number consists of four numbers separated by periods (e.g., 125.115.125.48). The first three numbers identify the network on which the computer is located; the remaining number identifies your computer on that network.

➤ **Your network's subnet masks for each network adapter on the net work** The subnet mask is a number mathematically applied to the IP address to determine which IP addresses are a part of the same sub network as the computer applying the subnet mask.

➤ **Your server's default gateway** The gateway is the computer that serves as a router, a format translator, or a security filter for a network.

▶ **The domain name server for the network** This is a computer that serves as an Internet host, which performs translation of fully qualified domain names into IP addresses.

▶ **Any DHCP and WINS information about your network** If you already have these services configured, the process of configuring TCP IP is greatly eased.

If you did not install TCP/IP upon the initial installation of Windows NT Server, you must perform the following steps to install and configure this protocol suite:

1. Open the Control Panel (Start|Settings|Control Panel).

2. Double-click the Network icon.

3. In the Network window, click the Protocols tab.

4. Click the Add button.

5. Select TCP/IP from the list of available protocols. NT may request the installation CD or the location of the installation files.

6. In the Network window, click the Close button.

7. Either enter the TCP/IP address of the computer or select Obtain An IP Address From A DHCP Server, whichever is appropriate for the installation. Then, specify the subnet mask and default gateway.

8. If your network has a DNS server or a constant Internet connection, click the DNS tab, and enter the DNS address.

9. If your network has a WINS server, click the WINS tab, and enter the WINS address.

10. Click OK to close the TCP/IP Properties dialog box. If you did not specify a primary WINS address, NT will display a warning.

11. Click the Close button.

12. Click Yes when NT asks to restart the computer.

This concludes the installation process for the TCP/IP protocol suite. Now, let's take a look at some of the TCP/IP utilities.

TCP/IP Utilities

The Windows NT version of TCP/IP is bundled with many useful command-line utilities to aid in the configuration and administration of a TCP/IP-based network. Here is a list of those utilities, a brief description, and the syntax (obtained by the /? parameter):

➤ **arp** Address Resolution Protocol. The **arp** utiliity displays the IP address mapped to a MAC node address. (See Figure 8.1.)

➤ **hostname** Displays the name of the current computer host.

➤ **ipconfig** Displays IP configuration details. (See Figure 8.2.)

➤ **lpq** Displays the status of a print queue only on a computer running DLC.

➤ **nbtstat** Displays NetBIOS of TCP/IP status. (See Figure 8.3.)

➤ **netstat** Displays TCP/IP status and statistics. (See Figure 8.4.)

➤ **ping** Provides a means to test and verify network connections.

➤ **route** Interacts with routing tables. (For syntax details, see the section titled "Routing And IP RIP," later in this chapter.)

➤ **tracert** Details the route used by TCP/IP.

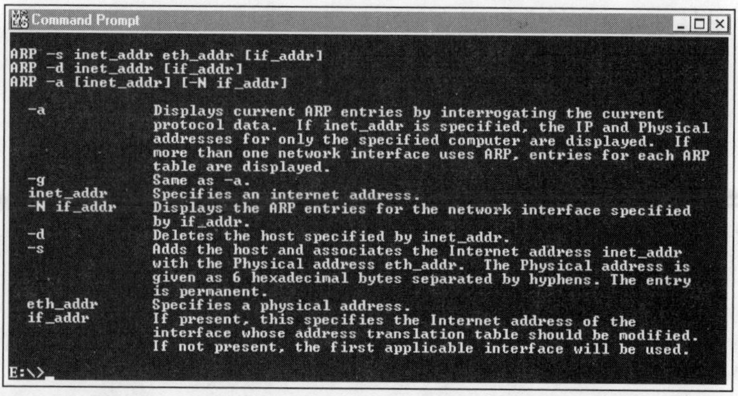

Figure 8.1 The syntax of **arp**.

```
Command Prompt                                                    _ □ ×
E:\>ipconfig /?

Windows NT IP Configuration

usage: ipconfig [/? ¦ /all ¦ /release [adapter] ¦ /renew [adapter]]

       /?         Display this help message.
       /all       Display full configuration information.
       /release   Release the IP address for the specified adapter.
       /renew     Renew the IP address for the specified adapter.

The default is to display only the IP address, subnet mask and default gateway
for each adapter bound to TCP/IP.

For Release and Renew, if no adapter name is specified, then the IP address
leases for all adapters bound to TCP/IP will be released or renewed.

E:\>
```

Figure 8.2   The syntax of **ipconfig**.

```
Command Prompt                                                    _ □ ×
Displays protocol statistics and current TCP/IP connections using NBT
(NetBIOS over TCP/IP).

NBTSTAT [-a RemoteName] [-A IP address] [-c] [-n]
        [-r] [-R] [-s] [-S] [interval] ]

   -a   (adapter status) Lists the remote machine's name table given its name
   -A   (Adapter status) Lists the remote machine's name table given its
                         IP address.
   -c   (cache)    Lists the remote name cache including the IP addresses
   -n   (names)    Lists local NetBIOS names.
   -r   (resolved) Lists names resolved by broadcast and via WINS
   -R   (Reload)   Purges and reloads the remote cache name table
   -S   (Sessions) Lists sessions table with the destination IP addresses
   -s   (sessions) Lists sessions table converting destination IP
                   addresses to host names via the hosts file.

   RemoteName   Remote host machine name.
   IP address   Dotted decimal representation of the IP address.
   interval     Redisplays selected statistics, pausing interval seconds
                between each display. Press Ctrl+C to stop redisplaying
                statistics.

E:\>
```

Figure 8.3   The syntax of **nbtstat**.

```
Command Prompt                                                    _ □ ×
E:\>netstat /?

Displays protocol statistics and current TCP/IP network connections.

NETSTAT [-a] [-e] [-n] [-s] [-p proto] [-r] [interval]

   -a         Displays all connections and listening ports. (Server-side
              connections are normally not shown).
   -e         Displays Ethernet statistics. This may be combined with the -s
              option.
   -n         Displays addresses and port numbers in numerical form.
   -p proto   Shows connections for the protocol specified by proto; proto
              may be tcp or udp. If used with the -s option to display
              per-protocol statistics, proto may be tcp, udp, or ip.
   -r         Displays the contents of the routing table.
   -s         Displays per-protocol statistics. By default, statistics are
              shown for TCP, UDP and IP; the -p option may be used to specify
              a subset of the default.
   interval   Redisplays selected statistics, pausing interval seconds
              between each display. Press CTRL+C to stop redisplaying
              statistics. If omitted, netstat will print the current
              configuration information once.

E:\>
```

Figure 8.4   The syntax of **netstat**.

A cursory knowledge and awareness of these utilities will suffice for the exam. The exact details of syntax are not required knowledge but may help you understand the information these utilities display and modify.

NetBEUI Connectivity Issues

NetBEUI is a common protocol for small networks. Here, we'll step through the installation of NetBEUI as a network protocol.

Installing NetBEUI

NetBEUI is by far the easiest protocol to install and configure on an NT network. To install this protocol, perform the following steps:

1. Open the Control Panel (Start|Settings|Control Panel).

2. Double-click the Network icon.

3. In the Network window, click the Protocols tab.

4. Click the Add button.

5. Select NetBEUI from the list of available protocols, and click OK.

6. Enter the path to the installation CD or the location of the installation files.

7. If you have RAS installed, NT asks if you want to support it with this protocol. Click Cancel to leave it unsupported.

8. In the Network window, click the Close button.

9. Select Yes when NT asks to restart the computer.

That's it for the installation of NetBEUI.

Now that we have discussed the common networking protocols and their special requirements, let's move on to discuss a few general protocol principles. This discussion includes issues such as protocol bindings and routing.

Protocol Bindings

Protocol binding is the process NT uses to link network components from various levels of a network architecture to enable communication among the components. To set the binding order for network protocols, double-click the Network icon in Control Panel, and click the Binding tab. This is where the bindings of installed network components are listed, in order of upper-layer services and protocols to lower-layer network adapter drivers.

Binding should be ordered to enhance a system's use of the network. As an example, if your network has both TCP/IP and NetBEUI installed, and most network devices use TCP/IP, workstation bindings should be set to bind TCP/IP first and NetBEUI second. In other words, the most frequently used protocol should be bound first. This speeds network connections. Servers use whatever protocol is sent to them by each workstation, so the binding order only needs to be changed on the workstations. Network speed is affected by the binding order on the workstations, but not on the servers.

Routing With Windows NT

It is rare for a network to remain isolated. More often than not, multiple networks are aggregated to improve communication and share resources, such as files, applications, and hardware. Microsoft designed Windows NT Server 4 to act as a router to simplify the interconnection of multiple networks. The Multiprotocol Router (MPR) is a service that can dynamically route traffic between different subnets over IPX and TCP/IP. However, to use MPR, the server must have two or more NICs installed and configured in such a way that each NIC is part of a different subnet. In other words, a server must be "multihomed" to implement MPR.

MPR is comprised of:

➤ RIP (Routing Information Protocol) For TCP/IP (a.k.a. IP RIP)

➤ RIP For IPX

➤ BOOTP Relay Agent For DHCP (a.k.a. DHCP Relay Agent)

RIP is a protocol used to dynamically exchange routing information between routers. Once RIP is installed, NT routes RIP protocols and dynamically exchanges routing information with other routers running the RIP protocol. Additionally, the BOOTP Relay Agent forwards DHCP requests to DHCP servers located on other subnets over the NT router. Thus, a single DHCP server can support or service multiple subnets.

Routing And IP RIP

A router can exchange routing information with neighboring routers if RIP is enabled. Alterations in the network layout, such as a downed router, are broadcast by routers to neighboring routers. Routers also transmit descriptions of all known routing information by using periodic broadcasts. RIP routers share routing information dynamically.

Windows NT can be a dynamic IP router or a static IP router. Dynamic routers share routing information with other routers to automatically build routing tables. Static routers employ manually configured routing tables.

Dynamic routing is enabled when you install RIP For IP. This is done through the Services tab of the Network applet in the Control Panel. Once it is installed, no further configuration is necessary. The service is started, and the Enable IP Routing option in the Advanced TCP/IP Configuration dialog box is checked automatically. RIP For IP runs as a service. It can be started and stopped via the Control Panel Services icon.

Static routing has the benefit of reduced network traffic. Network traffic is reduced because the static routers don't communicate with each other. The disadvantage of static routing is that the routing tables have to be maintained and created by hand.

To enable static routing, execute the following steps:

1. Go to the Control Panel, and click the Network icon.

2. Select the Services tab.

    If RIP For IP is installed on your computer, you must remove it before enabling static routing.

3. Highlight RIP For IP in the Network Services list located on the Services tab, then click Remove to remove RIP For IP. (If RIP For IP remains installed, dynamic routing will occur.)

4. Select the Protocols tab, highlight TCP/IP Protocol, then click Properties.

5. Select the Routing tab, enable IP Forwarding by marking the checkbox, then click OK.

Using static routing requires manual configuration of the static routing tables. This is done through the command-line command **route**, with syntax of:

```
route [-f] [-p] [command [destination] [MASK netmask] [gateway]
[METRIC metric]]
```

The options are:

- ➤ **-f** Removes all gateway entries from the routing table. If this parameter is used with a command, the tables are cleared before the command is run.

- ➤ **-p** Implements persistent routes by automatically sustaining routing changes through computer reboots.

- ➤ **command** One of the following commands:

  - ➤ **print** Prints a route.

  - ➤ **add** Adds a route.

  - ➤ **delete** Deletes a route.

  - ➤ **change** Modifies an existing route.

- ➤ **destination** Indicates the host or network to which you want to route.

- ➤ **MASK** Specifies that the next parameter is to be interpreted as the *netmask* parameter.

- ➤ **netmask** Specifies the subnet mask value to be associated with this route entry. If the value is not specified, this parameter defaults to **255.255.255.255**.

- ➤ **gateway** Specifies the default gateway.

- ➤ **METRIC** Specifies that the next parameter be interpreted as the *metric* parameter.

- ➤ **metric** Defines the hop count for the specified destination. If not defined, metric is set to **1** by default.

A few important items to note about the route utility:

➤ The subnet mask value of **255.255.255.255** is not accepted on the command line. To set this value, use the default by not specifying **MASK**.

➤ The NETWORKS file can be used to convert destination names to addresses, but the network numbers must be appended with trailing **.0** to comply with the full, four-octet, dotted, decimal notation.

➤ All gateways must be on the same logical network or the route will not be added to the table.

➤ Only one default gateway should be configured on a server with multiple NICs. Any secondary gateways are useless unless the primary default gateway fails.

➤ For each route to a new router, the new router must be instructed to reach back to the subnets hosted by the first router.

 The exam does not get specific enough that you must memorize the syntax of the route command, but you need to know its capabilities to interpret some questions.

Routing And IPX RIP

Windows NT 4 Server is also equipped with a RIP For NWLink (IPX/SPX) to enable routing over an IPX network. If you are using both TCP/IP and NWLink on your network, you can use both RIP For IP and RIP For IPX on the same network to route both protocols simultaneously.

 Enabling RIP For IPX is just as simple as it is for IP—just add the RIP For IPX service on the Services tab of the Network applet of the Control Panel. An additional configuration tab for the NWLink protocol, named "Routing," contains a checkbox labeled "Enable RIP Routing." This checkbox must be marked.

During the installation of RIP For IPX, a dialog box appears that states NetBIOS Broadcast Propagation (packets of broadcast type 20) is currently disabled. If you are using NetBIOS over IPX, click Yes to enable type 20 packet broadcasts.

The SAP Agent For IPX is automatically installed when RIP For IPX is enabled.

DHCP Relay Agent

DHCP (Dynamic Host Configuration Protocol) is used to assign an IP address to a workstation each time it boots. This allows a small set of IP addresses to support a larger number of computers. With the employment of the Windows NT DHCP Relay Agent, a single DHCP server can support multiple subnets connected by the NT Server MPR.

Without the DHCP Relay Agent, routers filter out the DHCP broadcasts instead of passing them through. The Relay Agent intercepts the DHCP broadcasts, then transmits the broadcasts directly to the DHCP server. The router still filters out the DHCP request, but the added Agent intervenes and sends the important boot message to the supporting server.

The following steps describe how to install the DHCP Relay Agent:

1. Add the DHCP Relay Agent through the Services tab of the Network applet in the Control Panel.

2. Specify the IP address of the DHCP server in the IP Address tab of the TCP/IP Properties dialog box.

   The DHCP Relay Agent is enabled automatically and installed as a service.

3. Choose the DHCP Relay tab in TCP/IP Properties dialog to change default values for the DHCP Relay Agent. The values are Seconds Threshold, Maximum Hops, and List Of DHCP Server Addresses.

AppleTalk Routing

If Macintosh clients are used on your network, you can route AppleTalk over NT Server. An NT server can be a seed router or a non-seed router for AppleTalk networks. A seed router must always be booted before any non-seed routers to establish the proper networking context. AppleTalk routing is a function of the Windows NT Services For Macintosh (SFM) and not part of the MPR. Any Macintosh client on an AppleTalk network routed over an NT server can access any other network routed through the NT server.

To enable AppleTalk routing, execute the following steps:

1. Open the Properties of the SFM from the Services tab of the Network applet in the Control Panel.

2. On the Routing tab, check the Enable Routing box.

3. If the Server is to be a seed router, check the Use This Router To Seed The Network box, identify the network range, and define the zones.

AppleTalk routing was not on any of the tests or preparation exams we encountered. So, you can be fairly assured that if you don't know what a seed router is or how to define a zone, there's no need to sweat it. There is a little coverage of this topic in the *Resource Kit*, but unless you use Macintosh clients in the real world, you don't need to know about AppleTalk routing.

Exam Prep Questions

Question 1

> There are two TCP/IP-based domains in your company: Market-
> ing and Sales. A Windows NT server acting as a router joins these
> two domains together. The Sales domain hosts the DHCP server
> that manages the IP addressing for workstations. What must be
> installed on the routing computer so the Marketing domain work-
> stations can obtain IP address assignments from the DHCP server
> located in the Sales domain?
>
> ○   a. NetBEUI
>
> ○   b. DHCP Relay Agent
>
> ○   c. RIP For IP
>
> ○   d. A proxy DHCP server must be installed in the Marketing
>   domain

NetBEUI is a non-routable protocol that does not support DHCP. Therefore, answer a is incorrect. The DHCP Relay Agent will intercept all DHCP
calls before they are filtered out by the router and direct them straight to
the DHCP server. Therefore, answer b is correct. RIP For IP enables routing between two domains, but it does not forward DHCP requests across
the link. Therefore, answer c is incorrect. There is no such thing as a proxy
DHCP server. The DHCP Relay Agent must be used to allow the Mar-
keting-based workstations to use the Sales-based DHCP server. Therefore, answer d is incorrect.

Question 2

> Your TCP/IP-based network is experiencing drastic increases in broadcast traffic. What is the best way to decrease the amount of broadcast traffic on your network?
>
> O a. Divide your network into two physical subnets, and install a bridge.
>
> O b. Divide your network into two logical subnets, and install a gateway.
>
> O c. Install a DHCP server.
>
> O d. Install a WINS server.

If a TCP/IP network does not have a WINS server, each computer on the network has to send a broadcast message to the other computers on the network, which increases network traffic. By making use of a WINS server, you provide computer-name-to-IP address resolution, which reduces the number of broadcast messages. Therefore, answer d is the correct answer.

Question 3

> You wish to locate information about the current usage statistics of TCP/IP. Which of the following TCP/IP command-line utilities will display this information?
>
> O a. lpq
>
> O b. arp
>
> O c. netstat
>
> O d. ping

The **lpq** utility will only display DLC-related print queue information. Therefore, answer a is incorrect. The **arp** utility will only display the mapping of an IP address to a MAC address. Therefore, answer b is incorrect. The **netstat** utility will display TCP/IP statistics when the -e parameter is used. Therefore, answer c is correct. The **ping** utility will only list the response time (if any) between the host and a remote system. Therefore, answer d is incorrect.

Question 4

> Of the following, which are required for access to a NetWare server
> from a Windows NT workstation running Client Service For
> NetWare? [Check all correct answers]
>
> ❏   a. A group on the NetWare server called "NTGATEWAY"
>   containing the Windows NT workstation's user account
>
> ❏   b. Gateway Service For NetWare
>
> ❏   c. A user account on the NetWare server
>
> ❏   d. The NWLink protocol

It is only necessary to place user accounts in the NTGATEWAY group on
the NetWare server if workstations are accessing the NetWare server via a
gateway, which is not the case in this question. Therefore, answer a is
incorrect. If an NT server is to act as a gateway to a NetWare server, the
Gateway Service For NetWare must be loaded onto a Windows NT server.
Because this scenario discusses an NT client accessing a NetWare server,
answer b is also incorrect. Any user accessing a NetWare server directly will
need a user account on that NetWare server. Therefore, answer c is correct.
An NT workstation running the Client Service For NetWare can access a
NetWare server directly by using the NWLink protocol. Therefore, answer
d is also correct. In this scenario, both answers c and d are the correct choices.

Question 5

> Your network uses multiple protocols. Where in NT is the binding
> order of the protocols changed to increase network speed?
>
> ○   a. Domain controllers only
>
> ○   b. Workstations only
>
> ○   c. Servers only
>
> ○   d. Both the workstations and servers (including the domain
>   controllers)

Because NT servers use the protocol sent to them by workstations, the binding order only needs to be changed on the workstations. Therefore, answer b is the correct choice. Network speed is affected by the binding order on the workstations, but not on the servers. Therefore, answers a, c, and d are all incorrect.

Question 6

Windows NT 4 Server is equipped to be a router between two or more subnets. This can occur only when multiple NICs are installed and configured on a single server computer. The facet of NT that provides the routing function is MPR, or Multiprotocol Router. What is the MPR comprised of? [Check all correct answers]

❑   a. NetBEUI

❑   b. RIP For IP

❑   c. DNS

❑   d. RIP For IPX

❑   e. DHCP Relay Agent

NetBEUI is not contained in MPR. MPR uses IP or MAC addresses to route traffic, not NetBEUI names. Therefore, answer a is incorrect. RIP For IP is part of MPR. Therefore, answer b is correct. DNS is a function of TCP/IP but is not part of MPR. Therefore, answer c is incorrect. RIP For IPX is part of MPR. Therefore, answer d is correct. DHCP Relay Agent is part of MPR. Therefore, answer e is correct. Thus, only answers b, d, and e are correct.

Question 7

> What is an advantage of SLIP over PPP?
>
> ○   a. SLIP supports security while PPP does not support security.
>
> ○   b. SLIP supports error checking while PPP does not support error checking.
>
> ○   c. SLIP supports flow control while PPP does not support flow control.
>
> ○   d. SLIP requires less system overhead than PPP.

SLIP does not support error checking, flow control, or security. These are features of PPP. Therefore, answers a, b, and c are incorrect. SLIP does, however, require less system overhead than PPP. Therefore, d is the correct choice.

Question 8

> You want to install TCP/IP on a member server in a non-routed network. You have already manually assigned an IP address to the server. What other parameter must you specify to install TCP/IP on the server?
>
> ○   a. Subnet mask
>
> ○   b. Default gateway
>
> ○   c. DHCP server IP address
>
> ○   d. WINS server IP address

When installing TCP/IP on a non-routed network, the IP address and subnet mask parameters must be specified. Therefore, answer a is the correct choice.

Question 9

You have a TCP/IP-based network that is divided into two subnets using the same cable segment. Your main server is named "SRVR1". The first subnet is comprised of workstations with permanently assigned IP addresses. The second subnet is comprised of workstations that are assigned new IP addresses by a DHCP server each time the workstations boot. What components of MPR should you install to enable routing between these two subnets? [Check all correct answers]

❑ a. RIP For IPX

❑ b. IPX/SPX

❑ c. RIP For IP

❑ d. DHCP Relay Agent

❑ e. None

The situation described in this question does not lend itself to routing based on MPR, because MPR requires two or more NICs in the server across which routing is to occur. This situation has two subnets but only one cable segment, thus, only a single NIC. Because MPR cannot be used on single NIC configurations, no part of MPR should be installed. Some alternate solution is required to route between these subnets. Therefore, only answer e is correct. RIP For IP, RIP For IPX, and DHCP Relay Agent are all part of MPR, but they cannot be used in this situation. Thus, answers a, c, and d are incorrect. IPX/SPX is a protocol and is not part of MPR. It should not be installed because it will not help with routing and the network is TCP/IP-based. Therefore, answer b is incorrect.

Question 10

Your Ethernet network consists of a Windows NT 4 server, several NT Workstation clients, a NetWare 3.12 client, and one NetWare 4.1 client. NWLink is running on the network. Each of the NetWare clients is using different frame types. How would you configure the NWLink IPX/SPX Properties dialog box on the Windows NT 4 server to enable the server to recognize both NetWare clients?

○   a. Enabling Auto Frame Type Detection

○   b. Selecting the Manual Frame Type Detection option, and adding a NetWare client's network number and frame type to the frame type configuration list

○   c. Selecting the Auto Frame Type Detection option, and adding both NetWare clients' network numbers and frame types to the frame type configuration list

○   d. Selecting the Manual Frame Type Detection option, and adding each of the NetWare clients' network numbers and frame types to the frame type configuration list

If frame types other than 802.2 are being used on a network, then Manual Frame Type Detection must be enabled. Frame types belonging to each client must be added to the frame type configuration list in the NWLink IPX/SPX Properties dialog box. Therefore, answer d is correct.

Question 11

Your network users need to access your network resources across the Internet. How can you allow Internet-based user access while still providing security?

○   a. Implement the SLIP protocol.

○   b. Implement the FTP protocol.

○   c. Implement the PPP protocol.

○   d. Implement the PPTP protocol.

The Point-To-Point Tunneling Protocol (PPTP) uses the Internet as a connection medium while maintaining network security. Therefore, answer d is the correct choice.

Question 12

To end the process of maintaining user accounts on two different types of servers, you have decided to migrate users from the NetWare server to a Windows NT server. What must be installed on the Windows NT server to provide the NetWare clients with access? [Check all correct answers]

❑   a. Gateway Service For NetWare

❑   b. NWLink protocol

❑   c. Client Service For NetWare

❑   d. SAP Agent

Gateway Service For NetWare must be installed on the Windows NT server. Therefore, answer a is correct. For the Windows NT server to communicate with the NetWare server, the NWLink protocol must be installed on the Windows NT server. Therefore, answer b is correct.

Need To Know More?

 Donald, Lisa and James Chellis: *MSCE: NT Server 4 In The Enterprise Study Guide*. Sybex Network Press, San Francisco, CA, 1997. ISBN 0-7821-1970-0. Chapter 13, "Internetwork Routing," gives brief but useful information regarding MPR. TCP/IP issues are discussed in Chapter 11. NWLink is covered in Chapter 9.

 Heywood, Drew: *Inside Windows NT Server*. New Riders, Indianapolis, IN, 1995. ISBN 1-56205-472-4. Chapter 9, titled "Using TCP/IP," discusses detailed issues relating to installing and configuring the TCP/IP protocol suite and routing for IP.

 Huitema, Christian: *Routing In The Internet*. Prentice Hall, Englewood Cliffs, NJ, 1995. ISBN 0-13-132192-7. This book deals with routing.

Perlman, Radia: *Interconnections*. Addison-Wesley Professional Computing Series, Reading, MA, 1992. ISBN 0-201-56332-0. This book deals with routing.

 Siyan, Karanjit S: *Windows NT Server 4 Professional Reference*. New Riders, Indianapolis, IN, 1996. ISBN 1-56205-731-6. Chapters 13 through 16 all discuss various aspects of protocol management. Appendix C, "Bridging and Routing," provides solid background information on routing as well as how to implement MPR.

 Search the TechNet CD (or its online version through www.microsoft.com) using the keywords "protocol management," "TCP/IP," "NWLink," "internetworking," and "routing."

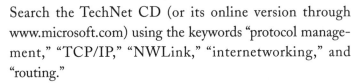   *The Windows NT Server Resource Kit* contains lots of useful information about shares and share permissions. Here again, you can search the TechNet (either CD or online version) or the *Resource Kit* CD using keywords like "protocols," "binding," "routing," and "networking services."

Windows NT Names And Name Services, Plus IIS

Terms you'll need to understand:

√ NetBIOS names

√ Dynamic Host Configuration Protocol (DHCP)

√ MAC address

√ Domain Name Service (DNS)

√ Windows Internet Name Service (WINS)

√ Internet Information Server (IIS)

√ Fully qualified domain name (FQDN)

Techniques you'll need to master:

√ Understanding network names and name resolution in Windows NT

√ Distinguishing between the uses for DNS and WINS

√ Familiarization with Internet Information Server (IIS)

Computers interact with each other using long strings of complicated address numbers. Fortunately, Windows NT hides most of these unfriendly references behind easy-to-remember names. This chapter discusses many of Windows NT's name resolution features and options. Plus, we include a brief discussion of IIS.

NT Names And Name Services

Name resolution is the activity of transforming a user-friendly (or otherwise) name for a computer or network share into a computer-friendly network address. This process enables networks to quickly locate and request resources while shielding users from complicated and difficult to remember—much less type in—hardware-level addresses. Within Windows NT, there are a base resolution service (NetBIOS), three protocol-specific services (NetBEUI, NWLink, and TCP/IP), and additional services for TCP/IP (DHCP, DNS, WINS).

NetBIOS Names In Windows NT

NetBIOS is automatically installed upon installation of NT. It is the underlying communication mechanism for many basic NT functions, such as browsing and interprocess communications between network servers. NetBIOS is an API used by all NT applications. It provides a uniform set of commands to access common low-level services.

All NT resources are identified by a unique NetBIOS name consisting of 15 characters or less. The NetBIOS namespace is not hierarchical, but flat. Thus, every machine on the same network must have a unique NetBIOS name, even if the machines are in different domains. Each time a computer connects to the network, it broadcasts its presence by "shouting" its NetBIOS name. The Master Browser "hears" this broadcast and attempts to register the new machine. If another machine is already using the name broadcasted by the newcomer, the registration is denied. That computer cannot go online until its NetBIOS name is changed or the other computer currently using the name goes offline.

A NetBIOS name is not the numeric same as a host name. A host name is a substitute for an IP address of an Internet host. These names are required for communication with the aliased machine (i.e., www.microsoft.com = 207.68.156.53). A NetBIOS name is a mandatory, unique name used by Windows NT for most network functions. Each time an Explorer interface is activated, such as an open file dialog box, you are interacting with NetBIOS names.

As discussed in Chapter 5 in the section on browsers, NetBIOS names are used to identify and list the resources currently available on a network. A computer announces itself and its resources upon booting up and once every minute thereafter. As it remains up and running, the interval increases to every 12 minutes. If a computer is gracefully shut down, it announces the removal of its resources as it leaves. If a computer goes offline otherwise, its resources may remain listed in the browser service up to 51 minutes until the Master Browser removes the entries and the Backup Browsers are updated. Computers rebroadcast their existence and all their resources every 12 minutes, so the level of traffic can be quite high, even for a small network.

NetBEUI And Name Resolution

All name resolution over NetBEUI is done through NetBIOS. Thus, there is no further configuration or installation required. Both users and computers use the NetBIOS name to call and access network system objects.

With NetBEUI, most of the network overhead is consumed by the NetBIOS announcement broadcasts. This is one of many reasons why NetBEUI should not be used on anything but the smallest of networks.

IPX And Name Resolution

IPX/SPX or NWLink uses NetBIOS over IPX (NBIPX) to resolve NetBIOS names into IPX addresses. Because IPX addresses contain the MAC address of the host, no further resolution is required. NWLink caches NetBIOS names to perform the IPX address mappings. NWLink does not use an address mapping file or name service. Unlike Novell's implementation of IPX/SPX, NWLink from Microsoft does not issue Service Advertisement Protocol (SAP) broadcasts. Thus, network overhead is greatly reduced.

IP And Name Resolution

Name resolution under TCP/IP is a complex but important issue. The resolution methods for IP include Dynamic Host Configuration Protocol (DHCP), Domain Name Service (DNS), and Windows Internet Name Service (WINS). These methods are discussed in the upcoming sections.

DHCP

DHCP, or Dynamic Host Configuration Protocol, is not exactly a name resolution system. Instead, it is an IP address-leasing system where a limited number of IP addresses can be shared among numerous computers, usually clients. DHCP dynamically assigns IP addresses to clients on a local subnet.

Fortunately, the details of installing and configuring a DHCP server are covered on the TCP/IP exam and not on the Enterprise exam. However, you need to be familiar with a few terms and the basic method of operation of DHCP.

When a client boots, it broadcasts a message requesting data from a DHCP server. The receiving DHCP server responds with an IP address assignment for a specified period of time. The client receives the data, integrates it into its configuration, and completes the boot process.

A DHCP server can also distribute subnet masks and default gateway addresses. Each assignment from a DHCP server is for a predetermined length of time, called a "lease period." When a lease expires, a DHCP server can reassign the address to another computer. An operating client can extend its lease simply by indicating that it is still using the address. When half of a lease period is reached, a client requests a lease extension, if needed. It continues to request an extension from the leasing DHCP server until 87.5 percent of its time period has expired. Then, it broadcasts the extension request to all DHCP servers. If no server responds by the time the lease expires, all TCP/IP communications of that client will cease.

A client's IP configuration and lease information can be displayed using **IPCONFIG** with the **/all** parameter. This utility can also release a lease by using the **/release** parameter or renew a lease by using the **/renew** parameter.

The 10,000-foot view of DHCP server installation is as follows:

1. Install the service through the Services tab of the Network applet.

2. Define a scope—a pool of valid IP addresses available for assignment.

3. Set the subnet mask.

4. Define any exclusions within the scope.

5. Set the lease duration.

Configuring a client to access a DHCP server is even simpler. To configure a client, all you have to do is open the TCP/IP properties dialog box from the Protocols tab of the Network applet. Then, on the IP Address page, select the radio button labeled "Obtain An IP Address From A DHCP Server."

If your DHCP server is located across a router, you'll need to use the DHCP Relay Agent to forward DHCP broadcasts. See Chapter 8 for details.

Any exam question that refers to a DHCP header is simply discussing the response packet from a DHCP server that contains special directional information for the requesting client. Because the client does not yet have an IP address, its MAC address is used to route the response package.

DNS

DNS, or Domain Name Service, is used to resolve host names into IP addresses. Host names are user-friendly conveniences to represent the dotted decimal notation of IP that are not required for operation of communication, unlike NetBIOS names. A host name (such as www.microsoft.com) is much easier to remember than its IP address (207.68.156.51).

Early DNS was a lookup table stored on every machine in a file called HOST. As networks expand, maintaining an updated and correct HOST file becomes increasingly difficult. To ease administration, centralized DNS was developed. A single server hosts the DNS data for the networks it supports, a hierarchy table of domains, and a list of other DNS servers to which it can refer requests.

DNS operates on user-friendly, fully qualified domain names (FQDN) to determine the location (IP address) of a system. For example, ftp2.dev.microsoft.com could represent the server named "FTP2" located in the ".dev" subdomain under the ".microsoft" domain within the ".com" top-level domain. This hierarchy structure enables DNS to quickly traverse its database to locate the correct IP address for the host machine.

DNS is essential on large networks, including the Internet. A client is configured to use a DNS server through the TCP/IP properties dialog box. The DNS tab contains fields to define the host name of the client, the domain where the client resides, the IP addresses of DNS servers, and a search order of domains.

Installing DNS servers is not a topic covered in depth on the Enterprise exam, because it is dealt with on the TCP/IP exam. However, familiarity with the basics will help to solidify your preparation for the Enterprise exam. The basic steps for a DNS server installation are as follows:

1. Install DNS through the Services tab of the Network applet.

2. After rebooting, launch the DNS Manager that now appears in Administrative Tools in the Start menu.

3. Add a new DNS server object through the DNS menu.

4. Create zones and host records.

The configuration of DNS is a very complicated and convoluted endeavor. Microsoft has done an excellent job of simplifying this task, but it is still difficult. Unix-based DNS, such as that most commonly used on the Internet, can be likened to building an Apollo rocket. Microsoft Windows NT-based DNS can be likened to building a high-performance race car.

WINS

WINS, or Windows Internet Name Service, is a name resolution service for NT-based TCP/IP networks. Similar to DNS, WINS maps NetBIOS names to IP addresses. But unlike DNS, WINS dynamically maintains the mapping database. WINS main functions include:

➤ Mapping NetBIOS names to IP addresses.

➤ Recognizing NetBIOS names on all subnets.

➤ Enabling internetwork browsing.

WINS reduced NetBIOS background tracking by eliminating the NetBIOS broadcasts. A WINS client communicates directly with a WINS server to send a resource notification, release its NetBIOS name, or locate a resource.

The original Microsoft solution to reduce NetBIOS broadcast traffic was the LMHOSTS file. This was a static file stored on each client that associated IP addresses with NetBIOS names. Just as with the DNS HOSTS file, it had to be manually maintained. Unfortunately, an LMHOSTS file is useless in a DHCP environment where relationships between IP addresses and NetBIOS names change.

WINS and DHCP work well together. Each time a DHCP client goes online, it can inform the WINS server of its presence. Thus, the dynamic relationship between IP addresses and NetBIOS names can be fully managed by these automatic services.

WINS clients are configured through the TCP/IP properties dialog box of the Services tab of the Network application. The WINS Address tab enables you to configure two WINS servers. The second server is for fault tolerance.

The installation and configuration of a WINS server is a TCP/IP exam topic and is not covered on the Enterprise exam. But, here are the basic steps for your own edification.

1. Add WINS from the Services tab of the Network applet.

2. After rebooting, launch the WINS Manager that now appears in Administrative Tools in the Start menu.

3. Add a WINS server object.

4. Set the renewal and extinction timeouts.

5. Set WINS database replication options.

6. Add static mappings.

7. Set additional preferences.

WINS Vs. DNS

WINS and DNS, while similar, have significant differences that define when each should be used for name resolution. Table 9.1 displays a comparison chart to highlight the differences between WINS and DNS.

Within many private networks, both DNS and WINS are installed. This provides support for both NetBIOS and FQDN resolution. Both DNS and WINS can be configured to pass resolution requests to the opposing resolution service if the referenced name is not listed in the respective database.

Now that we have detailed the various network naming schemes, let's move on to discuss how to hook your NT network to the Internet using Microsoft's Internet Information Server (IIS).

Table 9.1   Differences between WINS and DNS.

WINS	DNS
Maps IP addresses to NetBIOS names	Maps IP addresses to fully qualified domain names (FQDNs)
Automatic client data registration	Manual configuration
Flat database name space	Uses FQDN's hierarchical structure
Used on MS clients and networks	Used on TCP/IP-based hosts and networks
Only one entry per client	Each host can have multiple aliases
Enables domain functions such as logon and browsing	N/A

Internet Information Server

Another important component of NT that you need to be aware of is the Internet Information Server. NT ships with IIS version 2, but version 3 is the current standard for real-world implementation. For the Enterprise exam, you only need to know the basics of this application in its version 2 form. There is a separate test for IIS version 3 that covers this software in much greater detail.

IIS is a file and application server that provides Web, FTP, and Gopher services. If you are not already familiar with the Internet and these three services, you should reference:

➤ *Internet For Dummies*, by John R. Levine, Carol Baroudi, and Margy Levine-Young, Harper Audio, 1996. ISBN: 0-69451-667-8.

➤ *The Internet Complete Reference*, by Harley Hahn, Osborne McGraw-Hill, 1996. ISBN: 0-07882-138-X.

These resources will bring you up to speed on the topics considered as prerequisites for the NT Server and NT Server in the Enterprise exams.

IIS can be used to support the Internet services of Web, FTP, and Gopher within a private TCP/IP-based network or over the Internet. The bulk of the IIS material on the Enterprise exam focuses on the Web service, but you need to be at least minimally aware of the FTP and Gopher services.

Web

The Web, or World Wide Web, is a service based on the Hypertext Transfer Protocol (HTTP). HTTP is a client/server interprocess communications protocol that employs text and graphics as content. A Web server, such as IIS, sends out requested documents to a Web client, such as Internet Explorer. IIS's Web service offers numerous configuration options, including:

➤ Anonymous access

➤ NT user account restricted access

➤ Activity logging

➤ IP or domain name restricted/granted access

➤ Virtual server configuration

One important configuration feature of IIS's Web service is that of custom directory roots and virtual servers. Multiple Web sites can be hosted from a single installation of IIS. Each Web site is stored in its own root directory. In addition, each hosted Web site can be identified with its own FQDN and IP address. To host multiple IP addresses on the same IIS server, additional IP addresses are assigned to the server's NIC through the TCP/IP properties.

If IIS is used on a network with Internet connectivity, no additional ser-vices are required. DNS is handled by InterNIC (Internet-based) servers, and WINS will not be needed at all. However, if IIS is used within a pri-vate isolated network, both DNS and WINS might need to be installed to support local name resolution.

FTP

The File Transfer Protocol (FTP) is the service and protocol used on the Internet to transfer files from one machine to another. IIS offers this ser-vice to improve file distribution over the Internet and within large private networks. IIS's FTP service can host multiple sites, each stored in a sepa-rate directory, but they must all be referenced by a common base domain name. Version 2 of IIS does not support FTP virtual servers, so you may need to look elsewhere if you want to provide FTP services to your users (or get the newest version of IIS).

Gopher

Gopher is a text-based, menu-like hierarchical organization of data. This service was extremely popular before the development of the Web. Because of this, bastions of Gopher sites can still be found on the Internet. There is no compelling reason to use Gopher within a private network. Like FTP, multiple Gopher sites can exist, but they are all referenced by a common base domain name.

Exam Prep Questions

Question 1

> What is the primary function of a Dynamic Host Configuration
> Protocol server?
>
> O   a. To maintain a dynamic relationship database between IP
>   addresses and NetBIOS names
>
> O   b. To route IP packets across routers to other subnets
>
> O   c. To assign IP addresses to clients
>
> O   d. To resolve FQDNs into IP addresses

The service that maintains a dynamic relationship database between IP addresses and NetBIOS names is WINS. Therefore, answer a is incorrect. The service that routes IP packets is RIP for IP. Therefore, answer b is incorrect. The service that assigns IP addresses to clients is DHCP. Therefore, answer c is correct. The service that resolves FQDNs to IP addresses is DNS. Therefore, answer d is incorrect.

Question 2

> All Windows NT internal basic network server and service com-
> munications occur using what protocol?
>
> O   a. TCP/IP
>
> O   b. AppleTalk
>
> O   c. NetBIOS
>
> O   d. DLC

TCP/IP is a supported protocol of NT, but it is not the one used for basic internal communication. Therefore, answer a is incorrect. AppleTalk is a supported protocol, but it is not used in this manner. Therefore, answer b is incorrect. NetBIOS is the protocol or API used for all of NT's basic internal network communications. Therefore, answer c is correct. DLC is a protocol used for IBM mainframe and network-attached printers. Therefore, answer d is incorrect.

Question 3

What type of a frame header identifies network packets that contain information used to assign subnet masks and gateways to clients?

- ○ a. DNS header
- ○ b. DHCP header
- ○ c. WINS header
- ○ d. NetBEUI header

A DHCP header is the header type that identifies network packets used to assign subnet masks and gateways to clients. Therefore, only answer b is correct.

Question 4

A DNS server links what types of information together? [Check all correct answers]

- ❏ a. NetBEUI names
- ❏ b. FQDNs
- ❏ c. Subnet masks
- ❏ d. IP addresses
- ❏ e. MAC addresses

DNS maintains a relationship between FQDNs and IP addresses in such a way that both forward and reverse lookups are possible. Therefore, answers b and d are correct. NetBEUI names are stored by WINS. Therefore, answer a is incorrect. Subnet masks can be distributed by a DHCP server, but a link table does not exist. Therefore, answer c is incorrect. MAC addresses are linked through NWLink's and NetBEUI's cached name resolution. Therefore, answer e is incorrect.

Question 5

You need to set up four new virtual Web servers to be hosted on your private network using only a single installation of IIS. Each Web site will require its own directory, a unique URL, and a unique IP address. What should you do to implement this configuration? [Check all correct answers]

❏   a. Install RIP For IP on the IIS server.

❏   b. Assign each of the IP addresses to be used to the NIC in the IIS server, then associate each IP address with the appropriate Web directory.

❏   c. Set up the DHCP Relay Agent.

❏   d. Configure DNS so it contains the FQDN for each server and correlates that name to its IP address.

❏   e. Configure WINS by adding the NetBIOS names and IP addresses of the sites to the static list of servers.

RIP For IP should not be used in this situation, plus you do not know if there is more than one NIC in the server. Therefore, answer a is incorrect. Assigning the additional IP addresses to the server's NIC is an important step. Therefore, answer b is correct. The DHCP Relay Agent does not apply to this situation. Therefore, answer c is incorrect. Because this site is within a private network, you will need both DNS and WINS to support name resolution. Therefore, answers d and e are correct. Thus, answers b, d, and e are correct.

Question 6

What are the functions of WINS? [Check all correct answers]

❏   a. Enable internetwork browsing

❏   b. Map FQDNs to IP addresses

❏   c. Map NetBIOS names to IP addresses

❏   d. Map NetBIOS names to MAC addresses

❏   e. Assign clients IP addresses

Enabling internetwork browsing and mapping NetBIOS names to IP addresses are two of the three functions of WINS, the third function is recognizing NetBIOS names on all subnets. Therefore, answers a and c are correct. Mapping FQDNs to IP addresses is a function of DNS. Therefore, answer b is incorrect. Mapping NetBIOS names to MAC addresses happens in both NWLink and NetBEUI. Therefore, answer d is incorrect. Assigning clients IP addresses is a function of a DHCP server. Therefore, answer e is incorrect.

Question 7

What is an LMHOSTS file?

○ a. A static list of NetBIOS names mapped to IP addresses

○ b. A dynamic list of NetBIOS names mapped to IP addresses

○ c. A static list of FQDNs mapped to IP addresses

○ d. A dynamic list of FQDNs mapped to IP addresses

LMHOSTS is the predecessor to WINS and is a static list of NetBIOS names mapped to IP addresses. Therefore, answer a is correct. A dynamic list of NetBIOS names mapped to IP addresses is WINS. Therefore, answer b is incorrect. The HOST file is a static list of FQDNs mapped to IP addresses. Therefore, answer c is incorrect. There is no dynamic list of FQDNs mapped to IP addresses. Therefore, answer d is incorrect.

Question 8

Which of the following services are best matched for reducing administration of multiple clients? [Check all correct answers]

❑ a. DNS

❑ b. DHCP

❑ c. LMHOSTS

❑ d. WINS

❑ e. HOST

DHCP and WINS are the best matched pair of services for maintaining a dynamic list of changing client mappings. Therefore, answers b and d are correct. DNS, LMHOSTS, and HOST are all administrative intensive. Therefore, answers a, c, and e are incorrect.

Question 9

On a network with Internet access, you wish to host six Web sites from a single implementation of IIS. Which of the following must you do to accomplish this? [Check all correct answers]

❏   a. Install RIP For IP on the IIS server.

❏   b. Assign each of the IP addresses to be used to the NIC in the IIS server, then associate each IP address with the appropriate Web directory.

❏   c. Set up the DHCP Relay Agent.

❏   d. Configure DNS so it contains the FQDN for each server and correlates that name to its IP address.

❏   e. Configure WINS by adding the NetBIOS names and IP addresses of the sites to the static list of servers.

The only activity required to host multiple Web sites on IIS when connected to the Internet is to assign the multiple IP addresses to the server and the respective directories. Therefore, only answer b is correct. RIP For IP and DHCP Relay Agent are unrelated to this situation. Therefore, answers a and c are incorrect. DNS and WINS are not required because an Internet-hosted DNS will support the name resolution. Therefore, answers d and e are incorrect.

Question 10

On a private network not attached to the Internet, what are the benefits of using WINS over DNS? [Check all correct answers]

❏   a. Dynamic automated updates of NetBIOS and IP address correlation

❏   b. Reverse lookup capabilities

❏   c. Hierarchical database structure

❏   d. Supports domain functions

❏   e. Platform-independent

The advantages WINS has over DNS include the dynamic automated updates of its address correlation tables and its support for domain functions. Therefore, answers a and d are correct. WINS does not support reverse lookup, uses a flat namespace structure, and is limited to Microsoft platforms. Therefore, answers b, c, and e are incorrect.

Question 11

How are the HOST and LMHOSTS files different?

○ a. A HOST file maps host names to IP addresses, while an LMHOSTS file maps IP addresses to NetBIOS names.

○ b. An LMHOSTS file maps host names to IP addresses, while a HOST file maps IP addresses to NetBIOS names.

○ c. A HOST file maps host names to IP addresses, while an LMHOSTS file maps host names to NetBIOS names.

○ d. An LMHOSTS file maps host names to IP addresses, while a HOST file maps host names to NetBIOS names.

A HOST file maps host names to IP addresses, while an LMHOSTS file maps IP addresses to NetBIOS names. Therefore, answer a is correct.

Need To Know More?

 Donald, Lisa and James Chellis: *MSCE: NT Server 4 In The Enterprise Study Guide*. Sybex Network Press, San Francisco, CA, 1997. ISBN 0-7821-1970-0. Chapter 11 discusses TCP/IP-based name resolution, including DNS, WINS, LMHOSTS, HOST, and DHCP. Chapter 12 focuses on IIS.

 Heywood, Drew: *Inside Windows NT Server*. New Riders, Indianapolis, IN, 1995. ISBN 1-56205-472-4. Chapter 9 has a limited discussion of name resolution and DHCP. Chapter 18 looks at IIS.

 Siyan, Karanjit S: *Windows NT Server 4 Professional Reference*. New Riders, Indianapolis, IN, 1996. ISBN 1-56205-731-6. Chapters 13 through 16 discuss various aspects of protocol TCP/IP, name resolution, DHCP, and WINS. Chapter 23 discusses DNS. This book does not discuss IIS.

 Search the TechNet CD (or its online version through www.microsoft.com), and the *Windows NT Server Resource Kit* materials, using the keywords "name resolution," "DNS," "WINS," "LMHOSTS," "HOST," and "DHCP."

Windows NT Network Monitor

Terms you'll need to understand:

√ Network monitoring

√ Capture filters

√ Capture triggers

√ Buffer space

√ Dedicated mode captures

Techniques you'll need to master:

√ Installing and configuring Network Monitor

√ Analyzing Network Monitor data

√ Capturing network data by protocol, address, and data pattern

√ Recognizing security issues

Windows NT Server 4 is the first Microsoft operating system to include a network sniffer as a built-in utility. However, NT's Network Monitor is not a fully functional version. Instead, it is a scaled-down version of the Microsoft Systems Management Server Network Monitor tool.

Even with its limitations, Network Monitor is a handy tool for investigating network-related problems. For example, the Network Monitor can monitor the number of network frames that are dropped by a network card. Frames dropped by a network card might signify a faulty adapter. In this chapter, we examine the details of Network Monitor so you can successfully pass that portion of the Enterprise exam.

Installing And Configuring Network Monitor

Network Monitor is not one of the utilities automatically installed during the initial setup of NT. You must use the Services tab of the Network application in Control Panel to add Network Monitor Tools and Agent to your system. Once installed, Network Monitor appears in the Administrative Tools menu and the Monitoring Agent appears in the Control Panel.

You might notice that there is a Network Monitor Agent entry right beside the Network Monitor Tools and Agent. This allows you to install just the Agent portion of Network Monitor to help identify a system to a Network Monitor operating on another machine and to distribute Performance Monitor metrics when monitoring the performance of a system remotely. If you don't select the Tools version from the Services tab, you won't be able to capture and view data on the server.

Analyzing Network Monitor Data

Because the version of Network Monitor included with NT is a scaled-down version, it's not as functional as the SMS (Systems Management Server) version, and this limited functionality is not unexpected. On the other hand, this "limitation" offers a performance advantage. The server NIC does not have to be placed in promiscuous mode because all supported frame types are captured by the card due to the support for NDIS 4. This saves up to 30 percent in CPU performance over a system with a NIC in promiscuous mode.

 Network Monitor is only able to capture four types of data:
➤ Frames sent from the server
➤ Frames sent to the server
➤ Broadcast frames
➤ Multicast frames

To capture data using Network Monitor, simply launch the application, then select the Start command in the Capture pull-down menu (or press F10). At any time, you can stop or pause the data capture through this menu. Once the capture process has been stopped or paused, you can view the contents of any frame.

During and after the capture session, you can view four collections of information gathered by Network Monitor:

➤ Bar graphs

➤ Session statistics

➤ Station statistics

➤ Summary statistics

These options appear by default in the sectioned display window, as shown in Figure 10.1.

Bar graphs display information in realtime as it is gathered by the utility. The graphs include:

➤ Percent network utilization

➤ Frames per second

➤ Bytes per second

➤ Broadcasts per second

➤ Multicasts per second

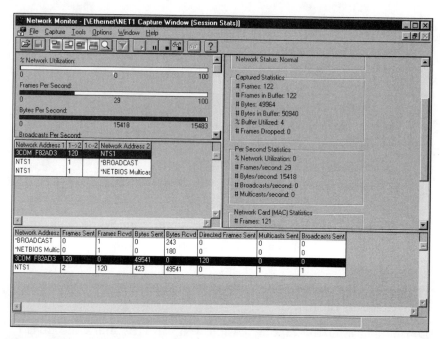

Figure 10.1 The Network Monitor.

The network utilization metric is significant because it gives you a direct visual guide to how traffic to and from the server is affecting overall network performance.

Session statistics detail the conversations going on over the network. This information is realtime and cumulative during each capture session. Remember, due to the limitations of this application, the network conversations listed in this section are only those that involve the server.

Station statistics are cumulative data on the dynamics of each network conversation. The information displayed here includes:

➤ MAC or network address (sometimes replaced by a NetBIOS name)

➤ Sent frames

➤ Received frames

➤ Bytes sent

➤ Bytes received

➤ Directed frames sent

➤ Multicasts sent

➤ Broadcasts sent

Summary statistics are cumulative data sets on a wide variety of metrics, including:

➤ Network

➤ Captured

➤ Per second

➤ MAC

➤ MAC errors

During a capture session, all of the intercepted frames are stored in the server's memory buffer. Once you complete your examination, wish to start another capture session, or are exiting Network Monitor, you can save the captured data to a CAP file for later investigation. By default, these files are placed in the \System32\Netmon\Capture directory. It is a good idea to name your captures by date to help identify them in the future.

Capture Filters

Capture filters are designed through the Capture Filter dialog box, reached by selecting the Filter command from the Capture drop-down menu (shown in Figure 10.2), or by pressing F8. This dialog box displays a decision tree that graphically represents the logic of the filter.

 The Network Monitor is only able to capture as much information as will fit in the available system memory. Capture information accumulates rapidly. If you attempt to gather all data points over an extended period of time, you'll have a difficult job of isolating (or even locating) any one element. Because of this, it is a good idea to limit the extent of the network capture. Through the use of filters, you can limit and fine-tune your gathering range to focus on one type of packet or data to and/or from one machine. A capture filter acts much like a database query: It specifies the results you want without dumping everything in your lap. Once you create a capture filter, it can be saved and reused later.

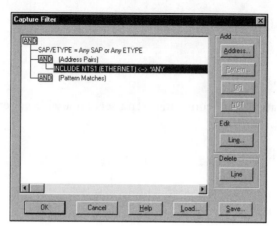

Figure 10.2 The Capture Filter dialog box.

Capture filters can gather data based on protocol, address pairs, and data patterns. The following sections discuss each technique available to filter and capture data.

Capturing By Protocol

A protocol-based filter is created by adding the filter line:

```
SAP/ETYPE={protocol}
```

The filter can be set to identify many different protocol types, including those listed in Table 10.1. The SMS version of Network Monitor supports additional protocols. Figure 10.3 shows the Capture Filter SAPs and ETYPEs dialog box.

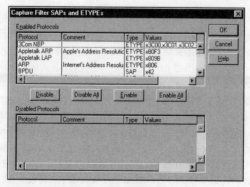

Figure 10.3 The Capture Filter SAPs and ETYPEs dialog box.

Table 10.1	The supported protocols for capture in Network Monitor.		
AARP	FINGER	NBT	RPC
ADSP	FRAME	NCP	RPL
AFP	FTP	NDR	RTMP
ARP_RARP	ICMP	NetBIOS	SAP
ASP	IGMP	NETLOGON	SMB
ATP	IP	NFS	SMT
BONE	IPCP	NMPI	SNAP
BPDU	IPX	NSP	SPX
BROWSER	IPXCP	NWDP	TCP
CBCP	LAP	OSPF	TMAC
CCP	LCP	PAP	TOKEN_RING
DDP	LLC	PPP	UDP
DHCP	MSRPC	PPPCHAP	XNS
DNS	NBFCP	PPPPAP	ZIP
ETHERNET	NBIPX	RIP	
FDDI	NBP	RIPX	

Capturing By Address

Communication between the server and a specific computer can be tracked using an address pair in the capture filter (see Figure 10.4). Up to four address pairs can be monitored simultaneously.

An address pair is:

➤ The MAC address of the two computers

➤ An arrow specifying the direction of traffic to monitor (<- -, - ->, or <- ->)

➤ The **INCLUDE** or **EXCLUDE** keyword to instruct Network Monitor to track the frame or to ignore it.

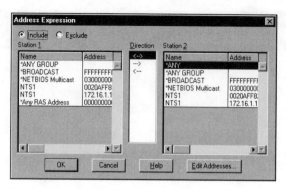

Figure 10.4 The Address Expression dialog box.

The order of the one to four address pairs is not significant. However, **EXCLUDE** statements are processed first. If the same frame is represented by both an **EXCLUDE** and an **INCLUDE** address pair, then it is ignored (i.e., **EXCLUDE** takes precedence).

If you do not specify an address pair, the default address pair of **<your computer> <- -> ANY** is used.

Capturing By Data Pattern

Communications can also be traced using pattern matching within the capture filter (see Figure 10.5). Pattern matching limits a capture to frames that contain a specific ASCII or hexadecimal pattern that occurs within the entire frame or a specified depth into the frame (called an "offset") in bytes (from either the beginning of the frame or the end of the topology header). Two logical operations can be used with pattern matching filters: OR and NOT. These operators enable you to identify multiple patterns to capture and ignore.

In addition to Pattern Matching, you can set Capture Triggers, as explained in the following section.

Capture Triggers

Capture triggers are defined through the Capture Trigger dialog box, shown in Figure 10.6. You access the Capture Trigger dialog box through the Trigger command in the Capture pull-down menu.

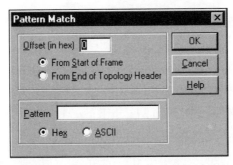

Figure 10.5   The Pattern Match dialog box.

 A capture trigger is a set of conditions that initiates an action when the conditions are met. Capture triggers allow you to automate some of the tasks associated with gathering network communications data, such as stopping the capture, executing a batch file, or even launching an application.

From this dialog box, the following selections can be used to define a custom trigger:

> ➤ **Nothing** Default setting of no trigger.

> ➤ **Pattern Match** Trigger is a matched pattern within a captured frame. The Pattern area is used to define the pattern matching conditions. The settings are the same as those present in the pattern match filter.

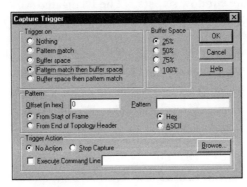

Figure 10.6   The Capture Trigger dialog box.

➤ **Buffer Space** Trigger is the percentage level of used buffer space. The Buffer Space area is used to set the percentage level.

➤ **Pattern Match Then Buffer Space** Trigger is a pattern match followed by a percentage of used buffer space.

➤ **Buffer Space Then Pattern Match** Trigger is a percentage of used buffer space followed by a pattern match.

Once the trigger has occurred, the settings in the Trigger Action area define what occurs:

➤ **No Action** By default, no action is taken other than a computer beep when the trigger occurs.

➤ **Stop Capture** Capture is halted.

➤ **Execute Command Line** A command line pointing to an application or batch file is launched.

Now that we have explained triggers, let's move on to discuss capturing in dedicated mode.

Dedicated Mode Captures

You can put the Network Monitor into dedicated mode to reduce the load on the CPU. This mode prevents the Network Monitor from updating and displaying Capture window statistics. The Dedicated Mode can be chosen from the Network Monitor Capture menu.

The Dedicated Mode dialog box only displays the total number of captured frames. In this dialog box, you will also find control buttons enabling you to stop, stop and view, or pause the capture. There is also a button called "Normal Mode" that takes the Network Monitor back to normal mode.

We have covered the details about Network Monitor you need to know to pass this section of the exam. Now let's move on and explore setting up security on your NT network.

Addressing Security Issues

Windows NT Network Monitor captures only the frames that are sent to or from the local computer (this includes multicast and broadcast frames). This is for security reasons. To prevent nonauthorized users from gaining access to Network Monitor's data, two passwords can be configured for this application.

 Through the Monitoring Agent utility in the Control Panel, a Display password and a Capture password can be set to restrict access. The Display password requires validation before any captured data files can be viewed. The Capture password requires validation before data can be gathered or viewed.

If the Network Monitor Agent is installed but no password is set, anyone using the SMS version of Network Monitor can connect to the machine and capture data.

As an added security precaution, you can use the Network Monitor to find different installations of Network Monitor on the local segment. This helps administrators limit unauthorized network monitoring. If the Network Monitor Agent is being used remotely, the Network Monitor detects all instances of this as well as SMS Network Monitor and Performance Monitor remote usage.

The Identify Network Monitor Users command on the Tools menu searches the local segment, then displays the computer's name, user name, state of the Network Monitor, version number, and network adapter address. This feature is not able to detect usage across routers that do not forward multicasts.

Displaying Data

Captured data can be examined on a frame-by-frame basis through the Display Captured Data command in the Capture menu. This command switches Network Monitor into Display Mode and presents an ordered list of all frames currently in the buffer. The frame captured number, time of capture, MAC source and destination address, protocol, description, and more can be viewed by scrolling through this list.

Any frame can be examined even closer by double-clicking it. This action opens two additional panes that display the protocol delivery details and a hexadecimal and ASCII representation of the captured data.

 Similar to capture filters, display filters can be used to limit or restrict the frames displayed to a specific source address, protocol, or various protocol-specific properties and values. Display filters are created through the Filter command in the Display menu. The Display menu only appears when Network Monitor is in Display Mode. The syntax for display filters is as follows (note that a GUI interface is present to simplify the construction of these expressions):

➤ **Protocol** Protocol == {INCLUDE or EXCLUDE list of protocols}

➤ **Address Filter** Address1 <- -> Address2 or Address1- -> Address2 (the default is ANY <- -> ANY)

➤ **Property** Protocol:Property [Relation] Value (each property can vary, but this is the standard syntax)

For a property filter, each of the supported protocols has a lengthy list of commands, properties, and events. Each of these properties often has two or more possible relations, such as ==, <>, >, =<, **CONTAINS, EXISTS, INCLUDES**, and so forth. Furthermore, the value is determined by the property and the relation. The most common value is a hex, decimal, or ASCII number, but it can also be a selection from a predefined list of expressions, events, or NetBIOS names. There may be a question or two about the construction of this type of display filter. We recommend you spend a little time reviewing the thousands of possible settings and then take your best guess if you get such a question on the test. Other than the common patterns listed previously, we can't offer any shortcut to this material.

Other Features

There are a handful of other features and functions of which you should be aware. We didn't see these highlighted on the test, but it never hurts to know more than you need:

➤ All of the addresses intercepted by Network Monitor can be viewed through the Addresses command in the Capture menu. From this dialog box, you can review all the addresses currently stored in Net work Monitor's database. You can edit entries to alter the type, address, name, or comment for each entry. Plus, you can manually add and delete entries. This address database is used to associate the MAC address with a user friendly name.

➤ The buffer size used by Network Monitor to store captured frames can be controlled through the Buffer Settings command in the Capture menu. By default, the buffer is set to 1 MB. The size of the buffer can be increased to a maximum of 8 MB less than the total amount of RAM installed on your server. Once the buffer is full, old frames are dropped to accommodate new ones, instead of storing the frames in the swap file. A further setting in this dialog box is the amount of data to store from each frame. This can be set to the entire frame or from 64 to 65,472 bytes. This does not change the size of frames used by the network, but changes how much of each frame is stored in the memory buffer.

➤ Through the Network command in the Capture menu, you can track multiple network segments attached to separate NICs. Each NIC installed on the server is listed in the Select Capture Network dialog box. Each listed NIC can be Connected (captured from) or Suspended (not captured from). To capture two networks simultaneously without combining the data requires two instances of Network Monitor, each set to watch a different segment.

➤ The Find All Names command from the Capture menu will search each captured frame for a NetBIOS name assigned to MACs. All names found are added to the address database and used in the display sections to simplify the identification of computers for humans. In other words, found names replace corresponding instances of MAC addresses in the statistics panes.

➤ The commands of Find Routers and Resolve Addresses From Name are not functional in the Network Monitor version that ships with NT. These are reserved for the SMS version.

Exam Prep Questions

Question 1

> While using the Network Monitor, you decide to implement a display filter to aid in your search for the NetBIOS Add Group Name command. What is the proper syntax of a properties-based display filter?
>
> ○   a. NETBIOS:Command == 0x0 (Add Group Name)
>
> ○   b. NETBIOS <= Add Group Name Command
>
> ○   c. Add Group Name > NETBIOS
>
> ○   d. NETBIOS<- ->Add Group Name

Answer a is the correct syntax for the properties display filter. It contains Protocol:Property [Relation] Value. Therefore, answer a is correct. Answer b is incorrect because the four elements of the properties-based display filter are scrambled. Answer c is incorrect because it is missing the property and the remaining elements are out of order. Answer d is incorrect because it is missing the property element, the other elements are out of order, and the relation is not valid for a property relation.

Question 2

> Which application is best suited for detecting which computer on a local segment is causing the most network traffic?
>
> ○   a. Performance Monitor
>
> ○   b. Network Monitor
>
> ○   c. Server Manager
>
> ○   d. Traffic Analyzer

The Performance Monitor is not able to identify a single machine from the bulk of network traffic. Therefore, answer a is incorrect. Network Monitor is able to identify individual machines based on their MAC addresses, and it can track their contributions to network traffic if that traffic is sent to the server. Therefore, answer b is correct. The Server Manager does not have the ability to monitor network traffic. Therefore, answer c is incorrect. There is no utility called Traffic Analyzer in NT. Therefore, answer d is incorrect.

Question 3

You are working with Network Monitor to evaluate your network usage. You want to capture all frames inbound to your server, except those sent from John's computer. The name of your server is "Admin1", and the name of John's computer is "Sales5". What is the best way to set up the capture filter?

○ a. INCLUDE Admin1 <- -> NOT (Sales5)

○ b. INCLUDE Admin1 <- -> ANY; EXCLUDE Admin - -> Sales5

○ c. EXCLUDE Admin1 <- - Sales5

○ d. EXCLUDE Admin1 <- -> Sales5

Answer a is not a proper construction. The relation indicates both inbound and outbound traffic, plus the **NOT** logical operator is used outside of the filter statement. Therefore, answer a is incorrect. Answer b lists the default **INCLUDE** statement, which does not need to be repeated, and the **EXCLUDE** statement applies to traffic sent to Sales5. Therefore, answer b is incorrect. Answer c is an **EXCLUDE** statement that restricts traffic from the Sales5 computer. Therefore, answer c is correct. Answer d excludes both inbound and outbound traffic from Sales5. Therefore, answer d is incorrect.

Question 4

What types of information can be tracked with Network Monitor? [Check all correct answers]

❑ a. Multicast packets

❑ b. All packets on a network

❑ c. Packets sent to or from the monitoring server

❑ d. Broadcast packets

❑ e. Packets from one workstation to another

❑ f. NetBIOS packets sent over a router

Answers a, c, and d are correct. Network Monitor can only track packets that include the monitoring server as the destination or origination address, this includes broadcast and multicast packets. Answers b, e, and f are incorrect. Network Monitor cannot capture packets that are not addressed to or from the server, plus NetBIOS is not a routable protocol.

Question 5

Which product from Microsoft also includes a Network Monitor, but the version shipped with this product has additional features and functions?

O a. SQL Server

O b. SNA Server

O c. Systems Management Server

O d. Exchange Server

SQL Server is a database system and does not include a Network Monitor. Therefore, answer a is incorrect. SNA Server is a mainframe integration product and does not include a Network Monitor. Therefore, answer b is incorrect. Systems Management Server includes a Network Monitor with more capabilities than the version shipped with NT. Therefore, answer c is correct. Exchange Server is an email system and does not include a Network Monitor. Therefore, answer d is incorrect.

Question 6

You installed Windows NT Server with the default configuration onto your C drive and subsequently installed Network Monitor Tools and Agent from the Services tab of the Network Control Panel application. When you save sets of captured data, where will the CAP files be placed by default?

O a. C:\Winnt\System32\Netmon\Capture

O b. C:\Program Files\Netmon\Capture

O c. C:\Admin\Netmon\Capture

O d. C:\Winnt\System32\Repl\Export\Netmon\Capture

The directory listed in answer a is the default location for storing the CAP files from Network Monitor. The directories listed in answers b, c, and d are not the default directories. Therefore, answers b, c, and d are incorrect.

Question 7

> Network Monitor's security feature of searching out other users of the Network Monitor Agent can detect what applications? [Check all correct answers]
>
> ❏   a. Network Monitor from SMS
>
> ❏   b. HP's OpenView
>
> ❏   c. Event Viewer from NT Workstation
>
> ❏   d. Network Monitor from NT Server
>
> ❏   e. Performance Monitor

Network Monitor can detect instances of Network Monitor from SMS. Therefore, answer a is correct. Network Monitor cannot detect HP's OpenView or Event Viewer, plus neither of these applications accesses the Network Monitor Agent. Therefore, answers b and c are incorrect. Network Monitor can detect both NT Server's Network Monitor and Performance Monitor. Therefore, answers d and e are also correct. Thus, answers a, d, and e are correct.

Question 8

> How would you protect captured data from being viewed by un-authorized users? [Check all correct answers]
>
> ❏   a. Set a Display password through the Monitoring Agent applet.
>
> ❏   b. Set an Access password on the Network Monitor application.
>
> ❏   c. Set a Capture password through the Monitoring Agent applet.
>
> ❏   d. Set a Display password through the Security menu of Network Monitor.
>
> ❏   e. There are no features to restrict Network Monitor access.

Setting a Display password through the Monitoring Agent applet will restrict users from viewing captured data. Therefore, answer a is correct. There is not a command named "Access Password." Therefore, answer b is incorrect. Setting a Capture password through the Monitoring Agent applet will restrict both capturing and viewing data. Therefore, answer c is correct. There is not a Security menu in Network Monitor. Therefore, answer d is incorrect. There are two passwords used to restrict access to Network Monitor configured through the Monitoring Agent applet in the Control Panel. Therefore, answer e is incorrect. Thus, only answers a and c are correct.

Need To Know More?

 Donald, Lisa and James Chellis: *MSCE: NT Server 4 In The Enterprise Study Guide*. Sybex Network Press, San Francisco, CA, 1997. ISBN 0-7821-1970-0. Chapter 16 is dedicated to the Network Monitor. Its coverage is mediocre, and details about filtering are virtually nonexistent.

 Heywood, Drew: *Inside Windows NT Server*. New Riders, Indianapolis, IN, 1995. ISBN 1-56205-472-4. This book completely overlooks the Network Monitor.

 Siyan, Karanjit S: *Windows NT Server 4 Professional Reference*. New Riders, Indianapolis, IN, 1996. ISBN 1-56205-731-6. This book also completely fails to include information about the Network Monitor.

 The Windows NT Server 4 manuals cover planning, configuration, and installation issues quite well. The *Concepts And Planning Manual* contains the only useful documentation we could find on the Network Monitor, in Chapter 10, "Monitoring Your Network."

For further details on the Network Monitor, please consult the inline help. It provides at least some details for each command.

Managing Windows NT Performance

11

Terms you'll need to understand:

√ Task Manager

√ Objects

√ Instances

√ Counters

√ Alerts

√ Logging

√ Baselining

√ Paging file

√ Process priorities

Techniques you'll need to master:

√ Using Task Manager to view and control system processes

√ Using Performance Monitor to capture and analyze network statistics

√ Monitoring and examining disk performance

√ Configuring administrative alerts

√ Viewing network statistics logs

√ Assigning process priorities

√ Optimizing NT Server settings

Performance management on Windows NT Server involves numerous applications and configuration screens. In this chapter, we look into many of the tools and methods used to monitor and increase performance, with a focus on the material covered on the exam. Specifically, we look at the Task Manager, Performance Monitor, and the NT paging file. In addition, we look at managing process priorities and optimizing server settings.

Task Manager

The Task Manager is a new utility to the Windows NT environment. This tool enables you to view and control the processes currently active on your machine. Three types of information are available through the Task Manager (each displayed on its own display tab).

The three types of information available through the Task Manager are:

➤ **Applications** This tab shows a list of the applications currently in use and their status, whether running or nonresponsive (see Figure 11.1).

➤ **Processes** This tab displays a list of all processes in memory, with details on the CPU and memory usage (see Figure 11.2).

➤ **Performance** This tab shows a graphical and numerical display of system performance metrics, including CPU and memory usage graphs; totals for handles, threads, and processes; physical memory stats; committed memory changes (memory allocated to the system or an application); and kernel memory stats (see Figure 11.3).

The Task Manager can be reached using two different methods:

➤ Press Ctrl+Alt+Del, then click the Task Manager button.

➤ Right-click over a blank area of the taskbar, then select the Task Manager from the pop-up menu.

The Task Manager is an invaluable tool for fast investigation of system activity and instant corrective actions, such as:

➤ Identifying nonresponsive applications, and terminating them to release their hostage resources (Applications tab).

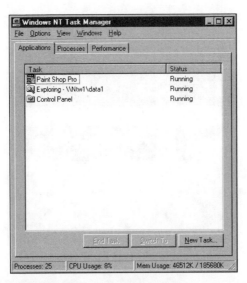

Figure 11.1   The Task Manager's Applications tab.

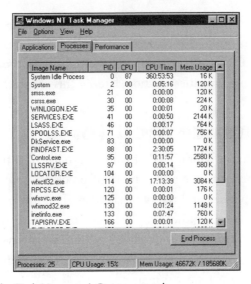

Figure 11.2   The Task Manager's Processes tab.

➤ Identifying runaway processes, and terminating them to return the system to normal operational levels (Processes tab).

➤ Ascertaining the memory use levels to determine the need for additional RAM (Performance tab).

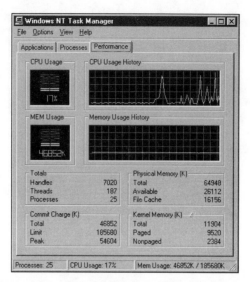

Figure 11.3   The Task Manager's Performance tab.

The Task Manager also enables you to launch new processes (applications), switch to a new foreground application, view separate graphs for each CPU, display the kernel access time, and alter the priority of processes (see the "Managing Process Priorities" section, later in this chapter).

Performance Monitor

The NT Performance Monitor (PerfMon) is a solid utility that you can use to inspect the performance and activity of processes, resources, physical components, networks, and remote machines. The use and operation of Performance Monitor is rather simple. However, knowing what metrics or counters to watch and what to do about them is not always so easy. We'll take a look at the controls and commands of PerfMon, then look into how to use it to evaluate NT's performance.

Performance Monitor has four views: Chart, Alert, Log, and Report.

➤ **Chart view**   Allows users to view realtime data in a line graph or histogram form (see Figure 11.4).

➤ **Alert view**   Allows users to set and view alerts and alert statistics.

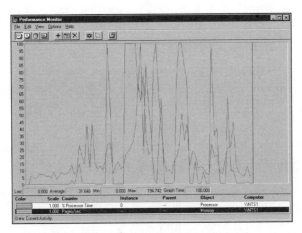

Figure 11.4   The Performance Monitor in Chart view monitoring processor time and memory page swaps.

> ➤ **Log view** Allows users to create and save a log of system performance.

> ➤ **Report view** Allows users to create custom reports of Performance Monitor data.

All four views revolve around counters. A counter is a measurable aspect of an object used to evaluate the performance of that object. No matter which view you use, the Add To command in the Edit menu is how you add counters. When you initiate this command, a dialog box appears that allows you to select counters based on the counter's computer, object, and instance.

➤ **Computer** Most computers on the network provide counters that PerfMon can read and display; however, as the OS gets farther away from NT, the number of useful counters decreases.

➤ **Objects** Any component on the specified computer that can be measured is listed as an object, such as processor, memory, physical disk, and so forth.

➤ **Instances** This identifies which instance of an object should be monitored. Instance 0 is the first or only occurrence of an object, instance 1 is the second occurrence, and so on. If it is not possible for an object to have multiple instances, such as the Server service, then this area is blank.

► **Counters** This identifies the available counters for a specific instance of an object on the chosen computer.

A cursory interaction with PerfMon may leave you baffled as to which counters are important. Because this book is geared toward passing the Enterprise exam, the next section only looks at counters that matter for the test.

Common Objects And Counters

In the real world of networking, you may have to be familiar with more counters than the ones listed in this section. Fortunately, if you don't quite understand any counter, you can highlight it in the Add To dialog box and click the Explain button to get a brief but helpful definition for each counter.

Most of the questions that refer to PerfMon seem to focus on the following counters, so if you have a good grasp of these, the test should be a breeze:

► **Processor: %Processor Time** When you suspect a processor upgrade may be necessary, measure this counter. If the processor counter measures 80 percent or more for an extended period of time, this could be a good indication that the processor is in need of an upgrade.

► **System: Processor Queue Length** This can also be measured to figure out if a processor upgrade is necessary. If the number of threads waiting to be processed is greater than two, the processor may be a bottleneck for the system.

► **Processor: Interrupts/sec.** When you suspect a hardware device is malfunctioning in the system, measure this counter. If the Processor-Interrupts/sec. increases and the processor time does not, a hardware device could be sending bogus interrupts to the processor. Locate the hardware device and replace it.

► **Memory: Cache Faults, Page Faults, and Pages/sec.** When you suspect that there is not enough memory in the system, these counters should be measured. They indicate the frequency your system needs to swap pages to the hard disk swap file. If this counter is high, chances are the need for memory is high as well.

➤ **PhysicalDisk/LogicalDisk: %Disk Time** When you suspect the hard disk is a system bottleneck, measure this counter. This counter shows you how much processor time is being spent servicing disk requests. Measure this counter against Processor: % Processor Time to see if the disk requests are using up a notable amount of processor time.

➤ **PhysicalDisk/LogicalDisk: Disk Bytes/Transfer** When you are trying to find out how fast your hard disks are transfer ring data, measure this counter.

➤ **PhysicalDisk/LogicalDisk: Current Disk Queue Length** When you are thinking about upgrading your hard disk, measure this counter. This counter shows you how much data is waiting to be transferred to the disk. If the disk queue is long, processes are being delayed by disk speed.

Note: The PhysicalDisk object counters apply to the entire physical storage device and are best used for suspected hardware troubleshooting. The LogicalDisk object counters focus on a specific volume and are best used for read/write performance investigations.

Monitoring Disk Performance

By default, the physical and logical disk counters are not activated. The process of gathering disk counters has a significant effect on the performance of storage devices. To turn on the disk counters, you need to execute **diskperf -y**, then reboot your system. Once you complete your monitoring, turn off the disk counters with **diskperf -n** and reboot. You must be logged on as the Administrator to execute either of these commands. Until **diskperf** is executed, all Physical and Logical Disk counters will display a reading of **0** (zero).

Using The PerfMon Views

In the following sections, we explore the various views you can use in Performance Monitor to examine network data. These views include Chart, Alert, Log, and Report.

Using Charts

Once you've selected and added counters to your Chart view, you can make some adjustments through the Options|Chart command. This brings up a dialog box where you can alter the maximum value of the vertical axis, change between graph and histogram, add grid lines, and change update intervals.

Configuring Alerts

You can use the Windows NT Performance Monitor to configure system alerts. For example, an administrator could be informed when a storage device approaches 85 percent capacity. To work with alerts, you must switch to the Alert view from the View menu. Just as in the Chart view, you add counters through the Edit|Add To Alert command. The Add To Alert dialog box is the same as that for a chart, with the addition of an alert trigger level and program/script to run when an alert occurs.

The remaining alert configuration options are accessed through the Options|Alert command. From there, you can instruct PerfMon to switch to Alert view when an alert is triggered, write the alert in the Application log, and send a notification message to a user or machine.

Working With Logs

The Log view is used to create a stored record of the performance of one or more objects to be analyzed or compared to at another time. Just as in the Chart view, you must use the Edit|Add To Log command to add objects for the Log to record. Note that Log does not offer a selection at the counter level. It records all possible counters for the selected objects.

Once you've selected the objects to log, you need to define the update interval and file name of the log file. This is done through the Options|Log command. You will be prompted for a file name and how often to capture the counters for the objects.

Creating A Report

A report of your gathered metrics can be created through the Report view. Counters to include in a report are added in a similar manner as counters are added in the other views, through the Edit|Add To Report command.

After you select the counters to list in the report, you need to set the update interval using the Options|Report command.

Miscellaneous Commands And Controls

All PerfMon view selections have numerous commands in common, including:

➤ **File|Save [View] Settings As** Saves a view's settings to be used at another time.

➤ **File|Save Workspace** Saves all view settings in a single file.

➤ **File|Export** Saves the current view's captured data in a tab- or comma delimited file.

➤ **Add|Edit** Edits the counter parameters or settings.

➤ **Add|Delete** Removes the counter.

➤ **Options|Data From** Displays data from the active network or from a log file.

> *Note: No matter which view is being used, Performance Monitor must remain up and running (i.e., as an active process) to display realtime charts, record a log, send alerts, or create reports.*

Now that we have discussed the Performance Monitor's views, let's move on to the process of baselining.

Baselining

Baselining, or establishing a baseline, is the process of recording the parameters of a fully functional system. This is done through the Log view. Once you've recorded a log of an operating system with "normal" parameters, you can use the log in the future to evaluate the performance of the system. Some objects you should include in your baseline are:

➤ Processor

➤ Physical disk

➤ Memory

➤ Server

➤ System

➤ Any installed protocols

However, just grabbing a short interval of data won't provide a useful baseline for comparison. Instead, you should record a log file for each counter over a 24-hour interval with a counter reading 5, 10, or 15 minutes, and repeat this for a few days or even a week. This provides you with a look into the network's performance during an entire day, covering both peak and off-peak hours. Furthermore, it is a good idea to repeat the process of collecting a baseline once a month. This not only establishes a timeline of "normal" performance, but provides a regular interval to investigate the activity of your network. The regular inspection may help reveal new bottlenecks or failures, which you would otherwise not be aware of until production came to a standstill.

NT Paging File

You should remember from the NT Server exam that NT uses disk space to expand the available memory for the system. The Virtual Memory Manager (VMM) swaps pages from physical RAM to the swap or paging file stored on a hard drive. Generally, the VMM handles everything about the paging file automatically, but you can control its maximum size and destination drive.

Changes to the paging file are made through the Performance tab of the System applet in the Control Panel. There is an area in the middle of this display tab labeled "Virtual Memory" (see Figure 11.5) that indicates the total size of the pagefile. Click the Change button to alter this setting.

Through the Virtual Memory dialog box, you can change the size of the paging file on any storage device. The paging file can reside on a single drive or in areas on multiple drives. However, the overall speed of NT is determined by how fast the VMM can swap sections of memory from physical RAM to the swap file. Thus, the speed of the storage device is important.

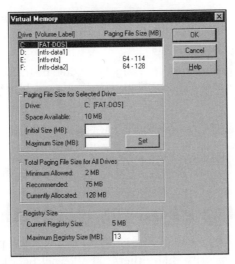

Figure 11.5 The Virtual Memory dialog box.

The two parameters you must define for each drive that will support a pagefile are "initial size" and "maximum size." The initial size is the space VMM initially allocates and uses for the swap file. The maximum size is the most space the VMM will use on the drive for the swap file. The VMM is able to expand and shrink the swap file as needed between these two settings. However, neither of these settings guarantees that the disk will have enough free space for a pagefile of the specified size.

Here are some hints on how to speed up the paging file:

➤ If your system is comprised of multiple physical disks, the paging file may be spread across these disks. This is called "disk striping," which automatically spreads the paging file across multiple physical disks. Disk striping increases the speed of the paging file because it uses the read/write heads of multiple disks instead of a single disk.

➤ If you move the paging file off the drive that contains the Windows NT system files, it keeps the paging files from competing with the operating system files.

➤ The pagefile should not be placed within a disk mirror because the double-writing of data in such a configuration causes a significant delay in pagefile access. Also, a pagefile shouldn't be placed in a duplex set because the temporary storage of memory data would require more CPU cycles to write twice (even over two controllers), once again increasing access time.

As a general rule, your pagefile should be the size of your physical RAM plus 12 MB. Thus, if your machine has 32 MB of RAM, you should set the pagefile to 44 MB.

While NT is operating, the PAGEFILE.SYS (the name of the swap file) cannot be deleted. If for some reason the swap file is deleted, NT will re-create it during boot-up.

Managing Process Priorities

NT's multiprocessing environment requires that some processes have a higher execution priority than others. The kernel handles the setting of priorities for each process and has the ability to increase or decrease the priority of a process to improve or alter how it executes. There are 32 priority levels (0 through 31). The higher-numbered priorities are executed before the lower numbered priorities.

Although the system has the ability to use all 32 levels directly, you have only a limited ability to set priorities. By default, all user and administrator-launched applications are assigned a base priority of **8** (/**normal**). However, users can launch applications with **4** (/**low**) or **13** (/**high**) priority and an administrator can launch with **24** (/**realtime**) priority. To launch an application with an alternate priority level, use the following syntax at a command prompt:

```
start [/low|/normal|/high|/realtime] application
```

NT offers two other priority controls to alter the levels of running processes. The first is a slide bar to control the performance boost for foreground applications. A foreground application is the process that is the active window on your screen, usually indicated by a colored title bar. This slide control is located on the Performance tab in the System applet in the Control Panel. By default, foreground applications have a priority of **10** (maximum). You can move the slider to set foregrounds with an additional priority level of **1** (middle tick) or **0** (none).

The second control is accessed via the Task Manager. By selecting any of the listed processes on the Process tab or any application on the Applications tab, you can change the priority to low, normal, high, or paused through the View|Update Speed command in the menu bar. On the Processes tab, you can change the priority of a selected process to low, normal, high, or realtime with the Set Priority command located in the right-click pop-up menu.

Optimizing Server Settings

The Server service is the process that distributes data to requesting clients. You can select one of four settings to fine-tune or optimize how this service operates.

 The dialog box shown in Figure 11.6 is reached through the Properties Of The Server Service listed on the Services tab of the Network applet in the Control Panel. The choices are:

➤ **Minimize Memory Used** This setting provides the best performance for less than 10 users.

➤ **Balance** This setting provides the best performance for 10 through 64 users.

➤ **Maximize Throughput For File Sharing** This setting provides the best performance for more than 64 users, by maximizing the memory available for file sharing. This is the default setting.

➤ **Maximize Throughput For Network Applications** This setting is used for supporting distributed applications, such as SQL Server.

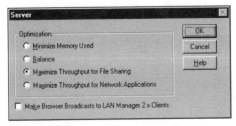

Figure 11.6   Selecting/Maximizing Throughput For File Sharing on an NT server.

Exam Prep Questions

Question 1

Which of the following is the best way to establish a baseline for Server service performance counters?

○ a. Capture performance counters from the Server object for 30 minutes during nonworking hours.

○ b. Capture performance counters from the Server object for 30 minutes during the peak hour, capture performance counters from the Service object for 30 minutes during a nonworking hour, then average these two measurements.

○ c. Capture performance counters from the Server object for 30 minutes each day at a pre-selected time for a week.

○ d. Capture performance counters from the Server object at regular intervals throughout the day for three days.

Answer a will not provide an adequate baseline because the captured data covers only a brief off-peak interval. Therefore, answer a is incorrect. Answer b will not provide an adequate baseline because the captured data represents only a brief off-peak and peak interval. Furthermore, the averaging of the times makes the data even more useless. Therefore, answer b is incorrect. Answer c will not provide an adequate baseline because recording a brief period every day does not reflect the overall picture of the network activity. Therefore, answer c is incorrect. Answer d will provide an adequate baseline because the data collected will represent all levels of use over a multiple-day period. Therefore, answer d is correct.

Question 2

You want to monitor the physical disk performance of a server remotely. With a standard installation of Windows NT Server on both machines, network connectivity, and membership in the same domain, what additional operation must be performed to enable the monitoring of the disk counters remotely?

○   a. Install Network Monitor Agent on the machine to be observed.

○   b. Run the **diskperf** utility with the **-y** option on the machine to be observed.

○   c. Install Network Monitor Agent, and run the **diskperf** utility with the **-y** option on the machine to be observed.

○   d. No additional operations are required. The physical disk counters are remotely accessible by default.

The Network Monitor Agent is not required to remotely monitor performance counters. It is only needed to access Network Monitor elements remotely. Therefore, answer a is incorrect. The **diskperf -y** command is needed to enable the physical disk counters, but all performance counters can be accessed remotely without further configuration. Therefore, answer b is correct. The Network Monitor is not required, but the **diskperf** command is. Therefore, answer c is incorrect. The **diskperf** command is required because all disk counters are not enabled by default. They must be turned on before PerfMon can access them locally or remotely. Therefore, answer d is incorrect.

Question 3

Users on your network are experiencing upwards of twice the normal time to access files from the NT server, but all other activities are relatively unaffected. Your server has three physical hard disks with two partitions on each. Which of the following is the best type of object counter to monitor to investigate this problem?

○   a. System object counters

○   b. Logical Disk object counters

○   c. Server object counters

○   d. Physical Disk object counters

○   e. Memory object counters

System, Server, and Memory object counters will provide little help toward a storage device performance problem. Therefore, answers a, c, and e are incorrect. Logical Disk object counters are the best selection because they will provide data on space usage and level of read/write activities on volumes. Therefore, answer b is correct. Physical Disk object counters are useful for hardware troubleshooting and affect an entire drive. The question focuses on the time to access files within a partition and not necessarily the entire drive, making the Logical Disk counters more effective. Therefore, answer d is incorrect.

Question 4

Which of the following utilities can be used to display the current level of CPU utilization? [Check all correct answers]

❑   a. Performance Monitor

❑   b. Network Monitor

❑   c. Task Manager

❑   d. Windows NT Diagnostics

❑   e. Server Manager

The Performance Monitor can display the Processor CPU Utilization counter. Therefore, answer a is correct. Network Monitor does not have a CPU utilization display ability. Therefore, answer b is incorrect. The Task Manager displays CPU utilization. Therefore, answer c is correct. Neither NT Diagnostics nor Server Manager can display CPU utilization. Therefore, both d and e are incorrect. Thus, only answers a and c are correct.

Question 5

Which view available through Performance Monitor should you use to create a baseline?

○   a. Chart

○   b. Log

○   c. Report

○   d. Graph

Chart view displays the realtime values of counters but cannot record the data as it is gathered. Therefore, answer a is incorrect. Log view records object counters and should be used to create a baseline. Therefore, answer b is correct. Report view creates a snapshot of the performance levels of counters from realtime gathering or a recorded log. Therefore, answer c is incorrect. Graph is not a view but a display selection in the Chart view. Therefore, answer d is incorrect.

Question 6

Which of the Server service optimization selections is recommended for use with fewer than 10 users?

○   a. Minimize Memory Used

○   b. Balance

○   c. Maximize Throughput For File Sharing

○   d. Maximize Throughput For Network Applications

Minimize Memory Used is the recommended setting for 10 users or less. Therefore, answer a is correct. Balance is the recommended setting for 10 through 64 users. Therefore, answer b is incorrect. Maximize Throughput For File Sharing is the recommended setting for more than 64 users. Therefore, answer c is incorrect. Maxamize Throughput For Network Applications is the recommended setting for a server hosting a distributed application. Therefore, answer d is incorrect.

Question 7

> After an application has been launched, which of the following are possible settings for the priority level on the Applications tab of the Task Manager? [Check all correct answers]
>
> ❑ a. Low
>
> ❑ b. Realtime
>
> ❑ c. System
>
> ❑ d. Normal
>
> ❑ e. Kernel
>
> ❑ f. High

Low, High, and Normal are three of the four selections available on the Applications tab; the fourth is Pause. Therefore, answers a, d, and f are correct. Realtime is only available on the Processes right-click pop-up menu. Therefore, answer b is incorrect. There is no such priority setting of System or Kernel. Therefore, answers c and e are incorrect. Thus, only answers a, d, and f are correct.

Question 8

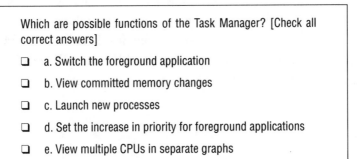

Which are possible functions of the Task Manager? [Check all correct answers]

❏   a. Switch the foreground application

❏   b. View committed memory changes

❏   c. Launch new processes

❏   d. Set the increase in priority for foreground applications

❏   e. View multiple CPUs in separate graphs

The Task Manager is able to switch the foreground application, view committed memory changes, launch new processes, and view multiple CPUs in separate graphs. Therefore, answers a, b, c, and e are correct. The Task Manager cannot set the increase in priority for foreground applications. This is done through the System applet. Therefore, answer e is incorrect.

Question 9

You just doubled the size of your server's physical RAM to 128 MB. If you have disk striping with parity implemented on a set of high-speed SCSI drives and are duplexing the boot partition, what change should you make to the pagefile settings?

○   a. No change to the pagefile size is recommended, but it should be placed on the stripe set.

○   b. The pagefile should be increased to 140 MB and placed on the boot duplexed drive.

○   c. The pagefile should be increased by 12 MB and placed on the stripe set.

○   d. The pagefile should be increased to 140 MB and placed on the stripe set.

The pagefile size is recommended to be the size of physical RAM plus 12 MB. Therefore, answer a is incorrect. The pagefile should not be placed within a duplex set, especially on the duplexed drive. Therefore, answer b is incorrect. The pagefile should be the size of physical RAM plus 12 MB. Therefore, answer c is incorrect. The pagefile should be 140 MB and placed on the fastest storage set available. Therefore, answer d is correct.

Need To Know More?

 Donald, Lisa and James Chellis: *MSCE: NT Server 4 In The Enterprise Study Guide*. Sybex Network Press, San Francisco, CA, 1997. ISBN 0-7821-1970-0. Chapter 15 contains information on Performance Monitor, Task Manager, and Server service optimizations. But, process priority settings are not listed.

 Heywood, Drew: *Inside Windows NT Server*. New Riders, Indianapolis, IN, 1995. ISBN 1-56205-472-4. The Performance Monitor is discussed in Chapter 13 on pages 561through 576. Virtual Memory is given a brief look in Chapter 12 on pages 509 through 510. The Task Manager and the Server service optimization settings are not discussed.

 Siyan, Karanjit S: *Windows NT Server 4 Professional Reference*. New Riders, Indianapolis, IN, 1996. ISBN 1-56205-731-6. A lengthy discussion of the Performance Monitor, Task Manager, process priority settings, and Server Service optimization is contained in Chapter 21.

 The Windows NT Server 4 manuals cover planning, configuration, and installation issues quite well. The *Concepts And Planning Manual* contains useful documentation on the Performance Monitor in Chapter 8, "Monitoring Performance."

 The *Windows NT Server Resource Kit* only mentions the Network Monitor in passing. It is not a useful resource for this topic. The *RK Supplement #1* contains many discussions on using Performance Monitor to investigate all aspects of a network.

 Little new information is available in either the Server manuals or the *Resource Kit* for the Task Manager, process priorities, Server service optimization, or pagefile management.

Advanced NetWare Topics

12

Terms you'll need to understand:

√ NetWare

√ NWLink Internetwork Packet Exchange/Sequenced Packet Exchange (IPX/SPX)

√ SubNetwork Access Protocol (SNAP)

√ Gateway Service For NetWare (GSNW)

√ Client Service For NetWare (CSNW)

√ File And Print Services For NetWare (FPNW)

√ NWCONV.EXE

Techniques you'll need to master:

√ Installing and configuring NWLink IPX/SPX

√ Configuring CSNW, GSNW, and FPNW

√ Using Microsoft's Migration Tool For NetWare

By making NetWare connectivity part and parcel of Windows NT Server, Microsoft makes it possible to integrate its products directly and easily with existing networks all over the world. Considering its built-in NetWare access capabilities, and the add-ins available at low cost from Microsoft for Windows NT Server to enhance these capabilities, it's clear that NetWare interoperability is an important concern in Redmond.

Even if you don't have any NetWare servers on your Windows NT network, you must still understand what Microsoft offers by way of NetWare compatibility and access to pass the Enterprise exam (as well as the Server exam). If you work in hybrid NetWare/Windows NT environments, much of this chapter's material might be familiar to you. On the other hand, if you don't have the benefit of direct exposure, you should study this chapter carefully. It will help you deal with NetWare-related exam questions, of which you're likely to confront at least one or two on the Enterprise exam.

Protocols And Compatibility Issues

To avoid paying royalties to Novell, Microsoft built its own implementation of the Internetwork Packet Exchange/Sequenced Packet Exchange (IPX/SPX) protocols. Surprisingly, comparisons between Novell's own IPX/SPX client implementations and Microsoft's NWLink (which is what it calls the protocols, to avoid using Novell trade names) show Microsoft's implementation as slightly faster than Novell's. In other words, these guys are serious about NetWare compatibility and have done a good job of it.

Although NetWare supports multiple protocols—primarily IPX/SPX and TCP/IP—it's most common to find IPX/SPX as the protocol used between NetWare's clients and servers. In fact, Novell itself supports no protocols other than IPX/SPX for versions of NetWare older than 3.x (which usually means version 2.2). Thus, if you see a test question that mentions NetWare 2.2, it's safe to assume that IPX/SPX is the protocol used to communicate between the NetWare server and its clients.

When Novell implemented IPX/SPX, it also used a special frame format for the protocol on Ethernet and other network types. Even though the emerging standard at the time (which has since become official) was to use 802.2 frame formats for networked communications, Novell elected to use what's often called a "raw 802.3" frame format for its implementation of IPX/SPX on Ethernet.

To make a long and complex story short, the upshot of Novell's initial decision and its subsequent divergence from industry standard frame types, introduced the possibility of a frame type mismatch when using IPX/SPX (or NWLink, in Microsoft parlance). You'll see one or possibly two questions on the test that deal with protocols.

 Here's what you need to know to deal with such questions:

➤ Although NWLink is provided primarily to enable NetWare access and interoperability, Windows NT-based networks can use NWLink, even when NetWare is absent.

➤ Until NetWare 3.12 shipped, NetWare's default frame type was raw 802.3, which Microsoft calls simply 802.3 frame type.

➤ For NetWare 3.12 and all 4.x versions (including Intra-netWare), the default frame type uses 802.2 headers, atop the native frame type for the network technology in use. Microsoft calls this the 802.2 frame type, without regard to technology.

➤ The total battery of frame types you're likely to encounter is:

  ➤ **802.2 frame type** Industry standard; default for NetWare 3.12 and higher-numbered versions.

  ➤ **802.3 frame type** So-called "raw 802.3 header" format, developed by Novell; default for older, pre-3.12 versions of NetWare.

  ➤ **802.3 with SNAP header** Sometimes called "Ethernet_SNAP" frame type in Microsoft terminology.

  ➤ **802.5 frame type** The native format for Token Ring networks.

➤ **802.5 frame type with SNAP header** Sometimes called Token_Ring_SNAP in Microsoft terminology.

Note: SNAP stands for SubNetwork Access Protocol, and it provides a mechanism to permit nonstandard, higher-level protocols to appear within a standard IEEE logical link control frame, like the frame types listed in the preceding bulleted item. SNAP is often used to transport AppleTalk or SNA in IP network environments. It's not necessary to understand the subtleties of this technology for this test.

➤ If any workstation (or server) is configured for an incorrect IPX frame type (one that doesn't match the rest of the population), an improperly configured machine can't interact with the network. This might occur even though the network otherwise works properly and all other machines communicate successfully.

➤ While Windows NT Server 4 can automatically detect 802.2 frame types, it cannot automatically detect any other type of IPX frame. This means that on networks where versions of NetWare older than 3.12 occur, Manual Frame Type Detection *must* be chosen when configuring NWLink. It also means that the IPX network numbers to which the Windows NT Server is attached and all IPX frame types in use must be explicitly identified as part of NWLink configuration.

➤ Windows NT Server can support a so-called SAP agent, which is necessary if the Server is to route IPX from one network interface to another as part of its duties. Otherwise, this functionality is not needed (we have yet to see a single correct answer to a question on this test that involves the SAP agent).

➤ For client/server applications (like SQL Server database access) or NetBIOS-based applications, native NetWare clients using IPX/SPX can communicate directly with a Windows NT Server running such an application. This can be done without requiring anything other than NWLink and the server side of the application to be installed on that machine. In essence, the client side of the client/ server application supplies everything clients need to communicate, with one requirement—the clients and servers must have a common protocol. Because the assumption is that native NetWare clients use IPX/SPX, a Windows NT Server must install NWLink to communicate with NetWare clients across a network.

Now that we've given you the heads-up on IPX/SPX compatibility issues, let's continue the NetWare discussion with some coverage on NT's Gateway Service For NetWare (GSNW).

Gateway Service For NetWare

Microsoft often refers to this software component by its acronym, GSNW. But there's more to GSNW than meets the eye, and it can be the occasion for some test confusion. Examine the listing in Figure 12.1 carefully. Notice that the complete name of the software component—Gateway (and Client) Services For NetWare—appears in the Add dialog box, generated from the Services tab on Network applet's Control Panel.

Unless you've actually looked at this on screen at some point or have been warned about it, you may be surprised to learn that GSNW includes Client Service For NetWare (CSNW), which is covered in detail later in this chapter. This means that any Windows NT Server with GSNW installed can also function as a NetWare client. This explains why you must remove existing NetWare client software—especially Novell's NetWare Client For Windows NT—from any Windows NT Server before installing GSNW.

Dealing with test questions that touch on GSNW requires that you understand what GSNW does and what's involved in installing the software. The next couple of sections provide key information aimed at increasing your understanding of GSNW features, installation procedures, and configuration issues.

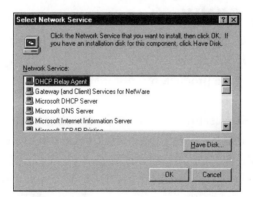

Figure 12.1   The unabridged expansion for GSNW is actually Gateway (and Client) Services For NetWare.

Understanding GSNW

Speaking generically, the term "gateway" refers to a software component that permits computers that do not share a common set of protocols and services to communicate with one another. In other words, a gateway translates between two incompatible protocol and service worlds.

GSNW is no exception. GSNW makes it possible for ordinary Microsoft network clients (be they PCs running Windows 3.x, Windows 95, or even Windows NT Workstation or Server) to access resources on a NetWare server. GSNW translates client requests stated in MS network terms into NetWare terms, and then translates the resulting responses of a NetWare server from NetWare terms back into MS network terms. The gateway is in the middle of any communication that goes from one protocol and service world to another.

 The "trick" that makes GSNW translations work is that the Windows NT Server where GSNW runs exports a logical volume from the NetWare server through a gateway that MS network clients can access as if it were any other NT-based network share. The gateway can also create a similar fiction for NetWare-based printers, making NetWare-based print services available to MS network clients. The chief selling point for GSNW is that it provides access to NetWare resources for MS network clients without requiring any additional software or software changes to be made to the clients themselves.

Installing, Configuring, And Enabling GSNW

Gateway Service For NetWare is an optional network service included as part of Windows NT Server 4. This means it's included with the distribution media for the product, but not installed by default when you install the core OS. To install GSNW, you must open the Network applet in Control Panel, select the Services tab, and then click the Add button in the resulting display. This produces the screen shown earlier in Figure 12.1, where GSNW appears as the second choice in the list. To begin installing GSNW, highlight its entry, then click the OK button at the bottom of the window. This prompts you for the NT Server CD, from whence it reads the necessary code.

Occasionally, a test question may reference NWLink separately from GSNW. It's important to note that if you elect to install GSNW on an NT Server that does not already have NWLink running, it automatically installs NWLink during GSNW installation. Thus, although NWLink is required for GSNW to run, it's not necessary to install it in advance, nor is it a problem if NWLink has already been installed when installing GSNW.

Here's a high-level overview of the GSNW installation process, emphasizing installation elements and information most likely to appear in GSNW-related test questions.

1. Before installing and configuring GSNW, you must create the following accounts on the NetWare server where the gateway will connect:

   a. User account on the NetWare server with rights to the NetWare file system directories that gateway users from the NT side will need.

   b. Group account named "NTGATEWAY" on the NetWare server with rights to all file and print resources that gateway users will need.

   Note: All users who share a GSNW gateway have the same access and rights to NetWare resources. The only way to create different collections of access and rights is to set up multiple gateways (keep in mind that only one instance of GSNW per individual Windows NT Server is permitted).

2. To install GSNW, you must log in to the Windows NT Server as an Administrator.

   a. In the Network applet in Control Panel, select the Services tab, click the Add button, and select the entry that reads "Gateway (and Client) Services For NetWare."

   b. Supply the NT Server CD or point to a copy of the \i386 directory where the necessary source code files reside. The software will more or less install itself.

3. To configure GSNW, double-click the GSNW icon in Control Panel. The Gateway Service For NetWare dialog box appears.

   a. Click the Gateway button to elicit the Configure Gateway dialog box.

   b. Check the Enable Gateway box to enable the Gateway service.

   c. In the Gateway Account field, enter the NetWare user name you created in Step 1a. Enter the password into the Password field, then confirm the password in the Confirm Password field.

   d. Click the Add button to create a NetWare share for use by Microsoft networking clients. A New Share dialog box appears.

   e. In the Share Name field, enter a name through which the NetWare directory will be shared.

   f. In the Network Path field, enter a UNC name for the NetWare directory that's being shared. For the SYS:Public directory on a server named "NETONE," the syntax is \\NETONE\SYS\PUBLIC.

   g. In the Comment field, you can add an optional descriptive phrase that will appear in the Browse window for MS clients on the network.

   h. In the Use Drive field, select a drive letter on the Windows NT Server to be assigned to the NetWare directory. This drive letter remains taken as long as GSNW runs on the Windows NT Server. By default, Z is the letter assigned to the first share name.

   i. The User Limit box permits administrators to limit the number of users who can simultaneously access the NetWare share. Because the gateway bogs down under increased loads, try to limit the number of users to 10 or so (unless the server's fast or only lightly loaded).

j. Click OK to save your configuration changes. You'll return to the Configure Gateway dialog box. Click OK again to exit the Gateway Service For NetWare dialog box. All changes will take effect upon the next system logon.

4. The only way to create NetWare shares is through the interface described in Steps 3d through 3j (not through Explorer or My Computer, as for normal Windows NT Server shares). Likewise, you must use the GSNW applet in Control Panel to set permissions for such shares.

    a. From an administrative logon, launch GSNW from Control Panel.

    b. When the Gateway Service For NetWare dialog box appears, choose the Gateway button.

    c. In the Configure Gateway dialog box that appears, highlight the NetWare share name, and choose the Permissions button. Use this interface to set permissions for the NetWare share.

5. Using NetWare Print Resources through the gateway requires no such special handling. Instead, configure NetWare print queues through the Printers icon in Control Panel (as with any other Windows NT Server-attached printer).

    a. From an administrative logon, launch the Printers applet. Select the Add Printer icon. This will display the Add Printer Wizard window.

    b. Select the Network Printer radio button, then click the Next button. This brings up the Connect To Printer dialog box.

    c. In this dialog box, you will see an icon labeled "NetWare Or Compatible Network" as well as "Microsoft Windows Network." You can expand and navigate this directory tree the same way you expand the Microsoft Windows Network tree, simply by double-clicking the network, selecting a server, double-clicking that server's name, and then selecting the printer you wish to manage. Otherwise, the procedure is exactly the same as installing an ordinary Windows NT network printer (covered in Chapter 13 of this book).

The important points to remember about this process are that it's necessary to map a drive on the Windows NT Server for the NetWare share and that NetWare shares and their permissions can only be managed through the GSNW applet (not through ordinary file management tools). NetWare printers, on the other hand, work like any other network printers through the Printers applet once GSNW has been installed.

That's it for the server side of dealing with NetWare, let's take a look at what needs to take place on the client end.

Client Service For NetWare

GSNW makes NetWare resources available to ordinary MS network clients. CSNW works with Windows NT machines so they can act as native clients to NetWare servers on the network. This system component is called CSNW only on Windows NT Workstation 4, which ships without GSNW. But, CSNW is part and parcel of GSNW on Windows NT Server. In either case, CSNW lets Windows NT machines link up to and browse NetWare resources alongside Microsoft Windows network resources.

Now, let's take a look at the requirements for sharing files and resources between NT and NetWare.

File And Print Services For NetWare

FPNW, as it's usually called, is not included with Windows NT Server 4. It must be purchased separately (but it only costs $100 in the U.S. market). What GSNW is to MS network clients, FPNW is to native NetWare clients—it makes resources from a Windows NT Server available to NetWare clients, without requiring additional software or configuration changes. Another way to think about FPNW is that it makes a Windows NT Server look like a NetWare 3.11 server to any native NetWare clients on a network.

Now that you know how to set up file and print sharing with NetWare, let's take a look at a handy tool Microsoft included with NT to help you migrate from the NetWare NOS to NT.

Microsoft's Migration Tool For NetWare

The name of this program, which ships as an optional element in the Windows NT Server 4 distribution media, is NWCONV.EXE. This program takes user and group data from a NetWare server, along with most of the associated rights and permissions that pertain to them, and re-creates that information on a Windows NT Server 4 machine.

Likewise, NWCONV can also grab volumes, directories, and files from a NetWare server and copy them to a Windows NT Server, while translating and preserving most of the file system permissions involved. This program is fairly sophisticated. It offers lots of bells and whistles for dealing with duplicate accounts and for converting information from its NetWare server incarnation to a reasonable Windows NT Server facsimile.

The aspects of NWCONV's behavior most likely to show up on the Enterprise exam touch on the Migration Tool's following capabilities:

➤ When duplicate account names are encountered during migration (which means identical account names already exist on both the NetWare and Windows NT Server machines), the default is to skip the account and not migrate any additional information from the NetWare server to the Windows NT Server.

➤ The Migration Tool includes options to permit duplicates to be transferred by adding a prefix to the old account name, thereby creating a unique name that captures the transferred information from the NetWare server on the Windows NT Server.

➤ If multiple NetWare servers that include identical account names are to be migrated to a single Windows NT domain controller, a mapping file that renames NetWare account names to Windows NT account names may be created to drive this process. Otherwise, only the first such account will transfer (if it's not already a duplicate). Microsoft recommends mapping files to achieve the best results when migrating account information from NetWare to Windows NT (consult the Siyan reference at the end of this chapter for details not covered here). One of the mapping file's most important functions is to preserve NetWare passwords on a Windows NT Server so that users need not learn another password once migration occurs. Because the Migration Tool cannot read NetWare passwords (they're encrypted), this is the only way to transfer such information successfully.

➤ If migration on a network involves replacing NetWare completely with Windows NT, it's important to remember that additional software changes may be necessary. To permit NetWare clients to browse Windows NT resources, it is necessary to install a Microsoft redirector on those clients. To permit NetWare clients to access resources on a Windows NT Server without replacing their client software completely, it is necessary to install FPNW on a Windows NT Server to permit it to look like a NetWare server to those clients.

➤ Only NTFS supports object-level file and directory security in the Windows NT environment; therefore, only NTFS can provide a reasonable equivalent to the file and directory security available from NetWare's own file system. In other words, NTFS provides the underlying support necessary to preserve as much security information from the NetWare environment as the two dissimilar security models will permit.

➤ For the Migration Tool to work, GSNW must be present on the Windows NT PDC where account and group information will be transferred.

Before you take the Enterprise exam, unless you work in a mixed NetWare/NT environment, please review the basics about GSNW, CSNW, FPNW, the Migration Tool, and NWLink, covered earlier in this chapter. If it sounds like gibberish, check the Glossary first, then reread this chapter (and at least one of the references listed at the end of this chapter) before you even *think* about taking an NT Server in the Enterprise test! For those who feel like they're better-prepared, here are some questions for you to study.

Exam Prep Questions

Question 1

Windows NT Server includes a Migration Tool to move data and accounts from NetWare to Windows NT servers. It can be especially helpful when moving user accounts from one or more NetWare servers to a Windows NT PDC. Which of the following requirements is most likely to benefit from use of a mapping file to guide the migration process?

○ a. When migrating unique user accounts from several NetWare servers to a Windows NT domain controller.

○ b. To make sure that existing domain accounts will not be affected by migration of identical user accounts from NetWare.

○ c. To migrate accounts from NetWare servers that do not have corresponding accounts in the Windows NT domain.

○ d. To supply passwords for migrated accounts in the Windows NT domain that match the previous NetWare passwords.

This is another question—and a corresponding set of answers—that requires careful reading to ferret out the "most likely" requirement. Answer a falls within the capabilities of a mapping file, but matches the default behavior of the Migration Tool, in that unique accounts (that is, those that are not duplicated, neither on the NetWare side nor the Windows NT side) are the easiest to migrate. Answer b relies on the default behavior of the Migration Tool where existing accounts will not be affected by identical accounts on a NetWare server. Answer c also works fine without a mapping file, because the Migration Tool can handle such accounts automatically. Answer d lets administrators supply the same passwords for NT accounts as NetWare accounts, which is not an automatic feature of the Migration Tool. This is the only behavior described in any of the answers that absolutely requires a mapping file. Therefore, answer d is definitely the best answer to this question.

Question 2

> To support a client/server application for NetWare clients to access a Windows NT Server on your network, which of the following additional software components must be present on the Windows NT Server?
>
> O   a. Gateway Service For NetWare
>
> O   b. File And Print Services For NetWare
>
> O   c. The Migration Tool For NetWare
>
> O   d. An NWLink SAP Agent
>
> O   e. The NWLink protocol

Client/server applications normally include whatever client- and server-side high-level capabilities and protocols that may be required within the applications themselves. The only absolute requirement is that clients and servers share a transport protocol in common. In this case, that protocol is NWLink. Thus, answer e is the only correct answer. Answer a, GSNW, is incorrect because it permits MS network clients to communicate with NetWare, not NetWare clients with Windows NT Server. Answer b, FPNW, is incorrect only because the client/server application itself provides the service-level access from NetWare clients to Windows NT Server. Answer c, the Migration Tool, is irrelevant because it applies only when moving accounts and data from a NetWare server to Windows NT Server. Finally, answer d, the NWLink SAP Agent, is incorrect because it is needed only when a Windows NT Server must be able to forward IPX Service Advertisement Protocol (SAP) packets from one network segment to another (which is not stated as a requirement in Question 2).

Question 3

> To facilitate a move from NetWare to Windows NT Server, XYZ Corp. plans to use the Migration Tool For NetWare. If the Tool encounters user account names on the NetWare server that match existing accounts in the target Windows NT domain, what will the Migration Tool do by default?
>
> ○ a. Prompt the administrator with an option to overwrite existing account information, or block the account information from the transfer.
>
> ○ b. The account will be transferred to the Windows NT domain, but a prefix will be added to all duplicate names.
>
> ○ c. All duplicate NetWare account information will be ignored.
>
> ○ d. The incoming NetWare account information replaces all existing Windows NT domain account information.

By default, the Migration Tool ignores any user account name on a NetWare server that matches an existing account name in the target Windows NT domain database. This makes answer c correct. Answer a is incorrect because the Tool does not prompt when duplicates are encountered. Answer b is incorrect because a mapping file must be defined to assign such prefixes (the Tool does not perform this action by default, nor would it know what prefix to assign). Answer d is flat wrong. The Tool has been designed to take the safest action by default, which is to leave existing domain database entries untouched.

Question 4

On a Windows NT Server where the Migration Tool For NetWare is to be run, which software components must be explicitly installed, assuming that no NetWare-related capabilities are already present on that machine? [Check all correct answers]

❑ a. NWLink

❑ b. Gateway Service For NetWare

❑ c. File And Print Services For NetWare

❑ d. The Migration Tool For NetWare

❑ e. Client Service For NetWare

As indicated in the discussion of the Migration Tool earlier in this chapter, Gateway Service For NetWare must be installed on a machine where the Tool is to be used. Thus, answers b and d are the only correct answers. Answer a is incorrect because installing GSNW on a machine where NWLink is not already installed will automatically install that protocol. Answer c is incorrect because the Migration Tool does not require NetWare clients to be able to access the Windows NT Server (although it might be a good idea to do so, after the migration is complete). Answer e is incorrect because installing GSNW on a Windows NT Server automatically installs CSNW (and CSNW is not available for installation on a Windows NT Server as a separate option). The trick in this question lies in remembering that GSNW includes CSNW, and that it will automatically install NWLink on a machine where the protocol is not already present.

Question 5

> XYZ Corp. has just finished migrating files and accounts from its NetWare server to a Windows NT Server on the network. That Windows NT Server already uses NWLink. NetWare clients complain that they cannot access the migrated files. What is probably missing on the Windows NT Server? [Check all correct answers]
>
> ❏   a. Gateway Service For NetWare
>
> ❏   b. Client Service For NetWare
>
> ❏   c. File And Print Services For NetWare
>
> ❏   d. Account permissions for the NetWare clients
>
> ❏   e. Microsoft redirectors for the NetWare clients

For NetWare clients to access files on a Windows NT Server, FPNW is the required software component. Therefore, answer c is one correct answer to this question. On the other hand, the NetWare clients must have a way to send requests to the Windows NT domain controller to browse available resources and request access to those resources. This is where the Microsoft redirectors for the NetWare clients come into play. These will permit the clients to browse network resources directly. Therefore, answer e is also correct. Answer a is incorrect because it lets MS network clients access a NetWare server, which is irrelevant to these circumstances. Answer b is incorrect because it lets Windows NT Workstations and Servers act as clients to a NetWare server, also irrelevant. Finally, answer d is incorrect because the question clearly states that accounts were migrated from NetWare to Windows NT.

Question 6

> Select all the protocols and file systems necessary on a Windows NT Server to accommodate the Migration Tool For NetWare when transferring files and folders, and their security information, from a NetWare server to a Windows NT Server. [Check all correct answers]
>
> ❑   a. NWLink
>
> ❑   b. TCP/IP
>
> ❑   c. NetBEUI
>
> ❑   d. FAT
>
> ❑   e. NTFS

Answers a and e are the only correct answers. NWLink provides the transport mechanism for moving files from the NetWare server to the Windows NT Server machine. NTFS provides the object-level security needed to accommodate NetWare's file and directory security information. Answer b is incorrect because the Migration Tool does not work with TCP/IP. Likewise for answer c, the Migration Tool doesn't work with NetBEUI. Answer d is incorrect because FAT does not support file- and folder-level security as a file system.

Need To Know More?

 Gaskin, James E.: *The Complete Guide To NetWare 4.11/ IntranetWare*, 2nd Edition. Sybex Network Press, Alameda, CA, 1997. ISBN 0-7821-1931-X. For a comprehensive look at NetWare networking, there's no better reference than this one. Use it to deal with NetWare specifics and the NetWare side of any NetWare-to-NT connection.

 Heywood, Drew: *Inside Windows NT Server*. New Riders, Indianapolis, IN, 1995. ISBN 1-56205-472-4. Chapter 16, "Windows NT Server And NetWare," explains the salient software, communications issues, and connectivity concerns likely to appear on the test.

 Minasi, Mark, Christa Anderson, and Elizabeth Creegan: *Mastering Windows NT Server 4*, 4th Edition. Sybex Network Press, Alameda, CA, 1997. ISBN 0-7821-2067-9. Minasi has been an NT guru since it all began. His experience and practical orientation show in Chapter 13, "Novell NetWare In An NT Server Environment."

 Siyan, Karanjit S: *Windows NT Server 4 Professional Reference*. New Riders, Indianapolis, IN, 1996. ISBN 1-56205-731-6. Chapter 12, "Integrating NetWare With Windows NT Server," brings Siyan's usual depth of coverage and details to this topic. It's the best available preparation material for NetWare questions on this test.

 Strebe, Matthew, Charles Perkins, and James Chellis: *MSCE: NT Server 4 Study Guide*. Sybex Network Press, San Francisco, CA, 1996. ISBN 0-7821-1972-7. Chapter 13, "Interoperating With NetWare," covers this ground well (only Siyan offers more details).

 Search the TechNet CD (or its online version through www.microsoft.com) using the keywords "NetWare," "NWLink," "Gateway Services," and related product names.

The Windows NT *Concepts And Planning Manual* also includes useful information on making NT-to-NetWare connections, and vice versa.

   The Windows NT Server Resource Kit contains lots of useful information about NetWare and related topics. Here again, you can search the TechNet (CD or online version) or the *Resource Kit* CD, using the same keywords mentioned in the preceding paragraph. Useful NetWare-related materials occur throughout the *Networking Guide* volume of the *Resource Kit*.

Advanced NT Printing

Terms you'll need to understand:

- √ Client application
- √ Connecting to a printer
- √ Creating a printer
- √ Network Interface Card
- √ Print client
- √ Print device
- √ Print job
- √ Print resolution

- √ Print server
- √ Print Server services
- √ Print spooler
- √ Printer/logical printer
- √ Queue/print queue
- √ Graphics Device Interface (GDI)
- √ Print auditing

Techniques you'll need to master:

- √ Installing and configuring a printer
- √ Managing printing clients
- √ Managing the print spooler
- √ Setting up print priorities
- √ Establishing logical printers and printing pools
- √ Creating and maintaining printer shares

The NT Server in the Enterprise examination requires you to know the material regarding printing covered in the Server exam plus a few additional topics. For your convenience, we've repeated most of the printing material from the Server Exam Cram book here, with additional enterprise-level printing topics. You should note that these additional topics are listed under the heading "Advanced Printing."

As a network administrator, it's your job to make sure that users have access to needed resources. One of the most often used resources is the printer. With many other network operating systems, one of the biggest complaints is the lack of the ability to effectively and efficiently handle printers. Microsoft developed an intuitive and simple way to manage these much-used resources. This chapter focuses on Microsoft's approach to printing and defines a few Microsoft-specific printing terms, with an eye toward preparing you for the printing section of the exam.

The Windows NT Print Lexicon

There is some Microsoft-specific printing terminology that must be mastered for successful exam taking. This section defines some terms as a prelude to the "meat and bones" discussion of printing with Windows NT Server 4.

These are the printing terms you will need to know for the exam:

> **Client application** A network program that originates print jobs (this can be located on a print server or client computer on the network).

> **Connecting to a printer** The process of attaching to a network share that resides on the computer on which the logical printer was created (performed through the Add Printer Wizard—accessed from the Start|Printers option).

> **Creating a printer** The process of naming, defining settings for, installing drivers for, and linking a printing device to the network. In Windows NT, this process is performed through the Add Printer application (also called the Add Printer Wizard).

➤ **Network Interface Card** These are built-in network interface cards for print devices that are directly attached to the network (such as the Hewlett-Packard JetDirect). The DLC protocol must be installed to communicate with directly attached print devices.

➤ **Print client** This is a computer on a network (called a "client computer") that transmits print jobs to the print server to be produced by the physical printing device.

➤ **Print device** The print device is what common terminology refers to as the printer. In other words, the print device is the physical hardware device that produces printed material. This is very confusing to most people. Just remember that the print device is the piece of hardware that actually spits out paper with your material printed on it.

➤ **Print job** This is the actual code that defines the print processing commands as well as the actual file to be printed. Windows NT defines print jobs by data type, depending on what adjustments must be made to the file for it to print accurately.

➤ **Print resolution** Resolution is the measurement of pixel density that is responsible for the smoothness of any image or text being printed. This is measured in dots per inch (DPI). When it comes to printing, the higher your DPI, the better the quality of the printed material.

➤ **Print server** This is the server computer that links physical print devices to the network and manages sharing those devices with computers on the network.

➤ **Print server services** These are software components located on the print server that accept print jobs and send them to the print spooler for execution. These components, such as Services For Macintosh, enable a variety of client computers to communicate with the print server to process print jobs.

➤ **Print spooler** The print spooler is the collection of dynamic link libraries (DLLs) that acquires, processes, catalogs, and disburses print jobs. Print spooling is the procedure of writing a print job to disk, called a "spool file." Print despooling is the process of reading what is contained in the spool file and transmitting it to the physical printing device.

➤ **Printer driver** This is a program that enables communication between applications and a specific print device. (Most hardware peripherals, like printers, require the use of a driver to process commands.)

➤ **Printer/logical printer** The logical printer (what Microsoft calls the "printer") is the actual software interface that communicates between the operating system and the physical printing device. The logical printer is what handles the printing process from the time the print command is issued. Its settings determine things such as the physical printing device that renders the file to be printed, as well as how the file to be printed is sent to the printing device (e.g., via a remote print share or local port, and so forth). Just remember that what Microsoft calls the printer is the software interface, not the physical printing device.

➤ **Queue/print queue** Literally defined, a queue is a line (that is, like standing in line). In printing terms, a queue is a series of files waiting to be produced by the printing device.

➤ **Rendering** The rendering process in Windows NT is as follows: A client application sends file information to the Graphics Device Interface (GDI), which receives the data, communicates that data to the physical printing device driver, and produces the print job in the language of the physical printing device. The printing device then interprets this information and creates a file (a bitmap) for each page to be printed.

It is very important for successful exam-taking that you know and fully understand all of these terms and concepts. Printing questions can be tricky, especially with this specialized terminology.

Printing With Windows NT Server

Windows NT print settings are managed through the Printers folder, which is accessible from the Control Panel or the Start menu. The Printers folder replaces the old Windows NT 3.51 Print Manager. This has simplified a number of printing aspects, such as print device installation and maintenance, as well as print permission management. This approach is extremely straightforward when compared to earlier versions of NT and other network operating systems.

Windows NT takes a modular approach to printing. Each component has a specific use and interfaces with the other components in the print architecture.

The following list defines each component of the NT printing architecture. Figure 13.1 shows a visual of the architecture:

> **Graphics Device Interface (GDI)** This component provides network applications with a system for presenting graphical information. The GDI works as a translator between an application's print request and the device driver interface (DDI) so the job is rendered accurately.

> **Print device** This is the physical hardware device that produces printed output.

> **Print driver** This is the software component that enables communication between the operating system and the physical printing device.

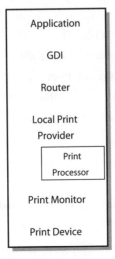

Figure 13.1 The Windows NT print architecture components work together to render print jobs for the user.

➤ **Print monitor** This component passes the print job (which has been translated to the print device's language) to the physical printing device.

➤ **Print processor** This component is responsible for making any necessary modifications to the print job before passing the job to the print monitor. NT actually has two print processors: one for the Windows platform and one for the Macintosh.

➤ **Print router** This component directs the print job to the appropriate printing device.

➤ **Print spooler** This component, also called the "print provider," accepts print jobs from the router, calls the processor to make any needed changes to the print job, and transfers the jobs one at a time to the print monitor.

Printing Clients

The following list examines how to set up printing for various types of clients:

➤ **Printing from Windows NT clients** This is where NT's approach to printing really shines. NT-based client computers need access to print devices, so they must add the printer (via the Add Printer Wizard). Previously, all client computers required that the print driver be installed on each client machine that needed access to a printing device. No more! All that is needed for printing from an NT client is that the driver be installed on the print server. This simplifies the printing process, because, if an updated print driver is released, it just needs to be installed on the server, not on every NT-based client machine.

➤ **Printing from Windows 95 clients** This process is the same as for NT clients. All that is needed is a connection between the Windows 95-based client computer and the print device, and for the print driver to be installed on the server.

➤ **Printing from MS-DOS and Windows 3.x clients** Unfortunately, the simplicity of printing from Windows NT and 95 clients does not extend to older client machines, such as DOS, Windows 3.x, and

Macintosh clients. The best idea for these computers is to create a central repository for print drivers. You can then use the central repository for any clients that must load the print drivers locally.

That's it for setting up clients to print to an NT print server. Now let's move on to some general printing topics, such as spooling issues and setting print priorities.

Spooling

As previously mentioned, when a user sends a print job, it goes to the print spooler. As a reminder, the spooler is the interface between the application and the print monitor. It is responsible for sending print jobs to the printing device. It is also responsible for tracking the print job through the printing process, routing jobs to the correct ports by tracking what printers are connected to what ports, and assigning priorities to print jobs. This section discusses spooling concepts pertinent to the exam, including setting print priorities, creating separate spool files, stopping and starting the spooler service, and changing the spool location.

Print Priorities

By default, the spooler prints jobs in the order in which they are received. It is possible, however, to ensure that print jobs from certain users are printed before any other job. To adjust priority levels for individual users or groups, you must create a different logical printer to a particular printing device (this is discussed in detail later in this chapter, in the section titled "Logical Printers And Printing Pools"). To assign higher priority to print jobs from certain users (such as the CEO, for example), perform the following steps on a logical printer:

1. Go to the Printers folder (Start|Settings|Printers).

2. Select Server Properties from the File menu for the logical printer to be adjusted.

3. Select the Scheduling tab.

4. Adjust the slide bar to assign a higher priority (this setting can range from 1 through 99, with 1 being the lowest, as well as the default, setting.

Separate Spool Files

If the printers on your network are hit pretty hard with many print jobs at a time, the print spooler can get to be fairly large. It is important to make sure that the spooler file is large enough to handle the jobs that are sent to it. Therefore, it may become necessary to create individual spool files for each printer on the network. This is performed through the Registry by creating files under the following Registry key:

```
HKEY_LOCAL_MACHINE\SYSTEM\CurrentControlSet\Control\Printers
```

Stopping And Restarting The Spooler Service

It is possible for print jobs to get stuck in the spooler. To remedy this situation, you may be required to stop and restart the spooler service.

To stop and restart the spooler service, performing the following steps:

1. Go to the Control Panel (Start|Settings|Control Panel).

2. Double-click the Services icon.

3. Highlight the entry labeled "Spooler" in the list of services.

4. Click the Stop button, and confirm that you want to stop the service.

5. Click the Start button.

6. Click Close on the Services dialog box.

This should remedy the problem of stalled print jobs in the spooler.

Changing The Spool Location

The default directory for the print spooler is \SystemRoot\System32\Spool. To change the location of the spooler directory, perform the following steps:

1. Go to the Printers folder (Start|Settings|Printers).

2. Select Server Properties from the File menu.

3. Select the Advanced tab.

4. Enter the path to the new spool directory in the Spool Folder text box.

One reason you might want to change this setting is that the drive for the default path has limited storage space for storing print jobs. Note that you must restart the print server before these changes take effect.

Now that we have covered spooling and priorities issues, let's move on to discuss setting up multiple printers and grouping print devices.

Logical Printers And Printing Pools

As previously defined, a logical printer (the printer in Microsoft-speak) is the software interface that enables communication between Windows NT and the physical printing device. You can create multiple logical printers that send print jobs to a single print device (and, conversely, a single logical printer that sends jobs to multiple print devices).

It is necessary to create different logical printers (with different share names) to assign varying priorities for print jobs from various groups and users to a single print device. All of this is defined through the Add Printer Wizard in the Printers folder. You simply provide different settings (such as access rights, access times, and priorities) for different shares that attach to the same physical print device.

When a printer services multiple printing devices, this is called a "printer pool." Put simply, a single logical printer spools out jobs to the next available printing device in the printer pool. It is necessary for the print devices in a printer pool to be of the same type. With this setup, the printer assigns files to be printed to whichever print device is free in the printer pool.

Now that we have discussed basic printing issues, we'll move on to explain a few issues that must be understood for the printing section of the Enterprise exam.

Advanced Printing

The Enterprise exam builds on your existing knowledge of Server-level printing and adds a few twists. This section pinpoints these precocious topics, encompassing discussions concerning the following:

➤ Print commands and controls

➤ Print shares

➤ Multiple physical and logical printers

➤ Print auditing

➤ Ownership

➤ DLC

➤ TCP/IP and Unix printers

The Print Commands And Controls

Solid knowledge of the common print controls and Printers folder commands is important. Take the time to review the multiple tabs of printer controls found in the properties of any locally installed printer.

Here are a few items on which you need to focus:

General Tab

➤ **New Driver** Installs or replaces existing printer driver.

➤ **Print Processor** Changes the data type used by the print system.

➤ **Separator Page** Defines a document to be inserted between print jobs.

Ports Tab

➤ **Enable Printer Pooling** Assists in configuring identical printers to share a single print queue.

Scheduling Tab

➤ **Available** Defines the time frames when a printer is active. If a user sends a print job to a logical printer when it is not available, that job is stored in the spooler and printed in priority order when the available time period arrives.

➤ **Priority** Sets the priority of a logical printer against other logical printers for the same physical printer (priority has no effect if there is only one logical printer serving a physical printer).

➤ **Spool Print Documents So Program Finishes Printing Faster** Indicates to use the spooler to store print jobs on a hard drive before or during printing. The alternate selection, Print Directly To The Printer does not save the print job at all. To reduce the time a large print job occupies the printer, select Start Printing After Last Page Is Spooled. Thus, the printer doesn't have to wait for the application to completely send the job over the network. It is stored on the spool before printing begins.

Some of the Printers folder commands are just as important to remember as the controls, such as those listed in the file drop-down menu:

➤ **Pause Printing** Halts the activity of the selected logical printer when deselected activity resumes where it left off.

➤ **Purge Print Documents** Flushes all waiting, paused, and printing print jobs from the selected printer.

➤ **Server Properties** Launches a dialog box where you can create new forms (paper sizes), modify ports, or perform advanced configurations. The Advanced tab has six important controls:

➤ Path to the spool

➤ Log spool errors

➤ Log spool warnings

➤ Log spool events

➤ Beep on document errors

➤ Notify completion of remote printing

You should remember to take a look at the individual logical Printers folders, as well. The Printer menu contains some of the Pause Printing and Purge Print Documents commands, as does the main Printers folder. The Document menu is the most important drop-down menu at the individual logical Printers folder level.

The important commands on the Document menu are:

➤ **Pause** Halts a print job.

➤ **Resume** Continues printing where paused.

➤ **Restart** Starts current print job over. Any document can be restarted if it has not been deleted from the spooler.

Printer Shares

One of the most useful abilities of a network is that of sharing a single printer with multiple users. The process of enabling other network users to access a printer is just as simple as giving users network access to a directory or a drive—you create a printer share. This is done through the Sharing command located in the File menu of the main Printers folder or the Printer menu of the individual Printers folder. All you need to do is assign a share name. Now, everyone on the network can print to that printer (provided they has the printer drivers available).

To tighten security on a printer, you must access the Permissions button located on the Security tab of a printer's Properties dialog box. The Printer Permissions dialog box acts the same way as the File Permissions version. The only real change is the types of access possible with printers:

➤ **No Access** Grants absolutely no access other than viewing the Net BIOS name.

➤ **Print** Enables users to print and manage their own documents, but they can only see the documents of others.

➤ **Manage Documents** Allows users to print documents and manage all print jobs.

➤ **Full Control** Allows users to print, manage print jobs, change per missions, and install drivers.

The default settings for a newly created printer share are:

➤ **Full Control** Administrators, Server Operators, and Print Operators

➤ **Manage Documents** Creator owner

➤ **Print** Everyone

To restrict access to a printer, you must remove the Everyone group, and then add group(s) and user(s) as needed.

Multiple Printers: Physical And Logical

Many of the exam questions that deal with printers involve multiple groups requiring printer access, with one of the groups printing large non-urgent documents. These situations are often resolved by defining multiple logical printers for a single physical printer and altering the priority or access times.

Keep in mind that:

➤ A single physical printer can be served by multiple logical printers.

➤ A single logical printer can serve multiple physical printers (pooling).

➤ Multiple logical printers can serve multiple physical printers.

Print Auditing

A printer is just another NT object. Therefore, you can use NT's audit system to monitor access, use, and errors. (For more details about NT's audit system, refer to Chapter 7.) You need to enable File And Object Access level auditing (Success and/or Failure) to track printer events. To set the events to Audit By User/Group, go to the Audit button on the Security tab of the Properties of a printer. This dialog box operates the same as the File version.

The events you can audit are:

➤ Print

➤ Full Control

➤ Delete

➤ Change Permissions

➤ Take Ownership

Events captured through print auditing are listed in the System or Security log, depending on the nature of the event.

Ownership

The creator of a logical printer is the owner of that printer. Only an administrator or a user with Full Control can take ownership of a printer (just like every other object within NT). In addition to the ability to change permissions on an owned printer, the owner can also modify form-to-tray assignments, install font cartridges, and adjust the halftone settings.

DLC

The DLC protocol is typically used to interoperate with IBM mainframes, but it is also used to provide connectivity to network-attached print devices. Most commonly, and for the exam, the DLC protocol is used for Hewlett-Packard network-attached printers and/or JetDirect interfaces (e.g., a printer NIC).

The DLC protocol is installed using the Protocol tab of the Network Control Panel applet. There are no configuration options; however, the binding order of DLC is important. The order in which adapters are bound (i.e., priority) to DLC is the reference number used by DLC applications—the first adapter is value 0, the second is value 1, and so on. Windows NT DLC can support up to 16 physical adapters.

To use DLC for printing, you must install both the DLC protocol and the Hewlett-Packard Network Port monitor on the server designated as the print server. You can designate any server to be the print server because the print device is attached to the network directly and not through a parallel cable to a computer. The DLC protocol must be installed first, then the HP Network Port monitor (HPMON.DLL) should be installed through the Add Printer Wizard Add Port command. Once installation is complete, the logical printer on the print server can be shared across the network and used as any other printer.

The Hewlett-Packard Network Port monitor can be configured so the managed ports are either "job-based" or "continuous connection," which are set at port creation. A job-based setting disconnects from a printer when the print job is complete. Thus, other print servers can connect and print. A continuous connection setting does not release the printer, so other servers cannot connect.

TCP/IP And Unix Printers

If your network has Unix workstations, you can use Windows NT TCP/IP Printing service. TCP/IP only needs to be installed on the printer server hosting the physical printer. The path of the TCP/IP printing service is the LPD (Line Printer Daemon) and LPR (Line Printer Remote). LPD servers and LPR clients are often Unix systems, but these utilities are available for most platforms, including NT.

TCP/IP Printing service is installed through the Services tab of the Network Control Panel applet. After installation, you can change its startup settings in the Services applet from Manual (the default) to Automatic. If the printer is hosted on a Windows NT machine, use the New Printer Wizard to create a new port of type "LPR Port" and direct it to the proper location of the printer, whether an NT print share or a Unix-hosted queue.

Logical printers are created to send documents to the TCP/IP printer through the Add Printer Wizard by using the IP address print server and the name of the printer, as defined by the print server.

Exam Prep Questions

Question 1

A single printer is shared by the Sales, Marketing, and Accounting departments. The Accounting users print large documents that tie up the printer for hours, but these documents are rarely needed the same day they are sent to the printer. You want to alter the printing situation so that the print jobs of the Sales and Marketing users will take priority and the Accounting print job will not tie up the printer. Which of the following steps are necessary? [Check all correct answers]

❑ a. Give the Sales and Marketing groups Full Control over the printer.

❑ b. Create three logical printers, and assign each printer to a single department.

❑ c. Set the Accounting group's logical printer so that it is only available from 8 p.m. to 6 a.m.

❑ d. Set the Accounting group's printer to send directly to the printer.

❑ e. Set the Accounting group's print priority to 99.

Giving users Full Control over anything is a bad idea, but doing so over the printer will invite them to delete the Accounting group's print jobs. Therefore, answer a is incorrect. Creating separate logical printers isolates the print jobs of the departments, giving you finer control over access privileges. Therefore, answer b is correct. Setting the Accounting printer to print jobs overnight will prevent the tie up of the device during the day. Therefore, answer c is correct. Sending the files directly to the printer will take longer to print than if they were spooled. Plus, if the printer is not available (off hours only), the print job would be lost because it would not be stored in the spool. Therefore, answer d is incorrect. Giving the Accounting group top priority will place its long jobs at the front of the queue. Therefore, answer e is incorrect. Thus, only answers b and c are correct.

Question 2

You have a large bank of printers. You have enough money in the budget to purchase two printers to replace two of the existing printers. How can you determine which printers receive the most usage (page count and print jobs) so you can replace them?

○   a. Audit File And Object Access events.

○   b. Use Performance Monitor to create a Printer object report.

○   c. Set the Application log to tally printer events.

○   d. Use the Printer Wizard to gather statistics.

You must use File And Object Access audits to record print activities, which in turn can be used to tally the number of pages and jobs sent to each printer. Therefore, answer a is correct. The Performance Monitor does not have a Printer object that you can use to create a report. Therefore, answer b is incorrect. There is no way to set the Application log to tally anything. The Application log records information an application sends to it to record. Therefore, answer c is incorrect. The Printer Wizard is used to create logical printers. It does not have any statistical abilities. Therefore, answer d is incorrect.

Question 3

During the printing of a 43-page document, your printer jams on the second page. You pause the printer through the Printers folder. After you remove the jam and reset the physical printer, what command should you enter?

○   a. Open the Printers folder for the printer, and select Resume from the Document menu.

○   b. Open the Printers folder for the printer, and select Restart from the Document menu.

○   c. Open the Printers folder for the printer, and select Resume from the Printer menu.

○   d. Open the Printers folder for the printer, and select Restart from the Printer menu.

Resume will start printing from the last place in the print job and will not resend the destroyed page or the data lost from the printer buffer. Therefore, answer a is incorrect. Restart will start the print process over again from the beginning. Therefore, answer b is correct. Resume is located in the Document menu, not the Printer menu, and it is the wrong command. Therefore, answer c is incorrect. Restart is located in the Document menu, not the Printer menu. Therefore, answer d is incorrect.

Question 4

Both the Sales group and the regional sales manager's secretary use the same network printer. How can you adjust the printing environment so the secretary's print jobs are processed quickly so she can keep up with her boss's hectic routine?

- O a. Set the Sales groups print jobs to print directly to the printer.
- O b. Give the secretary Full Control over the printer.
- O c. Create a separate logical printer for the secretary, and assign it priority level 99.
- O d. Create a separate logical printer for the secretary, and set it to use the Print Processor data type of RAW.

Sending the Sales group's print jobs directly to the printer will not improve the print time of the secretary. Therefore, answer a is incorrect. Giving the secretary Full Control will allow her to rearrange the print queue, but the added manual control will only slow her down by requiring her to perform administrative functions. Therefore, answer b is incorrect. Creating a logical printer with priority level 99 will place her print jobs at the front of the print queue. Therefore, answer c is correct. Setting the logical printer to use the RAW data type may prevent some graphical data from printing correctly and will not improve the print time. Therefore, answer d is incorrect.

Question 5

> A user is attempting to print to a printer attached to the network
> using an HP JetDirect card. The print server and the user's client
> machine both have DLC properly installed. But the user is repeat-
> edly denied access to the printer, even after the printer has been
> physically reset. What is the most likely cause of this?
>
> ○ a. The print server is disconnected from the network.
>
> ○ b. The JetDirect card is not compatible with the DLC
>   protocol.
>
> ○ c. Another user is printing to the device using the
>   Microsoft TCP/IP Printing service.
>
> ○ d. Another print server is configured with DLC set to
>   continuous connection mode.

If the print server is offline, the NetBIOS name of the resource would not
be present instead of a denial of service. Therefore, answer a is incorrect.
The JetDirect card is designed specifically for the DLC protocol. Therefore, answer b is incorrect. The TCP/IP Printing service in use by another
user would not deny access via DLC. Therefore, answer c is incorrect. If
DLC is set to continuous connection mode, no other access to that printer
is possible. Therefore, answer d is correct.

Question 6

> Several users are trying to print to a print server. You receive many
> complaints from users that they have sent several jobs to the print
> server but the jobs have not printed and cannot be deleted. How
> do you resolve this problem?
>
> ○ a. Verify that the Pause Printing option is not checked on
>   the print server.
>
> ○ b. Delete the stalled printer from the print server, create a
>   new printer, and tell your users to resend their jobs to the
>   new printer.
>
> ○ c. Delete all files from the spool folder on the print server,
>   and tell your users to resend them.
>
> ○ d. Stop the spooler service, and then restart it.

This scenario is a quintessential case of stalled print spooler. To fix the problem, select Services in Control Panel, stop the spooler service, and then restart it. Choice d is the correct answer.

Question 7

You have a Windows NT Server that provides print services to 20 Windows NT computers on your network. You have an HP LaserJet attached to the Windows NT print server. Hewlett-Packard has just released an updated printer driver. What must be done to provide the updated driver for the computers that print to this print server?

O a. Install the updated driver on all client computers. There is no need to update the server.

O b. Install the updated driver on the print server, and do nothing more.

O c. Install the updated driver on the print server and on all client computers.

O d. Create a separate logical printer with the updated driver on the print server, and tell all your users to print to the new printer.

O e. Install the updated driver on the print server, and instruct all client computers to download the updated driver from the server.

The best way to update a printer driver is simply to update the driver on the print server. Therefore, answer b is the only correct answer. There is no need to manually update the driver on each client computer that is running NT. When a client computer sends a print job to the print server, the updated driver is automatically copied to the client.

Question 8

> You run a network for a small consulting firm. You only have a
> single printer on the network. The company executives have asked
> that you configure printing so documents from the executives print
> before other users' documents. How is this performed?
>
> O   a. Create a separate logical printer, assign rights to the
> executive group, and set the printer priority to **1**.
>
> O   b. Create a separate logical printer, assign rights to the
> executive group, and set the printer priority to **99**.
>
> O   c. Create a separate logical printer for the executive group,
> and configure the printer to start printing immediately.
>
> O   d. Create a separate logical printer for the executive group,
> and configure the printer to print directly to the physical
> print device.

It is possible to set priorities between groups of documents by creating
different logical printers for the same physical print device and setting different priority levels on the printers. To set printer priority, select the Scheduling tab in Printer Properties. The highest priority is **99**. Therefore, choice
b is the correct response.

Question 9

> You have just installed a new printer on your print server. You
> send a print job to the printer, but it comes out as pages of non-
> sense words. What is the most likely cause of the problem?
>
> O   a. The DLC protocol is not installed.
>
> O   b. The print spooler is corrupt.
>
> O   c. An incorrect printer driver is installed.
>
> O   d. There is not enough hard disk space for spooling.

If an incorrect printer driver is installed, then documents may print illeg-
ibly. Therefore, choice c is the correct answer.

Question 10

You want to create a printer pool with five print devices. Which must be true for you to create a printer pool?

❍   a. All print devices must use the same protocol.

❍   b. All physical print devices must be connected to the same logical printer.

❍   c. All print devices must use the same printer port.

❍   d. All print devices must be located in the same room.

To create a printer pool, all print devices must be connected to the same print server. Therefore, answer b is the correct choice. All print devices should also be identical.

Question 11

You have a printer pool that consists of Printer 1 and Printer 2. Printer 1 is printing a job, and Printer 2 is idle. A paper jam occurs on Printer 1's print device. What will happen to the rest of the job that was being printed?

❍   a. The print job will be completed on Printer 2.

❍   b. The print job is canceled.

❍   c. The print job will be completed on Printer 2 because Printer 2 has a higher priority level.

❍   d. The print job is held for completion by Printer 1 until the device is fixed.

If a physical print device in a printer pool fails in the middle of a print job, the print job is retained at that physical print device until the device is fixed. Therefore, choice d is the correct answer. Any other print jobs sent to the printer pool will continue to print to other physical print devices in the printer pool.

Question 12

You want to configure a Windows NT computer to be the print server for an HP network interface print device. However, you are unable to locate the option to install a port for the printer. Why is this?

○   a. PostScript printing is enabled on the print device and must be disabled.

○   b. You didn't install the print driver on the print server.

○   c. The print processor is corrupt and must be fixed.

○   d. The DLC protocol is not installed on the print server.

For Windows NT to provide support for HP network interface print devices, you must install the DLC protocol. Therefore, answer d is the correct choice. You can't install a printer driver if Windows NT cannot recognize the print device.

Need To Know More?

Donald, Lisa and James Chellis: *MSCE: NT Server 4 In The Enterprise Study Guide*. Sybex Network Press, San Francisco, CA, 1997. ISBN 0-7821-1970-0. Chapter 8 focuses on printing, print shares, and print management.

Heywood, Drew: *Inside Windows NT Server*. New Riders, Indianapolis, IN, 1995. ISBN 1-56205-472-4. Chapter 6, entitled "Managing Print Services," details the issues relating to printing and printer permissions and management.

Siyan, Karanjit S: *Windows NT Server 4 Professional Reference*. New Riders, Indianapolis, IN, 1996. ISBN 1-56205-731-6. A nice discussion of using Windows NT print services is located in Chapter 17, "Windows NT Printing."

Strebe, Matthew, Charles Perkins, and James Chellis: *MSCE: NT Server 4 Study Guide*. Sybex Network Press, San Francisco, CA, 1996. ISBN 0-7821-1972-7. Chapter 14 contains detailed information about creating and maintaining your printing environment.

Search the TechNet CD (or its online version through www.microsoft.com) using the keywords "printing," "logical printers," "print management," "print devices," "DLC," and "TCP/IP Printing services."

The *Windows NT Server Resource Kit* contains lots of useful information about printers and printer management. Some places to start out are: *The Networking Guide* Chapter 14, "Using DLC With Windows NT" and *The Resource Guide* Chapter 2, "Printing." There are scattered documents about the TCP/IP Printing service and DLC.

Advanced Remote Access Service (RAS)

Terms you'll need to understand:

√ Remote Access Service (RAS)

√ RAS clients

√ Telephony Application Programming Interface (TAPI)

√ RAS Phonebook

√ Encryption

√ AutoDial

√ Logging

√ Null modem

√ Name resolution

Techniques you'll need to master:

√ Installing and configuring RAS

√ Configuring the RAS Phonebook

√ Implementing RAS security measures

RAS is an important topic for both the Server and the Server in the Enterprise exams. Some of the material covered by the Server exam is repeated on the Enterprise exam. To facilitate your study, we have repeated some material from the Server book about RAS, plus added the few extra issues that enterprise-level use raises.

What Is RAS?

RAS, or Remote Access Service, is a secure and reliable method of extending a network across communication links to remote computers. Modems and other communication devices act just like a network interface card (NIC) over a RAS connection. Everything a standard network-attached client is able to access and operate, a remote RAS client can do as well.

RAS in Windows NT 4 is a significant improvement over the capabilities in 3.5x. Many of its advances are borrowed from Windows 95, including the ease of installation, process of configuration, and the look and feel. RAS is able to support 256 simultaneous connections; act as a firewall, a gateway, or a router; and maintain tight security.

The following is a list of communication links through which RAS can connect:

➤ Public Switched Telephone Networks (PSTN)

➤ Integrated Service Digital Networks (ISDN)

➤ X.25 packet switching network

Standard Local Area Networks (LAN) protocols are used over the RAS connection. Thus, TCP/IP, IPX, and NetBEUI can be used for network communication over the link established by RAS. Because the actual network protocol is used, the remote RAS client acts just as if it were connected locally to the network. The only difference is in speed of data transfer—the RAS connection is slower than a network-attached connection. On the exam, there are questions that test your understanding of this; always remember: A client is a client is a client, no matter if it is connected locally or uses RAS.

RAS Clients

A RAS client is any machine that is able to dial-in or connect to a RAS server and establish an authorized connection. Although optimized for the integration of Microsoft-based operating systems, other system types can gain access with the proper software, protocols, and configuration.

The links established between a client and a server using RAS are often called Wide Area Network (WAN) links. This is because RAS is most often used to connect a computer (or an entire LAN) to a centrally located network over a long distance. It should not be too much of a stretch to think of the communication protocols used to establish a RAS connection as WAN protocols. Windows NT supports two WAN protocols:

➤ **SLIP** The Serial Line Internet Protocol connection supports TCP/IP, but does not support IPX or NetBEUI. SLIP does not support DHCP. Thus, every client must have an assigned IP address. SLIP does not support encrypted passwords. It is provided only as a means for an NT Server to act as a client when dialing into a Unix server, and it cannot be used to accept inbound connections on NT.

➤ **PPP** The Point-To-Point Protocol supports several protocols, including AppleTalk, TCP/IP, IPX, and NetBEUI. It was designed as an improvement to SLIP. PPP supports DHCP and encrypted passwords, and it is the most common and most widely supported WAN protocol.

Windows NT Server can act as a RAS client whenever it dials out over a modem (or other communication link device) to establish a connection with another server or computer system. The most common situation where NT is a client is when a LAN connects to the Internet.

RAS Servers

Windows NT Server can support up to 256 simultaneous incoming RAS connections.

Here are the important points to remember about NT as a RAS server:

➤   Only supports PPP clients. SLIP is not supported for dial-up.

➤ A NetBIOS gateway is established between the server and PPP-attached RAS client to sustain standard NT network operations.

➤ Supports both IP and IPX routing.

➤ Supports NetBIOS and Windows Sockets applications.

➤ Supports Point-To-Point Tunneling Protocol (PPTP) connections, which makes it possible for Windows NT computers to communicate securely over the Internet.

➤ Supports Multilink PPP (MP), where numerous connections can be aggregated.

Let's discuss these last two bullets in more detail.

Point-To-Point Tunneling Protocol (PPTP)

PPTP enables "tunneling" of IPX, NetBEUI, and TCP/IP inside PPP packets in such a way as to establish a secure link between a client and server over the Internet. PPTP connections are useful for establishing VPN (Virtual Private Networks) in small companies that cannot afford to obtain expensive leased-lines for wide area network communications. PPTP provides users anywhere in the world with a secure connection back to the home office's network. PPTP uses a powerful encryption security scheme that is more secure than the standard communications over the network itself. Thus, all traffic over the Internet using PPTP is safe.

PPTP must be installed through the Protocols tab of the Network applet.

Multilink PPP (MP)

Windows NT has the capability to combine the bandwidth of multiple physical links, which increases the total bandwidth that could be used for a RAS connection. This aggregation of multiple communication links can be used as an inexpensive way to increase the overall bandwidth with the least amount of cost. MP must be supported by both the client and server systems.

MP cannot be used with the callback security feature (covered later in this chapter). The MP callback feature can only control a single modem device to return a client's call. The only exception to this rule is a multichannel

ISDN modem. A single ISDN line consists of three individual lines: a D channel and two B channels. An MP callback can reestablish a connection with both B channels of an ISDN line because a phone number is used and the linking process usually is the responsibility of the modem itself.

The checkbox to enable MP is located on the Network Configuration dialog box, which is displayed in Figure 14.1 (seen later in the chapter).

When you install a modem or the RAS components of NT, Telephony Application Programming Interface (TAPI) is automatically installed. TAPI is required to control any communications device.

Telephony API (TAPI)

In Windows NT, the Telephony Application Programming Interface provides a standard method of controlling communications over voice, data, and fax. Although the hardware is not provided with NT, TAPI can be used to control many PBX systems and communication devices for automated activity.

As mentioned, TAPI is required to control any communications device. This includes modems. Each time a system attempts a dial-out connection, TAPI controls the modem and moderates the connection. Once the connection is established, TAPI continues to oversee the operation of the communication link.

The Dialing Properties dialog box (reached through the Modems applet) controls how TAPI uses your modem to place calls. You can control long-distance dialing, calling card use, prefix numbers, and tone/pulse dialing. You can also define multiple configurations based on physical location. If you travel with an NT Server notebook, you can define a dialing property profile for each of the cities you visit regularly.

TAPI is also the controlling entity for the Phonebook entries used to establish RAS connections. All the functions and features of the modem and the communication types established over a modem are configured through a TAPI-controlled interface (see the section entitled "RAS Phonebook" later in this chapter).

Now that we have discussed the RAS basics, let's move ahead to RAS installation and configuration.

Installing RAS

RAS is installed through the Services tab of the Network applet. Installing RAS takes some preparation and know-how to perform correctly. Following are the important elements to remember when performing the installation:

➤ Physically install or attach the modem.

➤ Install RAS through the Services tab of the Network applet.

➤ During the installation, if a modem has not already been installed, you will be forced to install one.

➤ Part of installing a modem requires the selection of the communications port.

➤ An installed modem must be added as a RAS device.

➤ The port must be configured for:

  ➤ Dial out only

  ➤ Receive calls only

  ➤ Dial out and receive calls

➤ The LAN network protocols must be selected (see Figure 14.1).

  ➤ If dial out was selected, only the outbound protocols can be chosen.

  ➤ If receive calls was selected, only the inbound protocols can be configured.

  ➤ If dial out and receive calls was selected, both outbound and inbound protocols can be configured.

➤ Each inbound protocol requires protocol-specific configuration, as shown in Figures 14.2 and 14.3.

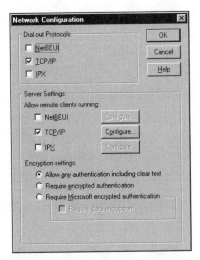

Figure 14.1   The Network Configuration dialog box for RAS.

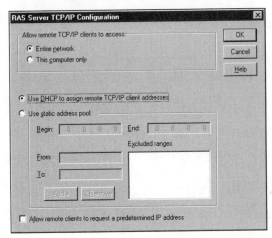

Figure 14.2   The TCP/IP inbound configuration dialog box for RAS.

➤ Once RAS itself is installed, you need to check your port and modem configuration through the Ports and Modems applets of the Control Panel.

➤ If RAS is configured to receive calls, the port and modem cannot be used by any other application. RAS locks the port to maintain control to monitor for inbound calls.

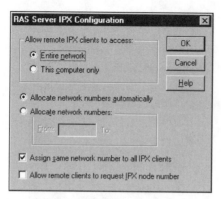

Figure 14.3 The IPX/SPX inbound configuration dialog box for RAS.

Now that we have discussed what RAS is and how to configure it, let's examine some RAS features.

RAS Features

RAS is a broad subject with many associated tie-ins to most of the standard network operations of NT. There is much more to RAS than what is listed in this chapter and what is covered on the exam. You'll need to review the reference materials listed at the end of this chapter for more RAS information. However, we have included some important features and options you need to know about RAS for the exam. The remaining sections in this chapter discuss topics such as RAS routing, gateways, and firewalls; the RAS Phonebook; RAS security, including encryption and callback features; RAS logon; AutoDial; and a number of other RAS features pertinent to the Enterprise exam.

RAS Routing, Gateway, And Firewall

On the dialog boxes to configure the network protocols for inbound calls, you can select whether to let RAS clients using the protocol to access just the RAS server or the entire network. If you allow RAS clients to access the entire network, you are using RAS as a router. When NetBEUI is the only protocol in use, RAS acts as a gateway to enable NetBEUI—a nonroutable protocol—to access the network. When you limit RAS clients to the RAS server, you are using RAS as a firewall. No access off of the RAS server of any kind is permitted.

RAS Phonebook

The dial-out capabilities of RAS are controlled and accessed through the RAS Phonebook. This utility is found in the Programs|Accessories folder of the Start menu, with the name Dial-Up Networking (DUN). The first time DUN is launched, you will be presented with the wizard to create your first Phonebook entry. Otherwise, the Phonebook dialog box will appear. Through this interface, you can create and modify dialup parameters for every RAS connection.

Phonebook entries consist of:

➤ Name

➤ Phone number

➤ Modem to use

➤ Server type

➤ Protocol settings

➤ Connection scripts

➤ Security settings

➤ X.25 settings (if applicable)

RAS Security

RAS has numerous levels and types of security to protect your network from unauthorized remote access. The following sections highlight RAS encryption and callback features.

RAS Encryption

Windows NT can be configured to increase or decrease connection security through the:

➤ Security Tab of a Phonebook entry for outbound RAS links.

➤ Network Configuration dialog box for inbound RAS links (shown earlier in Figure 14.1).

Three settings are available for RAS data encryption:

➤ **Allow any authentication including clear text** This is the most permissive setting. It should be used when the user is not concerned about passwords. This option allows a connection using any authentication provided by the server; therefore, it is useful when connecting to a non-Microsoft server. This selection uses PAP (Password Authentication Protocol), a clear-text authentication protocol.

➤ **Require encrypted authentication** This option is beneficial when the transmission of a clear-text password is not desired and when you're connecting to a non-Microsoft server. This selection uses CHAP (Challenge Handshake Authentication Protocol) or SPA (Shiva Password Authentication Protocol).

➤ **Require Microsoft encrypted authentication** For this setting, the Microsoft Challenge Handshake Authentication Protocol (MS-CHAP) must be used. Therefore, it is useful when calling a Microsoft server. (Also included here is Require Data Encryption. If this box is checked, data sent over the wire must be encrypted. Data encryption is provided by Windows NT using the RSA (Rivest-Shamir Adleman Data Security) Incorporated RC4 algorithm. If the data sent fails to encrypt, the connection is automatically terminated.)

RAS Callback

Callback is a security feature where a RAS connection is only established after the server has disconnected the inbound call and then called the user back. Setting callback is done via the properties of a user through the User Manager For Domains or the User|Properties command of the Remote Access Manager. The following three callback settings are available:

➤ **No Call Back** This is the default setting. No Call Back means that when users establish a RAS connection, they will not be called back.

➤ **Set By Caller** This means that callback can be set by the user. This is a good way to save on long-distance charges because the server calls the client back at the number that is set by the caller.

> ➤ **Preset To** This means you can configure the callback for a preset number. This heightens security because the user must call from a predetermined phone number.

The RAS Logon Process

In Windows NT Server 4, you can log on to a domain via RAS at the Logon prompt by selecting the Connect Via Dial-in and the proper domain. This allows you to establish a RAS connection to the remote network without requiring you to log on locally, first.

When you use TCP/IP via a slow RAS connection, an LMHOSTS file might speed up network access and name resolution. Place an LMHOSTS file on the RAS client. Ensure that LMHOSTS entries have the **#PRE** tag so that the IP addresses will be cached.

AutoDial

AutoDial is the ability of NT to remember the location of resources accessed over a RAS connection. NT maintains a map that correlates a network address to a Phonebook entry. When a resource is referenced, RAS reestablishes the WAN connection to regain access to the resource without additional user interaction. AutoDial is enabled by default. AutoDial does not yet function over IPX/SPX, but it works with TCP/IP and NetBEUI.

Logging

Troubleshooting RAS difficulties is much simpler when the logging capabilities are employed. There are two logging features of NT that record RAS-related activities. The first is the MODEMLOG.TXT file that records the modem's activities. This is enabled through a modem's properties in the Modems applet in the Advanced Connections Settings area. This file is placed in the NT root directory.

The second log file is DEVICE.LOG. DEVICE.LOG can only be enabled through the Registry. The "Logging" value located in \HKEY _LOCAL_MACHINE\SYSTEM\CurrentControlSet\ Services\ RasMan\Parameters should be set to 1. The DEVICE.LOG file is stored in the \%winntroot%\system32\ras directory.

The Event Viewer captures some RAS information that may be useful for troubleshooting and deciphering RAS. By default, all server errors, user connect attempts, disconnects, and so forth, are logged in the System Log.

Null Modem

A null modem is a serial cable that enables two computers to connect without the need for any modems. These special cables are common peer-to-peer attachment devices, but they can be used by NT RAS to establish a standard NT network connection. A null modem can be installed through the Modems applet by selecting it from the standard modems. A cable is not actually required for the setup, which offers you a way out when installing RAS if you don't already have the modem on hand. Once installed, a null modem cable can be used just like a modem, which is itself used by RAS just as if it was a NIC (meaning a null modem cable-attached workstation can fully participate in a domain, but at a slower data transfer rate).

Multiple Protocols

A RAS link uses both a WAN protocol and a LAN protocol to enable network communications. Most often, the WAN protocol is PPP. The LAN protocol can be any of the protocols installed on your RAS server, which may or may not be the same set of protocols on your LAN. However, even if you use multiple protocols on your LAN, only a single LAN protocol is used over the RAS connection. The first common protocol identified between the client and server is used. Therefore, the proper binding order of protocols to the RAS dial-up adapters should be configured so the most important protocol has the highest priority.

Name Resolution

In situations where static lookups occur, the most optimal configuration for resolution speed and WAN link traffic is to store the HOST (DNS) and the LMHOSTS (WINS) files on the local hard drives of the RAS clients. This presents some difficulty in maintaining the newest version of the files on multiple remote clients.

DUN Monitor

The Dial-Up Networking Monitor offers you a realtime assessment of the activity over RAS connections. Device statistics, connection statistics, and errors are some of the data sets presented by the utility.

Exam Prep Questions

Question 1

> If no standards are in place for the operating system, protocol, or the method of access for your remote clients, what is the highest level of security you can implement and still allow your users to connect via RAS?
>
> ○ a. Allow any authentication including clear text
>
> ○ b. Require encrypted authentication
>
> ○ c. PGP Encryption
>
> ○ d. Require Microsoft encrypted authentication

With nonstandardized configurations, implementing any encryption security other than Allow Any Authentication Including Clear Text results in some clients being restricted from accessing the network via RAS. Therefore, answer a is correct. Require Microsoft Encrypted Authentication and Require Microsoft Encrypted Authentication are encryption security schemes that require special configuration or operating systems. Therefore, answers b and d are incorrect. PGP Encryption is not a native option of NT. Therefore, answer c is incorrect.

Question 2

> Which of the following statements about PPP and SLIP are true? [Check all correct answers]
>
> ❑ a. PPP supports encrypted passwords. SLIP does not.
>
> ❑ b. SLIP supports NetBEUI, IPX/SPX, and TCP/IP. PPP only supports TCP/IP.
>
> ❑ c. PPP supports DHCP. SLIP does not.
>
> ❑ d. SLIP is used to access Unix servers.
>
> ❑ e. PPP is the most commonly used WAN protocol.

PPP supports encrypted passwords, and SLIP does not. Therefore, answer a is correct. PPP supports NetBEUI, IPX/SPX, and TCP/IP. SLIP only supports TCP/IP. Therefore, answer b is incorrect. PPP supports DHCP, and SLIP does not. Therefore, answer c is correct. SLIP is used to access Unix servers. Therefore, answer d is correct. PPP is the most commonly used WAN protocol. Therefore, answer e is correct. Thus, answers a, c, d, and e are correct.

Question 3

Which of the following NT networking activities are supported by a PPP RAS connection? [Check all correct answers]

❏   a. Printer share access

❏   b. Named pipes

❏   c. WinSOCK API applications over TCP/IP

❏   d. InterProcess Communications (IPC)

❏   e. User Logon Authentication

Because a RAS-connected client is no different from a directly connected client, other than speed of data transfer, all standard network activities still occur over the WAN link. Therefore, all answers—a, b, c, d, and e—are correct.

Question 4

While connected to the office LAN, you create a shortcut on your desktop that points to a documents folder located on the LAN's file server. After working with a few files from this folder, you close your RAS session. Later, you attempt to reopen one of the files you edited earlier. What happens?

◯   a. Access is denied because no link to the LAN exists.

◯   b. The file is pulled from the network cache.

◯   c. A file with a similar name on your local hard drive is accessed instead.

◯   d. RAS AutoDial attempts to reconnect to the office LAN.

Only answer d is correct. RAS maintains a map list of the resources accessed over WAN links. When one of these resources is referenced, RAS will attempt to AutoDial to regain a connection to the server hosting the resource. Answer a would be the result if AutoDial was not enabled, but you should always assume the default configuration for computers in Microsoft exam questions unless indicated otherwise. Therefore, answer a is incorrect. Answers b and c are fictitious activities that do not occur. Therefore, answers b and c are incorrect.

Question 5

Where can you find information related to RAS problems to aid in troubleshooting? [Check all correct answers]

❏ a. Event Viewer

❏ b. DEVICE.LOG

❏ c. Dr. Watson

❏ d. MODEMLOG.TXT

❏ e. NT Diagnostics

The Event Viewer, DEVICE.LOG, and MODEMLOG.TXT can be useful troubleshooting tools for RAS problems. Therefore, answers a, b, and d are correct. Dr. Watson does not track RAS events. Instead, it focuses on applications. Therefore, answer c is incorrect. NT Diagnostics will not provide useful information related to RAS. Therefore, answer e is incorrect.

Question 6

What is the best method for offering reliable and secure access to your network over the Internet for your remote users?

○ a. Internet Information Server (IIS)

○ b. Serial Line Interface Protocol (SLIP)

○ c. Point-To-Point Tunneling Protocol (PPTP)

○ d. Require encrypted authentication

IIS only offers WWW, FTP, and Gopher services, without access to the entire network or additional security. Therefore, answer a is incorrect. SLIP will not offer access over the Internet, it cannot be used to dial into an NT Server, and it does not support encryption. Therefore, answer b is incorrect. PPTP offers a reliable and secure network connection over the Internet. Therefore, answer c is correct. Require Encrypted Authentication is a midlevel security setting, but it does not directly offer connection over the Internet nor does this setting imply access to the network. Therefore, answer d is incorrect.

Question 7

> You have a field technician who travels extensively around the country. Her schedule changes often, and she rarely visits the same place twice. It is important that she is able to connect to the office LAN periodically, but your organization's security policy requires callback security on all RAS connections. How can you configure her account so she is able to gain access while supporting your organization's security?
>
> O   a. Set the callback security to No Call Back only for her account.
>
> O   b. Enable callback security with Set By Caller selected.
>
> O   c. Set the callback security to Preset To with her home phone number.
>
> O   d. Set the callback security to Roaming, and give her the page number to remotely configure the callback number.
>
> O   e. Turn on the callback Caller ID capture.

Setting the No Call Back option will violate the organization's security policy. Therefore, answer a is incorrect. Setting the Set By Caller option will allow the technician to input the callback number each time she needs to connect. Therefore, answer b is correct. Setting the Preset To number will not allow her to gain access to the network because she is never in the same place. Therefore, answer c is incorrect. There is not a Roaming callback setting. Therefore, answer d is incorrect. NT does not have a Caller ID capture setting, but this can be obtained through third-party software; however, Caller ID capture is not required for this situation. Therefore, answer e is incorrect.

Question 8

> Which protocols can be used over a RAS connection?
>
> ○ a. TCP/IP, NetBEUI, but not NWLink
>
> ○ b. TCP/IP, NWLink, but not NetBEUI
>
> ○ c. Only TCP/IP
>
> ○ d. TCP/IP, NetBEUI, and NWLink

TCP/IP, NetBEUI, but not NWLink is the restriction for the AutoDial feature but not a limitation of RAS as a whole. Therefore, answer a is incorrect. TCP/IP, NWLink, but not NetBEUI are the protocols that can be routed over RAS, but not a limitation as to which protocols can be used. Therefore, answer b is incorrect. Only TCP/IP can be used over SLIP, but RAS is not limited to SLIP. Therefore, answer c is incorrect. TCP/IP, NetBEUI, and NWLink can all be used over RAS. Therefore, answer d is correct.

Question 9

> What are the possible uses of a null modem cable? [Check all correct answers]
>
> ❑ a. Attach a workstation to a domain
>
> ❑ b. Enable subnet routing
>
> ❑ c. Test a RAS server locally
>
> ❑ d. Establish a VPN over the Internet
>
> ❑ e. Temporarily connect two LANs

Attaching a workstation to a domain is a use for a null modem cable. Therefore, answer a is correct. Subnet routing can only be implemented when two NICs are installed on the same machine. Therefore, answer b is incorrect. A RAS server can be tested using a null modem cable to simulate a remote client. Therefore, answer c is correct. A VPN over the Internet can only be established with PPTP and a connection to the Internet. An Internet connection requires a modem. Therefore, answer d is incorrect. Two closely adjacent LANs can be connected over a null modem cable. Therefore, answer e is correct. The correct answers are a, c, and e.

Question 10

Your LAN uses both NetBEUI and NWLink protocols. Your RAS server supports NetBEUI and TCP/IP, bound in that order. A RAS client also uses both NetBEUI and TCP/IP, bound in that order. Which of the following activities cannot occur over a RAS connection made between the client and the server?

○ a. Access a directory list of NetBIOS share names

○ b. Access resources on the LAN

○ c. Access resources on the RAS server

○ d. Access WinSOCK applications

The binding order of the protocols on both the client and server determines what single LAN protocol is used over the RAS connection. This situation will result in a NetBEUI connection. Thus, WinSOCK applications, those based on the Windows TCP/IP API, cannot be used because TCP/IP is not a protocol being communicated over the link. Therefore, answer d is correct. The other activities can occur using the NetBEUI protocol. Therefore, answers a, b, and c are incorrect.

Question 11

If static name resolution is used, what is the proper location of the HOST and LMHOSTS to optimize the lookup time?

○ a. Both HOST and LMHOSTS should be stored on the RAS clients.

○ b. HOST should be stored on the RAS server, and LMHOSTS should be stored on the RAS clients.

○ c. Both HOST and LMHOSTS should be stored on the RAS server.

○ d. HOST should be stored on the RAS clients, and LMHOSTS should be stored on the RAS server.

The fastest lookup time will occur when the HOST and LMHOSTS files are stored on the local hard drive of each RAS client because no WAN traffic needs to occur to resolve a resource location. Therefore, answer a is correct.

Need To Know More?

Donald, Lisa and James Chellis: *MSCE: NT Server 4 In The Enterprise Study Guide*. Sybex Network Press, San Francisco, CA, 1997. ISBN 0-7821-1970-0. Chapter 14 focuses on RAS use in the enterprise.

Heywood, Drew: *Inside Windows NT Server*. New Riders, Indianapolis, IN, 1995. ISBN 1-56205-472-4. Chapter 14 discusses the installation, configuration, and use of RAS.

Siyan, Karanjit S: *Windows NT Server 4 Professional Reference*. New Riders, Indianapolis, IN, 1996. ISBN 1-56205-731-6. Chapter 18 covers RAS in great detail.

Strebe, Matthew, Charles Perkins, and James Chellis: *MSCE: NT Server 4 Study Guide*. Sybex Network Press, San Francisco, CA, 1996. ISBN 0-7821-1972-7. RAS is examined in Chapter 11.

Search the TechNet CD (or its online version through www.microsoft.com) using the keywords "RAS," "Remote Access," "PPP," and "modems." The *Windows NT Server Resource Kit* contains some discussion of RAS, such as Appendix E, "RAS Reference," in the *Networking Guide*.

Advanced Troubleshooting

15

Terms you'll need to understand:

√ Troubleshooting

√ Boot failures

√ NTLDR

√ NTOSKRNL

√ BOOT.INI

√ BOOTSECT.DOS

√ NTDETECT.COM

√ Event Viewer

√ Last Known Good Configuration (LKGC)

√ Registry

√ Emergency Repair Disk (ERD)

√ Dr. Watson

√ Kernel Debugger

Techniques you'll need to master:

√ Understanding the troubleshooting process

√ Troubleshooting media errors, domain controller communication difficulties, STOP message errors or halt on blue screen, hardware problems, and dependency failures

√ Recognizing installation failures

√ Troubleshooting boot failures

√ Using NT's built-in repair tools

The arena of troubleshooting NT is both extensive and immense. Some of the issues covered on the Server exam are repeated in the Enterprise exam. In this chapter, we've tried to focus on the troubleshooting issues that appear on the Enterprise exam, including installation failures, boot failures, repair tools, printing solutions, and a collection of other pertinent issues.

Installation Failures

During the initial installation of NT, there are five common types of errors: media errors, domain controller communication difficulties, stop message errors or halt on blue screen, hardware problems, and dependency failures. Following is a short synopsis of each type of error:

> **Media errors** Media errors are problems with the distribution CD-ROM, the copy of the CD-ROM hosted on a network drive, or the communication between the installation and the distribution files. The only way to resolve a media error is to attempt to switch media, such as from one server's CD-ROM to another or copy the CD-ROM files to a network drive. If media errors are encountered, always restart the installation process from the beginning.

> **Domain controller communication difficulties** Not being able to communicate with the existing domain controller prevents the current installation from joining the domain. This is especially a problem when installing a BDC. This error is often due to a mistyped name, network failure, or the domain controller being offline. Verify the viability of the domain controller directly and with other workstations (if present).

> **Stop message errors or halt on blue screen** Stop messages and halting on the blue screen during installation are usually caused by the wrong driver for a controller card. If any information is presented to you about an error, try to determine if the proper driver is being used. If not or if you can't tell, double-check your hardware and the drivers required to operate them under NT.

> **Hardware problems** Hardware problems should only occur if you failed to verify your hardware with the HCL (Hardware Compatibility List) or a physical defect has surfaced in previously operational devices. In

such cases, replacing the device is the only solution. However, it is not uncommon for a device to be improperly configured or installed. Always double-check the setup of your hardware before purchasing a replacement.

➤ **Dependency failures** Dependency failures are when one or more dependent services fail due to the absence of a foundational service, hardware, or driver. An example of a dependency failure is when the server and workstation services fail because the NIC fails to initialize properly. If NT even boots with such errors, check the Event log.

Now that we have covered some caveats pertaining to installation, let's move on to discuss common errors in the boot process.

Boot Failures

Boot failures are problems during the startup of NT after a successful installation has completed. Some of the more common boot failures are presented in the sections that follow.

NTLDR Error Message

If the NTLDR executable is missing or if a floppy is in the A drive, then an error message is displayed as follows:

```
BOOT: Couldn't find NTLDR. Please insert another disk.
```

If the NTLDR is damaged or missing, you must use the ERD (Emergency Repair Disk) to repair or replace it. This process is detailed in a later section of this chapter. If there is a floppy disk in the drive, eject it, and continue the boot process.

NTOSKRNL Missing Error Message

If the NTOSKRNL (NT Operating System Kernel) is corrupt, missing, or the BOOT.INI points to the wrong partition, an error message like the following appears:

```
Windows NT could not start because the following
file is missing or corrupt:
```

```
\winnt root\system32\ntoskrnl.exe
Please re-install a copy of the above file.
```

This error can be resolved by repairing the NTOSKRNL file using the ERD repair process. Or, if BOOT.INI is wrong, you can edit it to correct the problem (see the discussion on ARC names in Chapter 6).

BOOT.INI Missing Error Message

If no BOOT.INI is present, the NTLDR will attempt to load NT from the default \winnt directory of the current partition. If this fails, an error message similar to the following appears:

```
BOOT: Couldn't find NTLDR. Please insert another disk.
```

To alleviate this problem, replace the BOOT.INI file from a backup or use the ERD to repair.

BOOTSECT.DOS Missing Error Message

If the BOOTSECT.DOS file is not present to boot to MS-DOS or another operating system (not NT), an error message appears as follows:

```
I/O Error accessing boot sector file
multi(0)disk(0)rdisk(0)partition(1):\bootsect.dos
```

This indicates that the BOOT.INI file has been changed, the partition numbering has changed, or the partition is missing, inactive, or inaccessible. To attempt to repair or replace the BOOTSECT.DOS file, use the ERD repair procedure.

NTDETECT.COM Missing Error Message

If the NTDETECT.COM file is not present, the following error message appears:

```
NTDETECT V1.0 Checking Hardware...
NTDETECT failed
```

This error must be repaired with the ERD repair process.

Repair Tools

Fortunately, NT does not leave you high and dry when you encounter errors. There is a handful of invaluable tools you can use to repair and correct operational difficulties. In the next few sections, we detail how to use the Event Viewer, Last Known Good Configuration, Registry, and ERD.

Event Viewer

The Event Viewer, located in Programs|Administrative Tools, is used to inspect the three logs created by NT automatically. These logs are:

> **System** Records information and alerts about NT's internal processes.

> **Security** Records security-related events.

> **Application** Records NT application events, alerts, and system messages.

Each log records a different type of information, but all the logs collect the same information about each event: date, time, source, category, event, user ID, and computer. Plus, each event recorded has, at worst, an error code number or, at best, a detailed description with a memory HEX buffer capture.

Most system errors, including stop errors that result in the blue screen, are recorded in the System log. This allows you to review the time and circumstances around a system failure.

Last Known Good Configuration

The Last Known Good Configuration (LKGC) is a recording made by NT of all the Registry settings that existed the last time a user successfully logged on to the server. Every time a login completes, NT records a new LKGC. If a system error occurs or the Registry becomes corrupted so that booting or logging in is not possible, the LKGC can be used to return to a previously operational state. The LKGC is accessed during bootup when the following message displays: "Press the spacebar to boot with the Last Known Good Configuration." A menu will appear where you can select to load using the LKGC (by pressing L) or other stored configurations.

The Registry

Editing the Registry by hand should be the last resort. A single, improperly configured Registry entry can render an installation of NT DOA. There are two Registry editing utilities: REGEDIT and REGEDT32. Both of these utilities must be launched from the Run command or a DOS prompt. REGEDIT displays all the hives of the Registry in a single display window, and the entire Registry can be searched at one time. REGEDT32 displays each of the five hives in a separate display window, but it offers more security- and control-related functions.

It is a good idea to regularly back up your Registry. This can be done using:

➤ NT Backup

➤ Disk Administrator (SYSTEM key only)

➤ Either Registry editing tool (REGEDIT or REGEDT32)

➤ REGBACK utility from the Resource Kit

The best times to make a backup are just before and after any significant changes are made to your system, such as hardware installation, software installation, or service pack application. If NT fails to operate properly but boots up, you can attempt a repair by restoring the Registry from a backup.

There are a few things you should note about working with the Registry. When you edit the Registry, you are working with it in memory. This means that the instant you make a Registry change, it goes into effect. However, in some cases, a reboot is required to correct memory settings and launch applications to fully comply with the changes. It is always a good idea to reboot after editing the Registry. Also, when a key of the Registry is saved (or backed up), you capture all the subcontents of that key. This is important to remember when restoring portions of the Registry from backup. All subkeys below the point at which restoration occurs will also be overwritten by the saved version. Any and all changes made since the backup will be lost in the sections restored.

Emergency Repair Disk

Emergency Repair Disk (ERD) is the miniature first-aid kit for NT. This single floppy contains all the files needed to repair system-partition and many boot-partition problems. The ERD is most often used to repair or replace files that are critical to the boot process of NT. An ERD is usually created during the installation of NT, but additional and updated ERDs can be created using the RDISK.EXE utility. At the Run command, **RDISK /S** will force NT to save to disk all current Registry settings in memory to \Winnt\System32\Config, then prompt you for a preformatted disk. The ERD will contain the files listed in Table 15.1.

The ERD does not contain the entire Registry but just enough to fix the most common errors. To use the ERD to make repairs, you need the three setup disks used to install NT. The repair process is depicted in the following steps:

1. Reboot the computer using Windows NT setup Disks 1 and 2.

2. Select "R" for Repair. A menu appears containing the following options:

   ➤ Inspect Registry files

   ➤ Inspect startup environment

   ➤ Verify Windows NT system files

   ➤ Inspect boot sector

Table 15.1   The contents of an ERD.

File	Contents
SYSTEM._	HKEY_LOCAL_MACHINE\SYSTEM compressed
SOFTWARE._	HKEY_LOCAL_MACHINE\SOFTWARE compressed
SECURITY._	HKEY_LOCAL_MACHINE\SECURITY compressed
SAM._	HKEY_LOCAL_MACHINE\SAM compressed
NTUSER.DA_	Default profile, compressed
AUTOEXEC.NT	%winntroot%\system32\autoexec.nt
CONFIG.NT	%winntroot%\system32\config.nt
SETUP.LOG	List of installed files and their checksums
DEFAULT._	HKEY_USERS\DEFAULT compressed

3. Deselect any options you do not wish to use, then continue.

4. Insert Disk 3 and the ERD when prompted.

Now that we have discussed some common system problems, let's move on to everyone's favorite—printing.

Printing Solutions

When working with printers, there seems to be an infinite number of issues to resolve before normal operation is restored after an error. Many printer problems are either simple or obvious, so always check the obvious before moving on to more complicated solutions. Here is a short list of tasks you can perform when digging for a printer solution:

➤ Always check the physical aspects of the printer—cable, power, paper, toner, and so on.

➤ Check the logical printer on both the client and server.

➤ Check the print queue for stalled jobs.

➤ Make sure the printer driver has not become corrupted by reinstalling it.

➤ Attempt to print from a different application or a different client.

➤ Print using Administrator access.

➤ Stop and restart the spooler using the Services applet.

➤ Check the status and CPU usage of the SPOOLSS.EXE using the Task Manager.

➤ Check the free space on the drive hosting the spooler file, and change its destination.

There are a number of topics that don't really fall into any one category, the following sections discuss this hodgepodge of troubleshooting considerations.

Miscellaneous Troubleshooting Issues

The following sections cover a handful of great troubleshooting items that just don't fit well into any particular section. Topics included here encompass issues such as permissions problems, re-creating setup disks, the master boot record, and other troubleshooting issues.

Permissions Problems

If a permissions problem is suspected, attempt the action using the Administrator account or temporarily add the user account to the Administrators group. Double-check group memberships for conflicting access levels, especially No Access. Check the access control list (ACL) on the object in question for group and No Access assignments. Check the permissions on the share if appropriate. Check user, group, or computer policies for access restrictions.

Re-creating The Setup Disks

If you need a new set of installation floppies, run the WINNT.EXE (or WINNT32.EXE) program from the installation CD with the /ox parameter. This will create the three floppies without initializing the actual installation process. However, you will need to preformat the diskettes beforehand.

Master Boot Record

If the Master Boot Record (MBR) fails on the system partition (the section of the disk that contains BOOT.INI, NTLOADER, and NT DETECT), the ERD will not help with its restoration. Instead, you'll need to use the first diskette from DOS 6.0 (or higher). Executing **FDISK / MBR** re-creates the MBR and allows the system to boot.

Dr. Watson

Dr. Watson is NT's application error debugger. It detects application errors, diagnoses the error, and logs the diagnostic information. Most of the information gathered by Dr. Watson is only useful when working with a Microsoft technical professional to diagnose an application error. Data captured by Dr. Watson is stored in the DRWTSN32.LOG file. Dr. Watson can also be used to create a binary crash dump file of the memory where the failing application operates.

Dr. Watson launches itself automatically whenever an application error occurs. However, to configure Dr. Watson, you can launch it by executing DRWTSN32 at the command prompt or in the Run dialog box. The configuration options of Dr. Watson are fairly obvious, the only two that may cause some confusion are:

➤ **Dump Symbol Table** Adds the corresponding symbol data to the dump file, greatly increasing its size.

➤ **Dump All Thread Contexts** Forces a dump file to be created for all active threads, not just those owned by the failed application.

BOOT.INI Switches

To improve the troubleshooting abilities of the bootup, you can use one of the following switches after each OS line in the BOOT.INI file (remember those are the ones with the ARC name followed by the displayable name in quotes):

➤ **/BASEVIDEO** Boots using the standard VGA video driver.

➤ **/BAUDRATE=***n* Sets the debugging communication baud rate when using the Kernel Debugger. Default is 9,600 for a modem and 19,200 for a null modem cable.

➤ **/CRASHDEBUG** Loads the debugger into memory, where it remains inactive unless a Kernel error occurs.

➤ **/DEBUG** Loads the debugger into memory to be activated by a host debugger connected to the computer. See the section titled "Kernel Debugger" later in this chapter.

➤ **/DEBUGPORT=** com*x* Sets the debugging COM port.

➤ **/MAXMEM:n** Sets the maximum amount of RAM that Windows NT can use.

➤ **/NODEBUG** Indicates that no debugging information is being used.

➤ **/NOSERIALMICE=[COM*x* | COM*x,y,z*...]** Disables serial mouse detection of the specified COM port(s).

➤ **/SOS** Specifies to display each driver name when it is loaded.

VGA Mode

If you set your video driver to something that prevents a readable display, you can select VGA Mode from the boot menu to boot with the standard VGA driver loaded. Then, you can modify the display drivers to correct the problem.

NTDETECT Debugged

If NTDETECT fails to detect the proper hardware, it may be corrupted or damaged or your hardware may not be functioning properly. A debugged or checked version of NTDETECT is stored on the CD in the Support \Debug\I386 directory. First, rename NTDETECT.COM to NT DETECT.BAK, then copy the file named NTDETECT.CHK to the system partition, and rename it to NTDETECT.COM. Then, you can reboot. This version of NTDETECT will give a verbose display of all detection activities to help isolate the problem. NTDETECT.COM has the attributes of Hidden, System, and Read Only set. You need to deselect these attributes before renaming the file, and reset them after the renaming process. Once you've solved the hardware detection problem, return the original NTDETECT from NTDETECT.BAK or the ERD.

ESDI Hard Drives

Some ESDI hard drives are not supported by NT. ESDI hard drives are pre-IDE type storage devices that have the ability of being low-level formatted with various values of sector per track. Due to special formatting geometry and drive controllers, NT may be able to access cylinders beyond 1,024. If NT has direct access to the above 1,024 cylinders, only NT, not DOS, can access these areas. If the controller handles a translation so that it is transparent, both NT and DOS can access above 1,024 cylinder areas.

A determination whether NT can even use an ESDI disk cannot be made until an installation is attempted. If NT fails to install properly on an ESDI disk, then a Fatal System Error:0x0000006b message will be displayed after NTLDR starts. When this occurs, you can deduce that the ESDI drive is not supported by NT.

Now that we've wrapped up many of troubleshooting's loose ends, let's take a look at some advanced troubleshooting issues.

Troubleshooting

In addition to the tools and utilities listed earlier in this chapter, there are three more troubleshooting mechanisms that require a professional support engineer to interpret. The three mechanisms—blue screen, Kernel Debugger, and memory dump—are listed here only for your general understanding.

Blue Screen

No matter what "they" tell you, NT has GPFs, but they aren't called that. When a GPF occurs under NT, the blue screen "of death" appears. This is a test display of the STOP message error. There are lots of details included on this screen, such as the location of the error, type of the error, and whether a memory dump is created. Unfortunately, most of the data is in hex or a strange acronym shorthand that you won't be able to read.

Kernel Debugger

The Kernel Debugger records the activity of NT during bootup and when a stop error occurs. To employ the Kernel Debugger, two computers with the same version of NT connected by a null modem cable or RAS must be used. One computer is designated as the host, and the other computer is the target. The host machine must have the symbol files installed from the NT CD-ROM (or the version associated with the installed Service Pack). The debugging software is located on the CD in the \support\debug\platform directory. This path must be copied onto the host machine, as well.

Memory Dump

A memory dump is the act of writing the entire contents of memory to a file when a STOP error occurs. The contents of this file can be inspected to determine the cause of the failure. Memory dumps are configured on the Startup/Shutdown tab of the System applet. The options are:

➤ Write the error event to the System log

➤ Send an Administrative alert

➤ Write a dump file

➤ Automatically reboot

The default location and the name of the memory dump file is %WINNTROOT%\MEMORY.DMP. The DUMPEXAM.EXE utility can be used to view the contents of a memory dump file. However, most of the contents will require a Microsoft technical professional to interpret.

Exam Prep Questions

Question 1

> Which of the following can be corrected by the repair process
> using the three installation disks and a recent Emergency Repair
> Disk? [Check all correct answers]
>
> ❏ a. Boot sector corruption
>
> ❏ b. Unable to locate Master Boot Record
>
> ❏ c. NTLDR not found
>
> ❏ d. Corrupt NTOSKRNL

The ERD repair process can often correct boot sector problems, replace
the NTLDR, and repair the NTOSKRNL. Thus, answers a, c, and d are
correct. The MBR cannot be repaired with the ERD or the installation
floppies—that requires a DOS setup disk. Therefore, answer b is incorrect.

Question 2

> Your NT Server experiences a STOP error due to a runaway pro-
> cess from a custom application developed in-house. Where can
> information about this error be found once the server has been
> rebooted?
>
> ○ a. Kernel Debugger
>
> ○ b. Performance Monitor
>
> ○ c. Event Viewer
>
> ○ d. NT Diagnostics

The Kernel Debugger is only able to view STOP error information when
specifically configured and installed on two connected machines. That situation was not indicated in this question. Therefore, answer a is incorrect.
The Performance Monitor and NT Diagnostics are not able to record any
information about a STOP error. Therefore, answers b and d are incorrect.
The Event Viewer can be used to view the System log where all STOP
errors are recorded. Therefore, answer c is correct.

Question 3

> Which two parameter switches are present by default on the VGA
> Mode selection ARC name line in the BOOT.INI file? [Check two
> answers]
>
> ❑　a. /nodebug
>
> ❑　b. /basevideo
>
> ❑　c. /noserialmice
>
> ❑　d. /sos
>
> ❑　e. /vgavideo

The parameters **/nodebug** and **/noserialmice** are not present on the VGA
Mode line by default. Therefore, answers a and c are incorrect. The parameters **/basevideo** and **/sos** are present on the VGA Mode line by default.
Therefore, answers b and d are correct. The parameter **/vgavideo** is not a
valid parameter. Therefore, answer e is incorrect.

Question 4

> The **SYSTEM** Registry key contains errors. You do not have a re-
> cent ERD, but you do have a copy of the **SYSTEM** key itself on
> floppy. Which of the following programs should you use to re-
> store the **SYSTEM** key from the floppy disk?
>
> ○　a. Disk Administrator
>
> ○　b. System applet
>
> ○　c. Network Client Administrator
>
> ○　d. Server Manager

The Disk Administrator is the correct utility to use to restore the
SYSTEM key if you have a stored copy. Therefore, answer a is correct. The
other three utilities do not offer Registry restoration options. Therefore,
answers b, c, and d are incorrect.

Question 5

Your NT Server has recently been experiencing numerous STOP
errors. Where should you configure NT so a memory dump will
occur before the system reboots to help pinpoint the problem?

○   a. The server properties within Server Manager

○   b. The recovery option in Dr. Watson

○   c. The Tracking tab of the Task Manager

○   d. On the Startup/Shutdown tab of the System applet

The Server Manager does not offer memory dump configuration options.
Therefore, answer a is incorrect. Dr. Watson is used to perform memory
dumps on application faults, not for NT Server itself. Therefore, answer b
is incorrect. The Task Manager does not have a Tracking tab nor does it
offer memory dump options. Therefore, answer c is incorrect. The Startup/
Shutdown tab of the System applet is the location of the memory dump
options for NT. Therefore, answer d is correct.

Question 6

After installing a new SCSI driver, NT will not successfully boot.
No other changes have been made to the system. What is the
easiest way to return the system to a state where it will boot
properly?

○   a. Use the repair process with the ERD.

○   b. Use the Last Known Good Configuration.

○   c. Launch the Kernel Debugger.

○   d. Boot to DOS, and run the setup utility to change the
       installed drivers.

The ERD repair process will restore the system so it can boot; however,
this requires a recent ERD and all three installation disks. In addition, this
process can take upwards of 30 minutes. Therefore, answer a is incorrect.
The LKGC is the fastest way to return to a bootable configuration, especially

because only a single change was made to the system. Therefore, answer b is correct. The Kernel Debugger will not help this situation, especially because it was not preconfigured to watch the boot process before the new driver was installed. Therefore, answer c is incorrect. There is no DOS setup utility, that utility was only available for Windows 3.x. Therefore, answer d is incorrect.

Question 7

During the boot process, you receive the following error message after the Last Known Good Configuration prompt:

"Windows NT could not start because the following file is missing or corrupt: \WINNT ROOT\SYSTEM32\NTOSKRNL.EXE. Please re-install a copy of the above file."

What are the possible explanations for this error? [Check all correct answers]

❏   a. NTOSKRNL.EXE is missing.

❏   b. BOOT.INI points to the wrong partition.

❏   c. NTOSKRNL.EXE is corrupt.

❏   d. BOOT.INI file is missing.

All of these explanations can result in the given error message. Therefore, answers a, b, c, and d are all correct. When the boot process cannot find NTOSKRNL.EXE, it does not indicate if the problem is with the file itself, its location, or the pointers to it.

Question 8

Which of the files on the ERD lists the files installed during setup and the checksums of each of these files?

○   a. INSTALLED.DAT

○   b. CONFIG.NT

○   c. DEFAULT._

○   d. SOFTWARE._

○   e. SETUP.LOG

INSTALLED.DAT is not a file present on an ERD. Therefore, answer a is incorrect. The CONFIG.NT, DEFAULT._, and SOFTWARE._ are all files on an ERD, but they do not contain installed file and checksum information. Therefore, answers b, c, and d are incorrect. SETUP.LOG is the only file on the ERD that lists the files installed during setup and their corresponding checksums. Therefore answer e is correct.

Question 9

Your NT Server experiences yet another STOP error. Fortunately, you enabled the memory dump option through the System applet. What utility can you use to view the contents of the DMP file?

○ a. Event Viewer

○ b. Debug Inspector

○ c. DUMPEXAM.EXE

○ d. NT Diagnostics

The Event Viewer and NT Diagnostics are not able to view the contents of a memory dump file. Therefore, answers a and d are incorrect. There is not a Debug Inspector. Therefore, answer b is incorrect. Only DUMP-EXAM.EXE can be used to view the contents of DMP files. Therefore answer c is correct.

Question 10

Which of the following are valid ways to make full or partial back-ups of the Registry? [Check all correct answers]

❏ a. Create an ERD using the **rdisk /s** command

❏ b. Use NT Backup

❏ c. Copy all of the contents of the \Winnt\System32\Config directory

❏ d. Use the Disk Administrator

❏ e. Use REGEDT32

All of these methods are valid ways to create full or partial backups of the NT Registry. Therefore, answers a, b, c, d, and e are all correct. However, it should be noted that the files stored in \Winnt\System32\Config are only as current as the last reboot or execution of **rdisk /s**.

Need To Know More?

Donald, Lisa and James Chellis: *MSCE: NT Server 4 In The Enterprise Study Guide*. Sybex Network Press, San Francisco, CA, 1997. ISBN 0-7821-1970-0. Chapter 18 covers most of the issues discussed in this chapter. It is a great resource for troubleshooting information. The remainder of the book contains some problem-resolving data.

Heywood, Drew: *Inside Windows NT Server*. New Riders, Indianapolis, IN, 1995. ISBN 1-56205-472-4. This book does not have a chapter focused on troubleshooting. However, tips and tricks about resolving problems are scattered throughout the text.

Siyan, Karanjit S: *Windows NT Server 4 Professional Reference*. New Riders, Indianapolis, IN, 1996. ISBN 1-56205-731-6. This book fails to include a focused chapter on resolving problems, but troubleshooting information is present in some chapters.

Strebe, Matthew, Charles Perkins, and James Chellis: *MSCE: NT Server 4 Study Guide*. Sybex Network Press, San Francisco, CA, 1996. ISBN 0-7821-1972-7. Chapter 17 contains lots of great troubleshooting information. In addition, other tips and tricks are scattered through the rest of the text.

Search the TechNet CD (or its online version through www.microsoft.com) and the *Windows NT Server Resource Kit* CD. Using the keyword "troubleshooting" will result in numerous hits on relevant materials. However, for more focused searching, use keywords associated with the topic or subject in question, such as "boot," "installation," "printing," "Emergency Repair Disk," or "Registry."

16

Sample Test

In this chapter, we give you an opportunity to really prepare for the test. The following sections provide numerous pointers for development of a successful test-taking strategy. This includes figuring out how to choose proper answers, decode ambiguity, work within the Microsoft framework, decide what to memorize, and prepare for the test. Then, we provide a number of questions that cover subject matter likely to appear on the Microsoft Windows NT Server in the Enterprise exam. Good luck.

Questions, Questions, Questions

There should be no doubt in your mind that you are facing a test full of questions. Each exam is composed of 50 to 70 questions. You are allotted 90 minutes to complete the exam. As discussed in Chapter 1, questions are of four basic types:

➤ Multiple choice with a single answer

➤ Multiple choice with multiple answers

➤ Multipart with a single answer

➤ Pick the spot on the graphic

Always read a question twice before selecting an answer. Also, be sure to look for an Exhibit (or Graphic) button. This button brings up graphics and charts used to help explain a question, provide additional data, or illustrate layout. You'll find it difficult to answer questions with exhibits if you fail to look at them.

It is easy to assume that a question only demands a single answer. However, there are lots of questions that require more than one correct answer. In fact, there are even some questions where all the answers should be marked. Read each question carefully enough to decipher how many answers are needed and look for additional instructions on marking your answers—these instructions usually appear in brackets.

Picking Proper Answers

It should be obvious that the only way to pass an exam is to select the correct answers. But the Microsoft exams are not standardized like SAT and GRE exams. They are much more diabolical and convoluted. In many cases, the question is so poorly worded that deciphering it is nearly impossible. In such cases, you might need to rely on answer elimination skills. There is almost always at least one answer that can be immediately eliminated because it:

➤ Doesn't apply to the situation.

➤ Describes a nonexistent issue.

➤ Is already eliminated by the question text.

Once obviously wrong answers are eliminated, you need to rely on your retained knowledge to eliminate further answers. Look for items that sound correct but refer to actions, commands, or features not present or unavailable in the described situation.

If, after elimination, you are still faced with a blind guess between two or more answers, reread the question. Try to picture in your mind's eye the situation and how each possible remaining answer would alter the situation.

If you have exhausted your ability to eliminate answers and you are still unclear about which remaining possible answer is correct, guess. An unanswered question offers you no points, but a guessed answer gives you a chance of getting a question at least partially right. But don't be too hasty to make blind guesses. Wait until your last round of reviewing marked questions before you start to guess (as mentioned in Chapter 1, guessing is best saved for the last five minutes of the exam). Guessing is a last resort, but always better than leaving a question blank.

Decoding Ambiguity

Microsoft exams have a reputation for being difficult, confusing, and ambiguous at times. In our experience with numerous exams, we can fully believe the reputation is well-deserved. The Microsoft exams *are* difficult. They are designed specifically to limit the number of passing grades to around 30 percent. In other words, Microsoft wants 70 percent of test-takers to fail.

The only way to beat Microsoft at its own game is to be prepared. You'll discover that many exam questions test your knowledge of many things not directly related to the issue raised in the text of the question. This means that the answers offered to you, even the incorrect ones, are just as much a part of the skill assessment as the question. If you don't know the material cold, you might not be able to eliminate an obviously wrong answer because it introduces an area that is unrelated to the question.

Questions often give away the answer, but you have to be sharper than Sherlock Holmes to see the clues. Often, subtle hints are included in the text in such a way that they seem like irrelevant information. You must realize that each question is a test in and of itself. You need to inspect and successfully navigate each question to pass the exam. Look for small clues, such as the mentioning of times, group names, configuration settings, and even local or remote access methods. Little items such as these can point out the right answer or, if missed, can leave you facing a blind guess.

Vocabulary is another common difficulty of the certification exams. Microsoft has an uncanny ability to name utilities and features very obviously on some occasions and completely inanely in others. Especially in the areas of printing and remote access—be sure to brush up on the terms presented in the printing and remote access chapters. You may also want to review the glossary before approaching the test.

Working Within The Framework

The test questions are presented to you in random order. Plus, many of the same elements or issues are repeated in multiple questions. It is not uncommon to find the correct answer to one question in the wrong answer of another. Take the time to read each answer, even if you know the correct one immediately. You may spark a memory through the reading that helps you on another question.

You can revisit any question as many times as you like. But searching for a single question that is unmarked is a waste of time. If you are uncertain of the answer to a question, mark the question in the box provided. Also, mark questions you think may offer data you can use to solve other questions. We marked 30 to 60 percent of the questions on exams we've taken. The testing software is designed to help you mark an answer for every question—use the framework to your advantage. Everything you want to see again should be marked. The software will help you return to marked items.

Deciding What To Memorize

The level of memorization you must perform for the exams depends on your ability to remember what you've read and interacted with. If you are a visual learner and can see drop-down menus and dialog boxes in your head, you won't need to memorize as much as those who can't. The tests stretch your recollection skills of command selections and feature locations for most of NT's utilities.

The important types of information to memorize are:

➤ Setup or configuration steps (in order).

➤ Features or commands found in pull-down menus and configuration dialog boxes.

➤ Applications found by default in the Start menu.

➤ Applets in the Control Panel.

➤ Names and purposes of the five main Registry keys.

If you work your way through this book while sitting at an NT Server machine, you should have little or no problem interacting with most of these important items.

Preparing For The Test

The best way to prepare for the test—after you've studied—is to take at least one practice exam. We've included a practice exam in this chapter. You can take this exam to help prepare you for the material as well as the test-taking process. The test questions are located in the "Sample Test" section later in this chapter. You should give yourself 90 minutes to take the test. Keep yourself on the honor system, and don't cheat by looking at the text earlier in the book. Once your time is up or you finish, the answers are listed inChapter 17, "Answer Key To The Sample Test," located in the next chapter.

If you want additional practice exams, visit the Microsoft Training And Certification site, and download the Self Assessment Practice exam utility at www.microsoft.com/train_cert.

Taking The Test

Relax. Once you are sitting in front of the testing computer, there is nothing more you can do to increase your knowledge or preparation. Take a deep breath, stretch, and attack the first question.

Don't rush, there is plenty of time to complete each question and repeat skipped questions. If you read a question twice and are clueless, mark it, and move on. Easy and hard questions are dispersed throughout the test in a random order. Don't cheat yourself by spending too much time on a difficult question early on. This might prevent you from answering numerous easy questions positioned near the end of the exam. Move through the entire test. Then, before returning to the skipped questions, evaluate your time in light of the number of skipped questions. As you answer a question, remove its corresponding mark. Continue to review the remaining marked questions until your time expires or you complete the test.

That's it for the pointers. Let's get to the questions.

•

Sample Test

Question 1

Which of the following are valid ways to make full or partial back-ups of the Registry? [Check all correct answers]

❑   a. Create an ERD using the **RDISK /s** command

❑   b. With NT Backup

❑   c. Copy all of the contents of the \Winnt\System32\Config directory

❑   d. Through the Disk Administrator

❑   e. Use REGEDT32

Question 2

A small company with a few departments wants to deploy a domain model network. It wants to be able to access all servers and resources from each department and maintain centralized management of user accounts. Which domain model is best suited for this purpose?

○   a. Single domain model

○   b. Master domain model

○   c. Multiple master domain model

○   d. Complete trust domain model

Question 3

Analyze the following scenario:

Your network includes two domains: Production and General. General is a master domain, and Production has a one-way trust with General. Each domain includes a single PDC, two BDCs, three member servers, and 100 workstations, all running Windows NT Workstation 4. To ensure the availability of data on the network, you need to create a group named "TotalBack" that can back up all the machines on the network—be they domain controllers, member servers, or workstations.

Required result:

- Members of the TotalBack group must be able to back up all domain controllers, in either Production or General.

Optional desired results:

- Members of TotalBack should be able to back up all member servers in both domains.

- Members of TotalBack should be able to back up all NT workstations in both domains.

Proposed Solution:

- Create a global group called "TotalBack" in the General domain, and add this group to the Backup Operators local group on every domain controller, member server, and Windows NT workstation in both domains.

Which results does the proposed solution produce?

- ○ a. The proposed solution produces the required result, and both of the optional desired results.

- ○ b. The proposed solution produces the required result, but only one of the optional desired results.

- ○ c. The proposed solution produces the required result, but neither of the optional desired results.

- ○ d. The proposed solution does not produce the required result.

Question 4

Which view available through Performance Monitor should you use to create a baseline?

○   a. Chart

○   b. Log

○   c. Report

○   d. Graph

Question 5

You want to track the activity around a new high-speed color laser printer so you can use the tracking information to restrict and grant privileged and priority access. Which of the following are required steps to implement printer auditing? [Check all correct answers]

❏   a. Set the auditing switches on the printer object to track the successful print events for the Everyone group.

❏   b. Grant the Everyone group the auditing right through the User Rights policy.

❏   c. Set the audit policy to Audit These Events through the User Manager For Domains.

❏   d. Set the audit switch of File And Object Access to Success under Audit These Events.

❏   e. Set the priority of the printer to 99 (maximum) under the Scheduling tab on the printer's Properties dialog box.

Question 6

You attempt to add new information into a document stored on a remote server. Using the Documents share, you are able to locate and open the document into your word processor. You have Full Control of the object. You are a member of the Sales group. The Sales group has Read access to the Documents share. You are unable to save your changes to the file. Why?

○   a. You cannot edit documents over a network.

○   b. Your resultant permissions for the file object are Read.

○   c. The Sales group has the Save privilege revoked.

○   d. Only administrators can save files over the network.

Question 7

You have a Windows NT server that provides print services to 20 Windows NT computers on your network. You have an HP LaserJet attached to the Windows NT print server. Hewlett-Packard has just released an updated printer driver. What must be done to provide the updated driver for the computers that print to this print server?

○   a. Install the updated driver on all client computers. There is no need to update the server.

○   b. Install the updated driver on the print server, and do nothing more.

○   c. Install the updated driver on the print server and on all client computers.

○   d. Create a separate logical printer with the updated driver on the print server, and tell all your users to print to the new printer.

○   e. Install the updated driver on the print server, and instruct all client computers to download the updated driver from the server.

Question 8

You have a network that has five domains in a master domain model configuration. Where should the logon scripts be placed for simplified administration?

○   a. On the PDC in the trusted domain

○   b. In the PDC's \%winntroot%\System32\Repl\
       Export\Scripts directory within each trusting domain

○   c. Within the NETLOGON share of each domain

○   d. On the local workstations

Question 9

ExecuCorp has 50,000 users and many branch offices. You have been hired to set the network up so that there is central adminis-tration of users but decentralized control of resources. Security is important. Which of the following domain models is best suited for this situation?

○   a. Single domain model

○   b. Master domain model

○   c. Multiple master domain model

○   d. Complete trust domain model

Question 10

You have two IDE hard drives on a single drive controller in your Windows NT Server computer. There is only one partition on each of the two drives. The first drive's partition is formatted with FAT, and the second drive's partition is formatted with NTFS. The boot files are located on the second drive. What is the ARC name for the boot partition?

○   a. multi(0)disk(1)RDISK(0)partition(1)

○   b. multi(0)disk(0)RDISK(1)partition(1)

○   c. multi(1)disk(0)RDISK(1)partition(1)

○   d. multi(0)disk(0)RDISK(1)partition(0)

○   e. multi(1)disk(0)RDISK(0)partition(1)

Question 11

A user is attempting to print to a printer attached to the network using an HP JetDirect card. The print server and the user's client machine both have DLC properly installed. But the user is repeatedly denied access to the printer, even after the printer has been physically reset. What is the most likely cause of this?

○   a. The print server is disconnected from the network.

○   b. The JetDirect card is not compatible with the DLC protocol.

○   c. Another user is printing to the device using the Microsoft TCP/IP Printing service.

○   d. Another print server is configured with DLC set to continuous connection mode.

Question 12

You have noticed that users complain of poor network performance in the morning and right after lunch—the times when users are authenticated by the domain controllers. Currently, there is one PDC and two BDCs within the domain. You inspect the performance levels of the domain controllers and determine that they are operating at acceptable levels. What is the best way to improve network performance?

○   a. Add additional BDCs.

○   b. Increase the RAM on all servers.

○   c. Decrease the Pulse Registry setting on the PDC.

○   d. Install an additional PDC in the domain.

Question 13

Which of the following NT networking activities are supported by a PPP RAS connection? [Check all correct answers]

❑   a. Printer share access

❑   b. Named pipes

❑   c. WinSock API applications over TCP/IP

❑   d. InterProcess Communications (IPC)

❑   e. User Logon Authentication

Question 14

You want to install TCP/IP on a member server in a non-routed network. You have already manually assigned an IP address to the server. What other parameter must you specify to install TCP/IP on the server?

○   a. Subnet mask

○   b. Default gateway

○   c. DHCP server IP address

○   d. WINS server IP address

Question 15

Windows NT Server includes a Migration Tool to move data and accounts from NetWare to Windows NT servers. It can be especially helpful when moving user accounts from one or more NetWare servers to a Windows NT PDC. Which of the following requirements is most likely to benefit from use of a mapping file to guide the migration process? [Choose the single best answer]

○   a. To migrate unique user accounts from several NetWare servers to a Windows NT domain controller.

○   b. To make sure existing domain accounts will not be affected by migration of identical user accounts from NetWare.

○   c. To migrate accounts from NetWare servers that do not have corresponding accounts in the Windows NT domain.

○   d. To supply passwords for migrated accounts in the Windows NT domain that match the previous NetWare passwords.

Question 16

Which of the following options are object attributes? [Check all correct answers]

❑   a. Data

❑   b. ACL

❑   c. Services

❑   d. Object name

Question 17

Which type of data should not be distributed via the Directory Replication service?

○   a. Logon scripts

○   b. User profiles

○   c. Relational database files

○   d. System policies

Question 18

To facilitate a move from NetWare to Windows NT Server, XYZ Corp. plans to use the Migration Tool for NetWare. If the Tool encounters user account names on the NetWare server that match existing accounts in the target Windows NT domain, what will the Migration Tool do by default?

○   a. Prompt the administrator with an option to overwrite existing account information, or block the account information from the transfer.

○   b. Transfer the account to the Windows NT domain, but add a prefix to all duplicate names.

○   c. Ignore all duplicate NetWare account information.

○   d. Replace all existing Windows NT domain account information with the incoming NetWare account information.

Question 19

You have a field technician who travels extensively around the country. Her schedule changes often and she rarely visits the same place twice. It is important that she is able to connect to the office LAN periodically, but your organization's security policy requires callback security on all RAS connections. How can you configure her account so that she is able to gain access while supporting your organization's security?

- ○ a. Set the callback security to No Call Back only for her account.
- ○ b. Enable callback security with Set By Caller selected.
- ○ c. Set the callback security to Preset To with her home phone number.
- ○ d. Set the callback security to Roaming, and give her the page number to remotely configure the callback number.
- ○ e. Turn on the Callback Caller ID Capture.

Question 20

An important new custom application is conflicting with an existing utility. The conflict seems to cause both programs to terminate prematurely. Which audit event type should be tracked to record some information about the conflict and which programs are affected?

- ○ a. File And Object Access
- ○ b. Security Policy Changes
- ○ c. Restart, Shutdown, And System
- ○ d. Process Tracking
- ○ e. Application Activity

Question 21

Your NT Server experiences a STOP error due to a runaway process from a custom application developed in-house. Where can information about this error be found once the Server has been rebooted?

O   a. Kernel Debugger

O   b. Performance Monitor

O   c. Event Viewer

O   d. NT Diagnostics

Question 22

Where does the Directory Replication service place distributed files by default?

O   a. \%winntroot%\System32\repl\Export of an import server

O   b. \Program Files\Replication of an export server

O   c. \%winntroot%\System32\repl\Import of an import server

O   d. \%winntroot%\System32\repl\Export of an export server

Question 23

The SYSTEM Registry key contains errors. You do not have a recent ERD, but you have a floppy of the SYSTEM key itself. Which of the following programs should you use to restore the SYSTEM key from the floppy?

O   a. Disk Administrator

O   b. System applet

O   c. Network Client Administrator

O   d. Server Manager

Question 24

What files should be placed on a boot disk in order to boot to the duplicate drive of a disk duplex from a floppy in the event of a failure of the original drive? Assume the drive controller is a SCSI that does not support BIOS translation. [Check all correct answers]

❏   a. NTDETECT.COM

❏   b. BOOT.INI

❏   c. NTLDR

❏   d. WINA20.386

❏   e. NTBOOTDD.SYS

Question 25

What are the functions of WINS? [Check all correct answers]

❏   a. Enable internetwork browsing

❏   b. Map FQDNs to IP addresses

❏   c. Map NetBIOS names to IP addresses

❏   d. Map NetBIOS names to MAC addresses

❏   e. Assign client IP addresses

Question 26

You are an administrator of a domain that consists of two groups of computers connected by a long-distance WAN link. There are multiple BDCs located in each group. The available bandwidth of the WAN link must be maximized. Which of the following changes to the domain controller synchronization will reduce the load placed on the link by the PDC and the BDCs? [Check all correct answers]

❏   a. Set Pulse to 60

❏   b. Set PulseConcurrency to 1

❏   c. Set PulseMaximum to 60

❏   d. Set MaintainServerList to Auto

❏   e. Set ReplicationGovernor to 50

Question 27

Of the following, which are required for access to a NetWare server from a Windows NT workstation running Client Service For NetWare? [Check all correct answers]

❏ a. A group on the NetWare server called "NTGATEWAY" containing the Windows NT workstation's user account

❏ b. Gateway Services For NetWare

❏ c. A user account on the NetWare server

❏ d. The NWLink protocol

Question 28

Tech Toys, Inc. has a network with three domains: Admin, Sales, and Production. Users from the Sales and Admin domains need access to resources from the Production domain, but they also need access to resources in each other's domains. How should you set up the trust relationships among the domains?

○ a. Define two-way trusts between all three domains.

○ b. Set up one-way trusts from Sales to Admin, Admin to Production, and Production to Sales.

○ c. Define a two-way trust between Sales and Admin, and another two-way trust between Production and Sales.

○ d. Set up two one-way trusts from Production to Sales and Production to Admin, and a two-way trust between Sales and Admin.

Question 29

All Windows NT internal basic network server and service communications occur using what type of communication?

○ a. TCP/IP

○ b. AppleTalk

○ c. NetBIOS

○ d. DLC

Question 30

You want to monitor the physical disk performance of a server remotely. With a standard installation of Windows NT Server on both machines, network connectivity, and membership in the same domain, what additional operation must be performed to enable the monitoring of the disk counters remotely?

○   a. Install Network Monitor Agent on the machine to be observed.

○   b. Run the **diskperf** utility with the **-y** option on the machine to be observed.

○   c. Install Network Monitor Agent, and run the **diskperf** utility with the **-y** option on the machine to be observed.

○   d. No additional operations are required. The physical disk counters are remotely accessible by default.

Question 31

While using the Network Monitor, you decide to implement a display filter to aid in your search for the NetBIOS Add Group Name command. What is the proper syntax of a properties-based display filter?

○   a. NETBIOS:Command == 0x0 (Add Group Name)

○   b. NETBIOS <= Add Group Name Command

○   c. Add Group Name > NETBIOS

○   d. NETBIOS<-->Add Group Name

Question 32

Assume two domains named "Users" and "Admin" are defined within an organization. Three members of the Users domain have been drafted to work with materials in the Admin domain prior to their general release to the user community. To assist with prerelease testing, these three users need access to a shared NTFS folder named "\Tests" on a server named "TEST1" in the Admin domain. Admin already trusts Users. Which of the following options is the best way to grant Full Control access to the \\TEST1\Tests share for those three individuals from the Users domain?

○   a. Remove the current trust relationship. Add a new trust wherein Admin trusts Users. Create a global group in the Users domain named "Utesters," and add the three individuals' accounts to that group. Create a global group named "Atesters" in the Admin domain, and add the global group Users\Utesters to Atesters. Give Atesters Full Control over the \\TEST1\Tests share.

○   b. Create a global group in the Users domain named "Utesters." Assign each of the three users' domain accounts to that group. Create a global group in the Admin domain named "Atesters," and assign Users\Utesters to Atesters. Give Atesters Full Control over the \\TEST1\Tests share.

○   c. Create a global group in Users called "Utesters." Add each of the three users' domain accounts to that group. Create a local group on TEST1 called "Utesters," and add the Users\Utesters global group to this local group. Grant Utesters Full Control to the \\TEST1\Tests share.

○   d. Remove the current trust relationship. Add a new trust wherein Admin trusts Users. Create a global group in Users called "Utesters." Add each of the three users' domain accounts to that group. Create a local group on TEST1 called "Utesters," and add the Users\Utesters global group to this local group. Grant Utesters Full Control to the \\TEST1\Tests share.

Question 33

Your Ethernet network consists of Windows NT 4 Server, several NT Workstation clients, a NetWare 3.12 client, and one NetWare 4.1 client. NWLink is running on the network. Each of the NetWare clients is using different frame types. How would you configure the NWLink IPX/SPX Properties dialog box on the Windows NT 4 Server to enable the server to recognize both NetWare clients?

O   a. Enabling Auto Frame Type Detection

O   b. Selecting the Manual Frame Type Detection option, and adding a NetWare client's network number and frame type to the frame type configuration list

O   c. Selecting the Auto Frame Type Detection option, and adding both NetWare clients' network numbers and frame types to the frame type configuration list

O   d. Selecting the Manual Frame Type Detection option, and adding both of the NetWare clients' network numbers and frame types to the frame type configuration list

Question 34

You need to set up four new virtual Web servers to be hosted on your private network using only a single installation of IIS. Each Web site will require its own directory, a unique URL, and a unique IP address. What should you do to implement this configuration? [Check all correct answers]

❑   a. Install RIP For IP on the IIS server.

❑   b. Assign each of the IP addresses to be used to the NIC in the IIS server, then associate each IP address with the appropriate Web directory.

❑   c. Set up the DHCP Relay Agent.

❑   d. Configure DNS so that it contains the FQDN for each server and correlates that name to its IP address.

❑   e. Configure WINS by adding the NetBIOS names and IP addresses of the sites to the static list of servers.

Question 35

You're asked to provide temporary access to resources in your Accounting domain for a group of auditors in the Auditors domain. For the same reason, you must also provide temporary access to the same group of users in other domains in the coming months. There is already a trust relationship in which Accounting trusts Auditors. Which of the following represents the best way to supply temporary access to Accounting for this group of auditors?

❑   a. Create a global group in the Accounting domain that includes the auditors' user accounts. Add this group to the Guests local group on all servers in the Accounting domain.

❑   b. Create a global group in the Auditors domain that includes the auditors' user accounts. Add this group to the local group on the server (or servers) in the Accounting domain that contain(s) the needed resources.

❑   c. Create a local group in the Accounting domain that includes the auditors' user accounts on each server where the needed resources reside.

❑   d. Create a local group in the Auditors domain that includes the auditors' user accounts. Add this group to the local group on the server (or servers) in the Accounting domain that contain(s) the needed resources.

Question 36

To end the process of maintaining user accounts on two different types of servers, you have decided to migrate users from the NetWare server to a Windows NT server. What must be installed on the Windows NT server to provide the NetWare clients with access? [Check all correct answers]

❑   a. Gateway Service For NetWare

❑   b. NWLink protocol

❑   c. Client Service For NetWare

❑   d. SAP Agent

Question 37

Where can you find information related to RAS problems to aid in troubleshooting? [Check all correct answers]

❑   a. Event Viewer

❑   b. DEVICE.LOG

❑   c. Dr. Watson

❑   d. MODEMLOG.TXT

❑   e. NT Diagnostics

Question 38

On a network with Internet access, you wish to host six Web sites from a single implementation of IIS. Which of the following must you do to accomplish this? [Check all correct answers]

❑   a. Install RIP For IP on the IIS server.

❑   b. Assign each of the IP addresses to be used to the NIC in the IIS server, then associate each IP address with the appropriate Web directory.

❑   c. Set up the DHCP Relay Agent.

❑   d. Configure DNS so that it contains the FQDN for each server and correlates that name to its IP address.

❑   e. Configure WINS by adding the NetBIOS names and IP addresses of the sites to the static list of servers.

Question 39

You installed Windows NT Server with the default configuration onto your C drive and subsequently installed Network Monitor Tools and Agent from the Services tab of the Network Control Panel application. When you save sets of captured data, where will the CAP files be placed by default?

○ a. C:\Winnt\System32\Netmon\Capture

○ b. C:\Program Files\Netmon\Capture

○ c. C:\Admin\Netmon\Capture

○ d. C:\Winnt\System32\Repl\Export\Netmon\Capture

Question 40

Your TCP/IP-based network is experiencing drastic increases in broadcast traffic. What is the best way to decrease the amount of broadcast traffic on your network?

○ a. Divide your network into two physical subnets, and install a bridge.

○ b. Divide your network into two logical subnets, and install a gateway.

○ c. Install a DHCP server.

○ d. Install a WINS server.

Question 41

You just doubled the size of your server's physical RAM to 128 MB. If you have disk striping with parity implemented on a set of high-speed SCSI drives and are duplexing the boot partition, what change should you make to the pagefile settings?

○   a. No change to the pagefile size is recommended, but it should be placed on the stripe set.

○   b. The pagefile should be increased to 140 MB and placed on the boot duplexed drive.

○   c. The pagefile should be increased by 12 MB and placed on the stripe set.

○   d. The pagefile should be increased to 140 MB and placed on the stripe set.

Question 42

During the boot process, you receive this error message after the Last Known Good Configuration prompt:

"Windows NT could not start because the following file is missing or corrupt: \WINNT ROOT\SYSTEM32\NTOSKRNL.EXE. Please re-install a copy of the above file."

What are the possible explanations for this error? [Check all correct answers]

❑   a. NTOSKRNL.EXE is missing

❑   b. BOOT.INI points to the wrong partition

❑   c. NTOSKRNL.EXE is corrupt

❑   d. BOOT.INI is missing

Question 43

If no standards are in place for the operating system, protocol, or method of access for your remote clients, what is the highest level of security you can implement and still allow your users to connect via RAS?

○ a. Allow any authentication including clear text

○ b. Require Microsoft encrypted authentication

○ c. PGP Encryption

○ d. Require encrypted authentication

Question 44

Your firm has five branch offices scattered across the globe. They are located in Houston, Moscow, Paris, Geneva, and Hong Kong. Each office has about 750 users. The corporate headquarters is located in Los Angeles. Each branch office is linked to the corporate office via a T1 WAN link. You have been asked to implement a domain model for this company.

Required results:

- All Los Angeles users must be able to access resources in Hong Kong and Moscow.

- Users in Houston, Paris, and Geneva must be able to access resources in Los Angeles.

- Security and logon validation traffic must be minimized over the WAN links.

Optional desired results:

- Centralized management of all user accounts.

- Each branch office is able to manage local resources.

Proposed Solution:

- Use a complete trust model.

- Place all users in the Los Angles domain.

- All branch office domains to be used as resource domains.

Which results does the proposed solution produce?

- ○ a. The required results and both of the optional results
- ○ b. The required results and only one of the optional results
- ○ c. The required results but none of the optional results
- ○ d. The required results are not all met

Question 45

XYZ Corp. has just finished migrating files and accounts from its NetWare erver to a Windows NT Server on the network. The Windows NT Server already uses NWLink. NetWare clients complain that they cannot access the migrated files. What might be missing on that Windows NT Server? [Check all correct answers]

❑ a. Gateway Service For NetWare

❑ b. Client Service For NetWare

❑ c. File And Print Services For NetWare

❑ d. Account permissions for the NetWare clients

❑ e. Microsoft redirectors for the NetWare clients

Question 46

You have a large bank of printers. You have enough money in the budget to purchase two printers to replace two existing printers. How can you determine which printers receive the most usage (page count and print jobs) so you can replace them?

○ a. Audit File And Object Access events.

○ b. Use Performance Monitor to create a printer object report.

○ c. Set the Application log to tally printer events.

○ d. Use the Printer Wizard to gather statistics.

Question 47

You are the administrator of domain ADMIN1. There are no BDCs within ADMIN1. A power outage destroys some system files on the PDC, and you attempt to correct the problem by reinstalling Windows NT onto the machine. After the installation, none of the workstations is able to connect to ADMIN1. What could be the problem?

○   a. The PDC was disconnected from the network.

○   b. A member server was automatically promoted to PDC status, and it is in conflict with the reinstalled PDC.

○   c. The new version installation of NT created a new SID for the PDC.

○   d. A BDC in a trusting domain promoted itself to act as the PDC in ADMIN1. The reinstalled PDC has caused a control conflict.

Question 48

There are two domains within an organization: Admin and Research. New beta software has been deployed on the Research domain for testing, but four members of the Admin domain need to gain access to the beta software to aid in the test process. The beta software resides in an NTFS-based share named "TEST2" on the BETA server in the Research domain. If the Research domain trusts the Admin domain, what additional steps are required to give the four Admin users access to the beta software?

○ a. Create a global group in the Admin domain called "Admin_Beta," and add the four Admin users to this group. Create a local group called "Soft_Test" on server BETA with Full Control over the TEST2 share. Add the Admin_Beta global group to the Soft_Test local group.

○ b. Create new accounts for the Admin users in the Research domain.

○ c. Remove the existing trust. Establish a new trust where the Admin domain trusts the Research domain. Create a global group in the Admin domain called "Admin_Beta," and add the four Admin users to this group. Create a local group called "Soft_Test" on server BETA with Full Control over the TEST2 share. Add the Admin_Beta global group to the Soft_Test local group.

○ d. Create a global group in the Admin domain called "Admin_Beta," and add the four Admin users to this group. Create a global group called "Soft_Test" on server BETA with Full Control over the TEST2 share. Add the Admin_Beta global group to the Soft_Test global group.

Question 49

Your LAN uses both NetBEUI and NWLink protocols. Your RAS server supports NetBEUI and TCP/IP, bound in that order. A RAS client also uses both NetBEUI and TCP/IP, bound in that order. Which of the following activities cannot occur over a RAS connection made between the client and the server?

○   a. Access a directory list of NetBIOS share names

○   b. Access resources on the LAN

○   c. Access resources on the RAS server

○   d. Access WinSock applications

Question 50

You want to configure a Windows NT Server to be the print server for an HP network interface print device. However, you are unable to locate the option to install a port for the printer. Why is this?

○   a. PostScript printing is enabled on the print device and must be disabled.

○   b. You didn't install the print driver on the print server.

○   c. The print processor is corrupt and must be fixed.

○   d. The DLC protocol is not installed on the print server.

Question 51

You add 4 new drives to your Windows NT Server computer of sizes 800, 600, 500, and 300 MB. You wish to establish a disk stripe set with parity. What is the total size of the largest set you can create using any or all of these drives?

○   a. 1,200 MB

○   b. 1,000 MB

○   c. 800 MB

○   d. 1,500 MB

Question 52

You are working with Network Monitor to evaluate your network usage. You want to capture all frames inbound to your server, except those sent from John's computer. The name of your server is "Admin1," and the name of John's computer is "Sales5." What is the best way to set up the capture filter?

○ a. INCLUDE Admin1 <--> NOT (Sales5)

○ b. INCLUDE Admin1 <--> ANY; EXCLUDE Admin --> Sales5

○ c. EXCLUDE Admin1 <-- Sales5

○ d. EXCLUDE Admin1 <--> Sales5

Question 53

If no configuration changes have been made to a server, what prevents a standard user from logging on to a server by walking up to the local console?

○ a. There is no restriction to prevent users from logging on.

○ b. Servers don't allow anyone to log on to them.

○ c. Log on locally user right is not assigned to standard users.

○ d. The user has No Access permission set for the server object.

Question 54

Which items below describe disk striping with parity? [Check all correct answers]

❑ a. Requires three physical drives

❑ b. Can be implemented with FAT

❑ c. Provides fault tolerance

❑ d. Has faster read-write performance than disk mirroring

❑ e. Data cannot be recovered if a single drive within the set fails

Question 55

You have a printer pool that consists of Printer 1 and Printer 2. Printer 1 is printing a job, and Printer 2 is idle. A paper jam occurs on Printer 1's print device. What will happen to the rest of the job that was being printed?

○ a. The print job will be completed on Printer 2.

○ b. The print job is canceled.

○ c. The print job will be completed on Printer 2 because Printer 2 has a higher priority level.

○ d. The print job is held for completion by Printer 1 until the device is fixed.

17

Answer Key
To Sample Test

Here are the answers to the questions presented in the sample test in Chapter 16.

Question 1

All of the methods are valid ways to create full or partial backups of the NT Registry. Therefore, answers a, b, c, d, and e are correct. However, it should be noted that the files stored in \Winnt\System32\Config are only as current as the last reboot or execution of **RDISK /s**.

Question 2

The single domain model is the best solution for this situation. It offers centralized management, access to all resources, and support for small networks. Therefore, answer a is correct. The master domain model has separate domains for resources and users. This design is too much work for a small network. Thus, answer b is incorrect. The multiple master domain model is too complicated for this size of a network. Therefore, answer c is incorrect. The complete trust domain model is also an unnecessarily complex design for this situation. Thus, answer d is incorrect.

Question 3

The answer to any "proposed solution" question on a Microsoft test is *pro forma* and nearly always follows the formula shown in Chapter 16. The key to dealing with such a question lies in analyzing the proposed solution and deciding where it fits the matrix of possibilities. In this case, defining a global group in General is exactly the right action to take because global groups in a trusted domain can be included in local groups in General and in any other domains that trust General. Production trusts General, so the global TotalBack group can be referenced in local groups in both domains. Finally, because all flavors of Windows NT mentioned—domain controllers, member servers, and Windows NT workstation machines—support the local Backup Operators group, placing a reference to General\TotalBack creates a situation where members of that group can back up all domain controllers, member servers, and NT workstations in either domain. Thus, answer a is correct because the required result and both optional desired results will be produced by the proposed solution.

Question 4

Chart view displays the realtime values of counters but cannot record the data as it is gathered. Therefore, answer a is incorrect. Log view records object counters and should be used to create a baseline. Therefore, answer b is correct. Report view creates a snapshot of the performance levels of counters from realtime gathering or a recorded log. Therefore, answer c is incorrect. Graph is not a view but a display selection in the Chart view. Therefore, answer d is incorrect.

Question 5

Setting the auditing switches on the object is required to enable printer tracking. Therefore, answer a is correct. There is not an auditing user right. Therefore, answer b is incorrect. Setting the master auditing switch to Audit These Events is required to track printer access. Therefore, answer c is correct. Setting the event type switch of File And Object Access to Success is required to track printer usage. Therefore, answer d is correct. Setting a printer's priority has nothing to do with tracking access. Therefore, answer e is incorrect. Thus, the correct answers are a, c, and d.

Question 6

It is possible to edit documents over a network. The only stipulation is that you must have the proper access level to modify remote objects. Therefore, answer a is incorrect. Accessing objects through shares results in the most restrictive shared permissions. Thus, answer b is correct. There is not a Save privilege in the NT environment. The Sales group merely has Read access to the share. Therefore, answer c is incorrect. The ability to save documents (i.e., modify objects) is not limited to administrators. Therefore, answer d is incorrect.

Question 7

The best way to update a printer driver is simply to update the driver on the print server. Therefore, answer b is the only correct answer. There is no need to manually update the driver on each client computer running NT. When a client computer sends a print job to the print server, the updated driver is automatically copied to the client.

Question 8

The PDC of the trusted domain (i.e., the user domain) is the best place for administration control of user scripts. Therefore, answer a is correct. The PDCs within the trusting domains (i.e., the resource domains) are not used to authenticate users. Plus, there are many of these machines, thereby increasing the administration difficulty. Therefore, answer b is incorrect. The NETLOGON share within each domain is the same problem presented in answer b—multiple administration sites within non-authenticating domains. Therefore, answer c is incorrect. A local workstation is not the correct place to store logon scripts, especially for easy administration. Therefore, answer d is incorrect.

Question 9

The single domain model cannot support 50,000 users. Therefore, answer a is incorrect. The master domain model cannot support 50,000 users in its single user domain. Therefore, answer b is incorrect. The multiple master domain model can support 50,000 with its multiple user domains, and each branch office can manage its own local resources. Thus, answer c is correct. The complete trust domain model does not offer centralized management of user accounts and does not adequately support security. Therefore, answer d is incorrect.

Question 10

Answer a displays an improperly composed ARC name—when **multi** is used, the **disk(n)** number must be set to zero. Therefore, answer a is incorrect. Answer b indicates the first partition of the second hard drive on the first multi type drive controller. Because this is indeed the location of the system partition for this configuration, answer b is correct. Answer c points to a second drive controller that doesn't exist in this example. Consequently, answer c is incorrect. Answer d supplies an incorrect number for the partition element. Partitions are numbered cardinally, so a partition number can never be zero. Because the first partition is numbered one, answer d is incorrect. Answer e names a second, nonexistent drive controller, and points to the first drive on that controller. Because the system partition for this question is attached to the first (and only) disk controller on the second hard drive, answer e is incorrect.

Question 11

If the print server is offline, the NetBIOS name of the resource would not be present instead of a denial of service. Therefore, answer a is incorrect. The JetDirect card is designed specifically for the DLC protocol. Therefore, answer b is incorrect. The TCP/IP Printing service in use by another user would not deny access via DLC. Therefore, answer c is incorrect. If DLC is set to continuous connection mode, no other access to that printer is possible. Therefore, answer d is correct.

Question 12

Adding additional BDCs improves network performance by distributing the user-authentication load. Therefore, answer a is correct. Adding RAM to the servers will not improve the network performance because the performance levels are acceptable. Therefore, answer b is incorrect. The Pulse Registry setting would have a negative effect on performance by increasing background network traffic. Therefore, answer c is incorrect. Only one PDC can exist within a domain. Therefore, answer d is incorrect.

Question 13

Because a RAS-connected client is no different from a direct-connected client (other than speed of data transfer), all standard network activities still occur over the WAN link. Therefore, all answers—a, b, c, d, and e—are correct.

Question 14

When installing TCP/IP on a non-routed network, the IP address and subnet mask parameters must be specified. Therefore, answer a is the correct choice.

Question 15

This is another question and corresponding set of answers that requires careful reading to ferret out the best answer. Answer a falls within the capabilities of a mapping file, but matches the default behavior of the Migration Tool in that unique accounts (i.e., accounts that are not duplicated, neither on the NetWare side nor the Windows NT side) are the easiest to migrate. Answer b relies on the default behavior of the Migration Tool, where existing accounts will not be affected by identical accounts on a NetWare server. Answer c also works fine without a mapping file, because the Migration Tool can handle such accounts automatically. Answer d lets administrators supply the same passwords for NT accounts as NetWare accounts, which is not an automatic feature of the Migration Tool. Because this is the only behavior described in any of the answers that absolutely requires a mapping file, answer d is definitely the best answer to this question.

Question 16

The data of an object is an attribute. Therefore, answer a is correct. The ACL of an object is an attribute. Therefore, answer b is correct. The services of an object are services, not attributes. Thus, answer c is incorrect. The name of an object is an attribute. Therefore, answer d is correct. Thus, answers a, b, and d are correct.

Question 17

Logon scripts, user profiles, and system policies are the only files that should be distributed by the replication service. Therefore, answers a, b, and d are incorrect. Relational database files are often very large and would cause severe performance degradation to a network if their distribution was handled by the replication service. Therefore, answer c is correct.

Question 18

By default, the Migration Tool ignores any user account name on a NetWare server that matches an existing account name in the target Windows NT domain database. This makes answer c correct. Answer a is incorrect because the Migration Tool does not prompt when duplicates are encountered. Answer b is incorrect because a mapping file must be defined to assign such prefixes (the Migration Tool does not perform this action by default, nor would it know what prefix to assign). Answer d is flat wrong. The Migration Tool has been designed to take the safest action by default, which is to leave existing domain database entries untouched.

Question 19

Setting the No Call Back option will violate the organization's security policy. Therefore, answer a is incorrect. Setting the Set By Caller option will allow the field technician to input the callback number each time she needs to connect. Thus, answer b is correct. Setting the Preset To number will not allow the tech to gain access to the network because she is never in the same place. Therefore, answer c is incorrect. There is no Roaming call-back setting. Therefore, answer d is incorrect. NT does not have a Caller ID capture setting, but this can be obtained through third-party software; however, caller ID capture is not required for this situation. Thus, answer e is incorrect.

Question 20

File And Object Access is for tracking NTFS objects, such as files and printers. Therefore, answer a is incorrect. Security Policy Changes tracks modifications to security and policies. Therefore, answer b is incorrect. Restart, Shutdown, And System tracks system restarts. Therefore, answer c is incorrect. Process Tracking tracks threads and process (e.g., applications). Therefore, answer d is correct. Application Activity is not a valid selection. Therefore, answer e is incorrect.

Question 21

The Kernel Debugger is only able to view STOP error information when specifically configured and installed on two connected machines. The configuration was not indicated in this question. Therefore, answer a is incorrect. Performance Monitor and NT Diagnostics are not able to record any information about a STOP error. Therefore, answers b and d are incorrect. The Event Viewer can be used to view the System log where all STOP errors are recorded. Therefore, answer c is correct.

Question 22

The directory listed in answer a is not the default destination server on an import server. Therefore, answer a is incorrect. The directory listed in answer b is not the standard import directory on an import server. Therefore, answer b is incorrect. The directory listed in answer c is the correct default destination directory on an import server. Therefore, answer c is correct. The directory listed in answer d is the export directory on an export server. This is where files are accessed for distribution. Therefore, answer d is incorrect.

Question 23

The Disk Administrator is the correct utility to use to restore the SYSTEM key if you have a stored copy. Thus, answer a is correct. The other three utilities do not offer Registry restoration options. Therefore, answers b, c, and d are incorrect.

Question 24

NTDETECT.COM is required on the boot floppy. Therefore, answer a is correct. BOOT.INI is required on the boot floppy, making answer b correct. NTLDR is required on the boot floppy. Therefore, answer c is also correct. WINA20.386 is a Windows device driver that is not needed on the boot floppy, so answer d is incorrect. NTBOOTDD.SYS is the driver for SCSI translation required for non-BIOS controllers, making answer e correct as well. The full set of correct answers to this question is a, b, c, and e.

Question 25

Enabling internetwork browsing and mapping NetBIOS names to IP addresses are two of the three functions of WINS. The third function is recognizing NetBIOS names on all subnets. Therefore, only answers a and c are correct. Mapping FQDNs to IP addresses is a function of DNS. Therefore, answer b is incorrect. Mapping NetBIOS names to MAC addresses happens in both NWLink and NetBEUI. Therefore, answer d is incorrect. Assigning clients IP addresses is a function of a DHCP server. Therefore, answer e is incorrect.

Question 26

Setting Pulse low (60) causes updates to take place too frequently and places extra traffic on the WAN link. Therefore, answer a is incorrect. Setting PulseConcurrency low (1) updates a fewer number of BDCs on each Pulse interval, thus reducing WAN traffic. Therefore, answer b is correct. Setting PulseMaximum low (60) forces a full update more often. Therefore, answer c is incorrect. MaintainServerList is a browser setting, not a domain controller synchronization setting. Therefore, answer d is incorrect. Setting the ReplicationGovernor to 50 percent will reduce the packet size transmitted over the WAN. More packets will be required, but each one will use less bandwidth. Therefore, answer e is correct. Thus, only answers b and e are correct.

Question 27

It is only necessary to place user accounts in the NTGATEWAY group on the NetWare server if workstations are accessing the NetWare server via a gateway, which is not the case in this question. Therefore, answer a is incorrect. If an NT server is to act as a gateway to a NetWare server, the Gateway Service For NetWare must be loaded onto a Windows NT Server. Because this scenario discusses an NT client accessing a NetWare server, answer b is also incorrect. Any user accessing a NetWare server directly will need a user account on that NetWare server. Therefore, answer c is correct. An NT workstation running the Client Service For NetWare can access a NetWare server directly by using the NWLink protocol. Therefore, answer d is also correct. In this scenario, both answers c and d are the correct choices.

Question 28

One good way to eliminate possibilities is to see what's missing in the question when compared to the answers. This question says nothing about Production requiring access to anything in Sales or Admin. This automatically knocks out answer a because it includes two-way trusts from Sales and Admin to Production that are not required (and perhaps even unwanted). Likewise, this knocks out answer c because it includes a trust from Sales to Production, as well as the required trust from Production to Sales. Answer b must be eliminated because it fails to include the two-way trust between Sales and Admin implied by the key phrase "but they also need access to resources in each other's domains." Answer d is the only correct answer because it provides the two-way trust required between Sales and Admin, and establishes one-way trusts from Production to both Sales and Admin (thereby meeting the stated requirement that users from Sales and Admin need access to resources from Production). Production must trust both domains, as the answer indicates, by specifying two one-way trusts from Production to each of the other domains.

Question 29

TCP/IP is a supported protocol of NT, but it is not the protocol used for basic internal communication. Therefore, answer a is incorrect. AppleTalk is a supported protocol, but it is not used in this manner. Thus, answer b is incorrect. NetBIOS is the protocol or API used for all of NT's basic internal network communications. Therefore, answer c is correct. DLC is a protocol used for IBM mainframe and network attached printers. Therefore, answer d is incorrect.

Question 30

The Network Monitor Agent is not required to remotely monitor performance counters; it is only needed to access Network Monitor elements remotely. Therefore, answer a is incorrect. The **diskperf -y** command is needed to enable the physical disk counters, but all performance counters can be accessed remotely without further configuration. Therefore, answer b is correct. The Network Monitor is not required, but the **diskperf** command is. Therefore, answer c is incorrect. The **diskperf** command is required because all disk counters are not enabled by default. Disk counters must be turned on before PerfMon can access them locally or remotely. Therefore, answer d is incorrect.

Question 31

Answer a is the correct syntax for the properties display filter. It contains Protocol:Property [Relation] Value. Therefore, answer a is correct. Answer b is incorrect because the four elements of the properties display filter are scrambled. Answer c is incorrect because it is missing the property element and the remaining elements are out of order. Answer d is incorrect because it is missing the property element, the other elements are out of order, and the relation is not valid for a property relation.

Question 32

The key phrase in this question is "the best way" because two answers are actually correct. Answer d, while correct, requires removing and replacing the existing trust from Admin to Users. This is unnecessary and could break existing trusts established for other uses. Otherwise, d is the same as c, which is correct because it:

➤ Uses an existing trust.

➤ Creates a global group in the trusted domain.

➤ Puts the global group into a local group on the TEST1 machine in the trusting domain.

➤ Grants the local group the required access to the share.

Answer a fails because it breaks an existing trust unnecessarily and because it places one global group inside another (global groups can contain only users, not other groups of any kind, whether local or global). Answer b fails for the latter reason as well—it places one global group inside another.

Question 33

If frame types other than 802.2 are being used on a network, then Manual Frame Type Detection must be enabled. Frame types belonging to each client must be added to the frame type configuration list in the NWLink IPX/SPX Properties dialog box. Therefore, answer d is correct.

Question 34

RIP For IP should not be used in this situation, plus you do not know if there is more than one NIC in the server. Therefore, answer a is incorrect. Assigning the additional IP addresses to the server's NIC is an important step. Thus, answer b is correct. The DHCP Relay Agent does not apply to this situation. Therefore, answer c is incorrect. Because this site is within a private network, you will need both DNS and WINS to support name resolution. Therefore, answers d and e are correct. The correct answers for this question are b, d, and e.

Question 35

There are two legitimate ways to meet the stated requirements. One way simply entails adding the users from the Auditors domain into the local group (or groups) in the Accounting domain (where the needed resources reside). The other way to meet the stated requirements is to put a global group between the two domains by defining a global group in Auditors that can be placed into global groups in Accounting. Both options are legal because Accounting trusts Auditors. This makes answers b and c potentially correct. But because the question mentions a need to put the same group elsewhere in the future, creating a global group will ultimately be less work. That's because when the current temporary situation expires, the reference to the Auditor's global group only needs to be expunged from the local group (or groups) in Accounting. To add this same group into another domain, the global group only needs to be added to the local groups in that domain (provided, of course, that the necessary trust relationship from the new domain to the Auditors domain exists). Thus, answer b represents the best way to meet all requirements. Answer a fails because it assumes that Guests will be able to access the necessary resources, without indicating whether this is true. Answer d fails because it puts one local group within another (only global groups and users can occur within local groups).

Question 36

Gateway Service For NetWare must be installed on the Windows NTServer. Therefore, answer a is correct. For the Windows NT Server to communicate with the NetWare server, the NWLink protocol must be installed on the Windows NT Server. Therefore, answer b is also correct.

Question 37

The Event Viewer, DEVICE.LOG, and the MODEMLOG.TXT can be useful troubleshooting tools for RAS problems. Therefore, answers a, b, and d are correct. Dr. Watson focuses on applications and does not track RAS events. Therefore, answer c is incorrect. NT Diagnostics will not provide useful information related to RAS. Therefore, answer e is incorrect.

Question 38

The only activity required to host multiple Web sites on IIS when connected to the Internet is to assign the multiple IP addresses to the server and the respective directories. Therefore, only answer b is correct. RIP For IP and DHCP Relay Agent are unrelated to this situation. Therefore, answers a and c are incorrect. DNS and WINS are not required because an Internet hosted DNS will support the name resolution. Therefore, answers d and e are incorrect.

Question 39

The directory listed in answer a is the default location for storing the CAP files from Network Monitor. The directories listed in answers b, c, and d are not the default directories. Therefore, answers b, c, and d are incorrect.

Question 40

If a TCP/IP network does not have a WINS server, each computer on the network has to send a broadcast message to the other computers on the network. This increases network traffic. By making use of a WINS server, you provide computer-name-to-IP address resolution, which reduces the number of broadcast messages. Therefore, answer d is the correct answer.

Question 41

The pagefile size is recommended to be the size of physical RAM plus 12 MB. Therefore, answer a is incorrect. The pagefile should not be placed within a duplex set, especially on the duplexed drive. Therefore, answer b is incorrect. The pagefile should be the size of physical RAM plus 12 MB. Therefore, answer c is incorrect. The pagefile should be 140 MB and placed on the fastest storage set available. Therefore, answer d is correct.

Question 42

All the explanations can result in the given error message. Therefore, answers a, b, c, and d are correct. When the boot process cannot find NTOSKRNL.EXE, it does not indicate if the problem is with the file itself, its location, or the pointers to the file.

Question 43

With non-standardized configurations, implementing any encryption security other than Allow Any Authentication Including Clear Text results in some clients being restricted from accessing the network via RAS. Therefore, only answer a is correct. Require Microsoft Encrypted Authentication and Require Encrypted Authentication are encryption security schemes that require special configuration or operating systems. Therefore, answers b and d are incorrect. PGP Encryption is not a native option of NT. Therefore, answer c is incorrect.

Question 44

The correct answer is d. The complete trust model can be used as a modified master domain model with good success. However, this solution does not reduce validation traffic over the WAN links. By placing all users in the Los Angeles domain, each time a branch office user logs on, he will connect to the corporate domain. Thus, heavy loads on the WAN links will result from this security traffic. To make this solution work, a Los Angeles domain BDC should be physically placed in each of the branch offices. Then, all users would access the BDC for authentication and minimize WAN usage.

Question 45

For NetWare clients to access files on a Windows NT Server, FPNW is the required software component. Therefore, answer c is one correct answer to this question. On the other hand, the NetWare clients must have a way to send requests to the Windows NT domain controller, browse available resources, and request access to those resources. This is where the Microsoft redirectors for the NetWare clients come into play. The redirectors will permit clients to browse network resources directly. Therefore, answer e is also correct. Answer a is incorrect because it lets MS network clients access a NetWare server, which is irrelevant to the circumstances. Answer b is incorrect because it lets Windows NT Workstations and Servers act as clients to a NetWare server, also irrelevant. Finally, answer d is incorrect because the question clearly states that accounts were migrated from NetWare to Windows NT.

Question 46

You must use File And Object Access audits to record print activities, which in turn can be used to tally the number of pages and jobs sent to each printer. Therefore, answer a is correct. The Performance Monitor does not have a printer object that you can use to create a report. Therefore, answer b is incorrect. There is no way to set the Application log to tally anything. the Application log records information sent by an application. Therefore, answer c is incorrect. The Printer Wizard is used to create logical printers. It does not have any statistical abilities. Therefore, answer d is incorrect.

Question 47

The PDC was not disconnected from the network. Instead, the new SID of the PDC is the culprit. Therefore, answer a is incorrect. Member servers can never be domain controllers. Therefore, answer b is incorrect. The SID of the PDC is the defining element of a domain, not its name. Thus, the new SID created a new domain in which none of the workstations is a member. Therefore, answer c is correct. BDCs in trusting domains cannot authenticate users nor can they act as PDCs for a trusted domain. Therefore, answer d is incorrect.

Question 48

Answer a is the proper sequence of steps required to give the Admin users access to the beta software. Therefore, answer a is correct. Adding new accounts to the Research domain is insecure and will result in twice the administration to maintain two accounts for each user. Therefore, answer b is incorrect. The existing trust will allow Admin users to use Research resources, reversing the trust will prevent access and destroy other possible links currently relying on the trust. Therefore, answer c is incorrect. It is not possible to add a global group to another global group, plus Microsoft recommends using local groups to manage resource permissions. Thus, answer d is incorrect.

Question 49

The binding order of protocols on both the client and server determine what single LAN protocol is used over the RAS connection. This situation will result in a NetBEUI connection. Thus, WinSock applications based on the Windows TCP/IP API cannot be used because TCP/IP is not a protocol being communicated over the link. Therefore, answer d is correct. The other activities can occur using the NetBEUI protocol, thereby making answers a, b, and c incorrect.

Question 50

For Windows NT to provide support for HP network interface print devices, you must install the DLC (Data Link Control) protocol. Therefore, answer d is the correct choice. You can't install a printer driver if Windows NT cannot recognize the print device.

Question 51

1,200 MB would be the size of the set if you used all 4 drives with 300 MB on each one. Because this is not the largest possible sum using this set of drives, answer a is incorrect. 1,000 MB is indeed the amount of data that could be stored on the largest set created from these drives, but the question requested the total size of the set, making answer b incorrect. Likewise, although 800 MB represents the size of the largest individual drive, you must use 3 drives to create a disk stripe set with parity. Therefore, answer c is incorrect. As it happens, 1,500 MB is the total size of the largest set that can be created from these drives, using only the 800, 600, and 500 MB drives. Therefore, answer d is the correct reply.

Question 52

Answer a is not a proper construction. The relation indicates both inbound and outbound traffic, plus the **NOT** logical operator is used outside of the filter statement. Therefore, answer a is incorrect. Answer b lists the default **INCLUDE** statement, which does not need to be repeated, and the **EXCLUDE** statement applies to traffic sent to Sales5. Therefore, answer b is incorrect. Answer c is an **EXCLUDE** statement that restricts traffic from the Sales5 computer. Therefore, answer c is correct. Answer d excludes both inbound and outbound traffic from Sales5. Therefore, answer d is incorrect.

Question 53

There is a default restriction to prevent general users from logging in locally to a server—it is the log on locally right, and it is not assigned to users by default. Therefore, answer a is incorrect. Servers allow members of the Administrators, Server Operators, Backup Operators, Account Operators, and Print Operators groups to log on to them. Thus, answer b is incorrect. The log on locally right is not assigned to standard users specifically to prevent them from gaining easy access to the server. Therefore, answer c is correct. There is not a server object to set No Access permissions to. Thus, answer d is incorrect.

Question 54

Disk striping with parity requires a minimum of three physical drives, so answer a is correct. Disk striping with parity requires NTFS, not FAT, so answer b is incorrect. Because disk striping with parity is indeed a fault-tolerant storage method, answer c is also correct. Disk striping with parity offers better performance than disk mirroring because it spreads the load across more drives. Thus, answer d is correct, as well. Disk striping with parity can recover from a single drive failure. Therefore, answer e is incorrect. This means the correct answers are a, c, and d.

Question 55

If a physical print device in a printer pool fails in the middle of a print job, the print job is retained at that physical print device until the device is fixed. Therefore, choice d is the correct answer. Any other print jobs sent to the printer pool will continue to print to other physical print devices in the printer pool.

Glossary Of Terms

AATP (Authorized Academic Training Program)—This program authorizes accredited academic institutions of higher learning to offer Microsoft Certified Professional testing and training. The institutions are also allowed to use the Microsoft Education course materials and Microsoft Certified Trainers.

account—See *user account*.

account policy—A setting that establishes how passwords on a domain or a workstation are used.

ACL (access control list)—The attribute of each object that defines which users and groups have what level of services for an object.

Administrator—The person responsible for the upkeep, management, and security of a network. Also, the Administrator is a built-in user in Windows NT that has full control of the system.

advanced user rights—The set of user rights that are not commonly associated with normal network use. These rights aid with software development and specialized process operation.

alias—An alternate name for an email address.

AppleTalk—Apple Computer's networking protocols and software.

architecture—A network's setup and how the network's components interconnect.

ASCII (American Standard Code For Information Exchange)—A way of coding that translates letters, numbers, and symbols into digital form.

ASP (Active Server Pages)—A type of HTML or other Web document-distribution system used by IIS version 3. This topic only appears on the IIS 3 exam.

assessment exam—Similar to the certification exam, these tests give you the opportunity to answer questions similar to the questions appearing on the certification exams but, at your own pace. Assessment exams also utilize the same tools as certification exams, which allows you to familiarize yourself with the exam tools.

ATEC (Authorized Technical Education Center)—The location where you can take Microsoft Official Curriculum courses taught by Microsoft Certified Trainers.

auditing—In the Security log of a server or workstation, it is the method of tracking and recording the activities of various users.

Auto Frame Type Detection—A process in NT that automatically detects the frame types for a network. This setting must be changed for NWLink (IPX/SPX).

AUTOEXEC.BAT—A DOS batch file that is launched when a computer is started or booted.

backup—A method of fault tolerance where computer data is saved on some type of external storage media.

Backup Browser—Computer on an NT network that maintain a duplicate list of the network's resources and acts in a similar way within the Browser service as BDCs act within domain control.

backup operators—A designated group in Windows NT that has the permission to log on to a domain and back up a particular server or workstation.

basevideo—A command-line parameter switch used on the BOOT.INI file. It forces NT to boot using 16-color VGA video at 640×480. This setting appears by default on the ARC name line identified by "[VGA mode]".

BDC (Backup Domain Controller)—A backup server that protects the integrity and availability of the SAM database. BDCs are not able to make any changes or modifications, but they can use the database to authenticate users.

beta—A version of software released for general public testing. A beta is pre-final release and often contains unresolved issues, bugs, or undocumented features.

beta exam—A test exam given to participants at a Sylvan Prometric Testing Center before the development of the Microsoft Certified Professional certification exam. The final exam is based on the results of the beta exam.

BIOS (Basic Input/Output System)—A system that houses the buffers used to transfer information from a program to the hardware devices receiving the information.

blue screen—A screen that appears when a GPF occurs in NT. This is a test display of the STOP message error. There are lots of details included on this screen, such as the location of the error, type of error, and whether or not a memory dump is created.

blueprint survey—A part of the development process of the Microsoft certification exam where data is gathered from qualified job function experts. This survey determines the importance, required competence, and weighting for each individual exam objective.

boot disk—A hard drive or floppy with bootstrap files on it that enable an operating system to launch.

boot menu—The text menu that appears immediately after the hardware test on a Windows NT machine. It lists all known operating systems present. The OS listed first is booted by default when the timeout period expires unless an alternate OS is manually selected.

BOOT.INI—One of the files placed on the system partition that contains the location of the system files for each OS installed on the machine. The locations are listed using ARC names.

BOOTP—Protocol used by diskless workstations to obtain boot data on IP-based networks; precursor to DHCP (which remains backward compatible with BOOTP to this day).

BOOTSECT.DOS—The file containing DOS boot sector data, which appears in the system partition only on a multi boot machine that numbers DOS, Windows, Windows 95, or some other near-DOS equivalent among the list of boot options in BOOT.INI.

bottleneck—The effect of trying to force too much information through a system with inadequate bandwidth, causing the system to slow significantly.

break mirror—The first step in repairing a mirrored set. This is accomplished in the Disk Administrator utility, using the Break Mirror option in the Fault Tolerance drop-down menu.

broadcast packets—The information packet sent from one user to all other users on a network.

browse list—The list of available computers and resources on an NT network. This list is never viewed directly by the user; however, numerous applications pull data from this list to offer users a context-based selection of resources.

Browser service—A utility that maintains a list of network resources within a domain, and provides lists of these domains, servers, and resource objects to any Explorer-type interface that requests it (e.g., browse lists).

buffer settings—Controls the buffer size used by Network Monitor to store captured frames.

buffer space—In the Capture Trigger dialog box, it is the area used to set the accepted percentage levels for usage of system objects.

cache—A specified area of high-speed memory used to contain data that is going to be or recently has been accessed.

callback—A security feature in which a RAS connection is only established after the server has disconnected the inbound call and then called the user back.

capture—The process of recording data for later perusal. Network Monitor captures frames to be viewed for protocol-level inspection.

change permissions—In NTFS file systems, it is one of the standard access file permissions. It allows an object's access permissions to be altered.

Chart view—In Performance Monitor, it is the view that allows users to peruse realtime data in a line graph or histogram form.

checksums—The sum of a group of data. The sum is used to guarantee that data is transmitted without any errors.

command line—A DOS prompt that accepts DOS-based commands.

computer name—The name of a computer on a LAN that is specific to an individual workstation or server.

CONFIG.POL—In the NETLOGON share, this is the file where all policies are stored.

Control Panel—In Windows, this is the area where you modify system settings, such as fonts, screen color, SCSI hardware, and printers, among others.

CPU (Central Processing Unit)—The "brains" of your computer. This is the area where all functions are performed.

CSNW (Client Service For NetWare)—Designed for Windows NT workstations that require a direct link to NetWare servers, CSNW lets Windows NT machines link up to and browse NetWare resources alongside Microsoft Windows Network resources.

cut score—On the Microsoft Certified Professional exam, it is the lowest score a person can receive and still pass.

default—A factory-enabled setting placed in effect until a user specifies otherwise.

device driver—Software that gives NT the ability to use hardware connected to the computer. This hardware includes modems, printers, mouse, monitor, even the computer itself.

DEVICE.LOG—A log file used by RAS to capture communications between software and a modem when attempting to establish a dial-up connection. This file is located in \%winnt root%\system32\ras.

DHCP (Dynamic Host Configuration Protocol)—A service that enables the assignment of dynamic TCP/IP network addresses, based on a specified pool of available addresses.

Dial-Up Networking—A utility found in the RAS Phonebook|Programs |Accessories folder of the Start menu that controls the dial-out capabilities of RAS.

directory replication—A service designed to disseminate often-used and regularly updated data (such as user profiles, logon scripts, and system policies) to multiple computers to speed file access and improve reliability.

disaster recovery—A plan that determines how to reinstate computer operations if a disaster or catastrophe occurs.

disk administrator—An administration application in the Administrative Tools group that lets an administrator create and delete stripe sets and various disk partitions, change the assignment of drive letters, and display facts about a partition's size and setup.

disk duplexing—A fault tolerance method used by Windows NT that uses a duplicate physical and logical drive on a separate hard disk where the drive is connected to the system via a separate controller. If the original drive or controller fails, the system continues to operate using the duplexed drive.

disk mirroring—A fault tolerance method used by Windows NT that creates an exact duplicate of one physical and logical storage device on a separate physical storage device.

disk partition—A portion of a hard disk that acts like a physically separate unit.

disk striping—A fault tolerance method used by Windows NT that stores data across multiple physical storage devices.

distribution files—The 80+ MB of files used to install Windows NT. These are located on the CD in the \i386 directory for the Intel platform, \mips for MIPS, \alpha for DEC Alpha, and \PPC for the Macintosh Power PC. This can also refer to the additional driver library stored in the \drvlib directory.

DLC (Data Link Control)—A protocol used to interoperate with IBM mainframes and provide connectivity to network-attached print devices.

DLLs (Dynamic Link Libraries)—Small executable program routines or device drivers stored in separate files and loaded by the OS when called upon by a process or hardware device.

DMB (Domain Master Browser)—In Windows NT networks, a browser that communicates resource lists across subnets within the same domain.

DNS (Domain Name Service)—A system used to resolve host names into IP addresses.

domain—A group of computers and peripheral devices that share a common security database.

domain controller—A computer that authenticates domain logons as well as manages the Security Accounts Manager (SAM) database.

domain database—A database maintained by a PDC or BDC that stores three types of information: user accounts, computer accounts, and group accounts. Each user account requires 1 K, each computer account requires 5 K, and each group account requires 4 K.

domain guest—A group in which the members are given the minimal level of user access to all domain resources. The Guest account is automatically a member of this group.

domain model—A tool used by Microsoft to describe and define organizational schemes for networks. In theory, the domain model can scale up to handle any size network.

DOS (Disk Operating System)—Software that regulates the way a computer reacts with its floppy or hard disks.

drivers—Software that bonds a peripheral device to the operating system.

election packet—The electronic communication used by a browser (Master, Backup, or Potential) to initiate a new selection of a Master Browser when the current Master Browser is no longer accessible or when a new machine goes online.

encryption—The method of coding data so a person has to have a decoding key to decipher the information.

ERD (Emergency Repair Disk)—A miniature first aid kit for NT. This single floppy contains all the files needed to repair system partition and many boot partition related problems.

Ethernet—The most widely used type of LAN, developed by Xerox.

Event log—An option in the Event Viewer in the Administrative Tools group that displays the events that have taken place on a particular computer.

Event Viewer—An application in Windows NT that displays log files and lets you modify them.

Everyone—A default group that lists each user within a domain as a member. This group cannot be deleted or renamed.

Exam Preparation Guides—Guides that provide information specific to Microsoft Certified Professional exams to help students prepare for the exam.

Exam Study Guide—Short for *Microsoft Certified Professional Program Exam Study Guide*, it contains information about more than one of the Microsoft Certified Professional exams.

FAT (File Allocation Table)—A table originally used by the DOS file system to keep information about the properties, location, and size of files being stored on a disk.

fault tolerance—The ability of a computer to work continuously, even when there is a system failure.

firewall—A barrier between two networks made of software and/or hardware that permits only authorized communication to pass.

FPNW (File And Print Services For NetWare)—A service that makes resources from a Windows NT Server available to NetWare clients, without requiring additional software or configuration changes.

FQDN (fully qualified domain name)—The complete site name of an Internet computer system.

FTP (File Transfer Protocol)—A protocol that transfers files to and from a local hard drive to an FTP server located elsewhere on another TCP/IP-based network (such as the Internet).

Full Control—In Windows NT Server, a permission that grants a person general permissions in addition to the authority to change permissions.

GDI (Graphics Device Interface)—Provides network applications with a system for presenting graphical information. The GDI works as a translator between an application's print request and a device driver interface (DDI) so a job is rendered accurately.

global groups—Groups that apply to all computers within a network. A global group needs to be defined only once for each domain. Global groups can have only users.

Gopher services—Provides text-only information over the Internet, most suited to large documents with little or no formatting or images.

graphics—Pictures and images created on a computer.

groups—Collections of users defined together with a common name and resource permissions.

GSNW (Gateway Service For NetWare)—A service that enables Windows NT Server to map a drive to a NetWare server and provides access to NetWare server resources for Windows NT workstations (via a gateway).

GUI (Graphical User Interface)—A computer interface that uses graphics, windows, and a trackball or mouse as the method of interaction with the computer.

HAL (Hardware Abstraction Layer)—In the NT operating system, it creates a bridge between the Windows NT operating system and a computer's CPU.

hard drive—Permanent storage area for data. It is also called the hard disk.

hardware—The physical components of a computer system.

HCL (Hardware Compatibility List)—A list that comes with Windows NT Server that tells you what hardware is compatible with the software. The most updated versions of this list can be found on the Microsoft Web site or on the TechNet CD.

hive—A section of the Windows NT Registry.

HOST file—A static list of FQDNs mapped to IP addresses.

HTML (Hypertext Markup Language)—Based on SGML, it is the markup language used to create Web pages.

HTTP (Hypertext Transfer Protocol)—This is the World Wide Web protocol that allows for the transfer of HTML documents over the Internet or intranets that respond to actions like a user clicking on hypertext links.

I/O error—A computer malfunction relating to the communication between one component and another. I/O errors usually relate to storage devices or modems.

IDE (Integrated Device Electronics)—A type of storage device interface where the electronics required to operate the drive are stored on the drive itself, thus eliminating the need for a separate controller card.

IEEE (Institute Of Electrical And Electronic Engineers)—A group of technical professionals who sponsor technical conferences worldwide, publish over 25 percent of the world's technical papers, and contribute significantly to the establishment of technical standards.

IIS (Internet Information Server)—A Web server software by Microsoft. It is included and implemented with Windows NT Server.

instructor-led course—Usually held in a classroom setting, a course led by an instructor.

interdomain trusts—Another, more descriptive name for a trust. A trust is established between two domains connected only by electronic network pathways. Thus, any trust within NT is an interdomain trust.

Internet—The collection of TCP/IP-based networks around the world.

intranet—An internal private network that uses the same protocols and standards as the Internet.

IP address—Four sets of numbers separated by decimal points that represent the numeric address of a computer attached to a TCP/IP network, such as the Internet.

IPC (Interprocess Communications)—Within an operating system, it is the exchange of data between applications.

IPCONFIG—In the Windows NT version of TCP/IP, a command-line utility that displays IP configuration details.

IPX/SPX (Internetwork Packet Exchange/Sequenced Packet Exchange)—The name of Novell's NetWare protocol that was reinvented by Microsoft and implemented in Windows NT under the name NWLink. This protocol is fully compatible with Novell's version and, in many cases, is a better implementation than the original.

IRQ (Interrupt Request)—On a PC, it is a hardware interrupt.

ISA (Industry Standard Architecture)—An acronym that refers to the design of the 16-bit AT bus developed by IBM.

ISDN (Integrated Services Digital Network)—A dedicated form of digital communication that has a bandwidth of 128 Kbps.

ISO (International Standards Organization)—An association based in Paris that is responsible for setting international data communications standards.

job function expert—A person who knows just about everything about a particular job function and the software products/technologies related to that job. Typically, a job function expert is performing the job, has recently performed the job, or is training people to perform the job.

kernel—The essential part of an operating system that provides basic services.

Kernel Debugger—A feature that records the activity of NT during boot up and when a STOP error occurs.

LAN (Local Area Network)—A network confined to a single building or geographic area and comprised of servers, workstations, peripheral devices, a network operating system, and a communications link.

LAN Manager—A network operating system product developed by Microsoft that is deployed as a server application under OS/2.

Last Known Good Configuration—A recording made by NT of all the Registry settings that existed the last time a user successfully logged in to a server.

LMHOSTS—The predecessor to WINS, it is a static list of NetBIOS names mapped to IP addresses.

local group—A group of users on a single domain that is set up and given privileges and rights to local resources on that domain.

lockout—In Windows NT security, it is a feature used to prevent compromised accounts from being used.

logical partitions—The segments created when a physical hard drive is divided. Each segment can be used independently of the others, including belonging to separate volumes and hosting different file systems. Most logical partitions have a drive letter assigned to them and can be referred to by an ARC name.

logical printers—The software component used by NT to direct print jobs from applications to a print server. A physical printer can be serviced by numerous logical printers.

logoff—The process by which a user quits using a computer system.

logon—The process by which a user gains access or signs onto a computer system.

logon scripts—Files that consist of a set of network commands that must be carried out in a particular order.

LPD (Line Printer Daemon)—Originally a Unix component, the LPD service receives documents from LPR clients and sends them to a printer. An LPD is essentially a print server.

LPR (Line Printer Remote)—A command-line utility provide by Windows NT used for directing and monitoring print jobs aimed for Unix host printers.

MAC (Media Access Control)—In the IEEE 802 network, it is the lowest of the two sublayers of the data-link layer.

Master Browser—A tool used to maintain the main list of all available resources within a domain (including links to external domains).

master domain model—An organizational structure in which user management is centralized in a single domain, resource management is centralized into separate resource domains, and trusts are set up between the domains to provide user access to resources.

MBR (Master Boot Record)—A BIOS bootstrap routine used by low-level, hardware-based system code stored in Read-Only Memory (ROM) to initiate the boot sequence on a PC.

MCI (multiple-choice item)—An item within a series of items that is the answer to a question (single-response MCI) or one of the answers to a question (multiple-response MCI).

MCP (Microsoft Certified Professional)—An individual who has taken and passed a series of certification exams, thereby earning one or more of the following certifications: Microsoft Certified Trainer, Microsoft Certified Solution Developer, Microsoft Certified Systems Engineer, or Microsoft Certified Product Specialist.

MCPS (Microsoft Certified Product Specialist)—An individual who has passed at least one of the Microsoft operating system exams.

MCSD (Microsoft Certified Solution Developer)—An individual who has taken and passed a series of certification exams, thereby classified as qualified to create and develop business solutions using the Microsoft development tools, technologies, and platforms.

MCSE (Microsoft Certified Systems Engineer)—An individual who has taken and passed a series of certification exams, thereby classified as an expert on Windows NT and the Microsoft BackOffice integrated family of server software. This individual can also plan, implement, maintain, and support information systems associated with these products.

MCT (Microsoft Certified Trainer)—An individual who has taken and passed a series of certification exams, thereby qualified by Microsoft to instruct Microsoft Education courses at sites authorized by Microsoft.

Microsoft certification exam—A test created by Microsoft to verify the mastery of a software product, technology, or computing topic.

Microsoft Certified Professional Certification Update—A newsletter for Microsoft Certified Professional candidates and Microsoft Certified Professionals.

Microsoft official curriculum—Microsoft education courses that support the certification exam process and are created by the Microsoft product groups.

Microsoft Roadmap To Education And Certification—An application based on Microsoft Windows that takes you through the process of determining your certification goals and planning how you can achieve them.

Microsoft Sales Fax Service—A service provided by Microsoft where you can obtain Exam Preparation Guides, fact sheets, and additional information about the Microsoft Certified Professional program.

Microsoft Solution Provider—An organization not directly related to Microsoft that provides integration, consulting, technical support, and other services related to Microsoft products.

Microsoft TechNet Technical Information Network—A service provided by Microsoft that provides helpful information via a monthly CD-ROM. TechNet is the primary source of technical information for people who support and/or educate end users, create automated solutions, or administer networks and/or databases.

mirror set—A pair of disks that have been duplicated in the Windows NT disk mirroring fault tolerance method.

modems applet—An application you use to install and maintain a modem.

MOLI (Microsoft Online Institute)—An organization that offers training materials, online forums, user groups, and online classes.

motherboard—A term that refers to the main circuit board in a computer system.

MPR (Multiprotocol Router)—A device that converts various email formats.

MRI (multiple-rating item)—An item that gives you a task and a proposed solution. Every time a task is given, an alternate solution is provided, and the candidate must choose the answer that gives the best results produced by one solution.

MSDN (Microsoft Developer Network)—The official source for Software Development Kits (SDKs), Device Driver Kits (DDKs), operating systems, and programming information associated with creating applications for Microsoft Windows and Windows NT.

multicasts—Transmitting a message to several recipients simultaneously.

multichannel—Having more than a single inbound or outbound communications port, link, or connection.

Multilink PPP (MP)—The combining of the bandwidth of multiple physical links, which increases the total bandwidth that can be used for a RAS connection.

multiple master domain model—A domain model that has two or more master domains that trust each other via two-way trust relationships. The model also provides centralized administration of user accounts.

multitasking—The ability to run more than one computer application on a system at a time.

NDA (nondisclosure agreement)—A legal agreement signed by both Microsoft and a vendor that renders certain rights and limitations.

NDIS (Network Driver Interface Specification)—A device driver specification developed by both Microsoft and 3Com that provides hardware and protocol independence for network drivers. NDIS is used by LAN Manager and Vines, and it is supported by several vendors of network cards.

net commands—The collection of DOS-based commands used to modify and operate a network. A net command is the leading executable "net" followed by parameters indicating the function to be performed.

NetBEUI—A simple network layer transport protocol that was developed to support NetBIOS networks.

NetBIOS—Originally developed by IBM in the 1980s, this protocol provides the underlying communication mechanism for some basic NT functions, such as browsing and interprocess communications between network servers.

NETLOGON—An administrative share that is created and used within domain controllers for authenticating users who are logging on to the enterprise domain.

netmask—When using static routing, it is one of the options presented in the command-line command **route**. It specifies the subnet mask value to be associated with the **route** entry.

Netstat—A utility that displays TCP/IP status and statistics.

NetWare—A popular network operating system from Novell.

Network Client Administrator—Located in the Administrative Tool's Start menu, it's used to create a boot disk or a set of startup disks for DOS workstations.

Network Monitor—A tool used for investigating network-related problems.

NIC (Network Interface Card)—An adapter card used to connect a computer to a network.

non-seed router—A Macintosh term referring to an AppleTalk router (usually a software implementation) that is unable to distribute new network addresses to clients.

NTFS—A naming file system used in Windows NT.

NTLDR file—The executable program launched by the boot files that load the NT kernel. The name is a shortened version of "NT Loader."

null modem cable—An RS-232 cable used to enable two computers within close proximity to communicate without a modem.

NWLink—Microsoft's "clean room" implementation of Novell's IPX/SPX protocol suite for NetWare networks.

ODI (Open Data-link Interface)—Developed by Novell, this is a device driver standard that lets you run several protocols on the same network adapter card.

operating system—A software program that controls the operations of a computer system.

OSI (Open Systems Interconnect)—A standard by the ISO that defines the framework required to implement seven-layer protocols within worldwide communications.

pagefile—The file used by the virtual memory manager to temporarily store segments or pages of memory to hard disk.

PAP (Password Authentication Protocol)—A clear-text authentication protocol.

parity—Redundant segments of data used to provide fault tolerance for stored information. Within NT, this term is most commonly used when discussing stripe sets with parity. Parity is a disk storage configuration where additional data is written in separate drives in 64 K blocks so that in the event of a single drive failure, all data can be reconstructed.

partition—A portion of a hard disk or memory.

passwords—A word used by an individual to gain access to a particular system or application.

PDC (Primary Domain Controller)—The central storage and management server for the SAM database.

Performance Monitor—A graphical application that lets you set, graph, log, and report alerts. It is also referred to as PerfMon.

permissions—A setting configuration assigned to files and folders to determine who has access rights to the resources.

PGP (Pretty Good Privacy)—An encryption program that is not native to Windows NT.

Phonebook entry—A collection of settings used by RAS to establish a connection with a remote dial-up server. A phonebook entry contains details such as phone number, name, password, protocol settings, and encryption type.

physical disk—The hardware component that adds additional storage space. A physical disk must be partitioned and formatted with a file system before data can be stored on it.

PING—A TCP/IP command used to verify the existence and connect to remote hosts over a network.

policies—A set of specifications or limitations that delimit the environment of a user. NT has three policies: account, user rights, and audit.

Potential Browser—A computer that can participate in the support of the list of resources for a domain. A Potential Browser is automatically elected to a position of Backup or Master browser by the Browser Service as needed.

power users—A user group found on NT Workstation. Also, a user who is well versed in the operation and modification of a computing system—someone who pushes an operating system to its limits.

PPP (Point-To-Point Protocol)—An industry standard protocol used to establish network-protocol-supporting links over POTS lines using modems.

PPTP (Point-To-Point Tunneling Protocol)—Enables "tunneling" of IPX, NetBEUI, and TCP/IP inside PPP packets in such a way as to establish a secure link between a client and server over the Internet.

primary partition—A logical designation on a physical hard drive where the main files for an operating system can reside. Under NT, a physical disk might contain four primary partitions or three primary partitions and a single extended partition.

print device—The physical hardware device that produces printed output.

print driver—The software component that enables communication between the operating system and a physical printing device.

print jobs—A document or image sent from a client to a printer. A print job is typically in Windows EMF or the RAW language of the printer.

print operators—A default group that has full control over all printers within a domain.

print queues—The list of print jobs waiting to be sent to a printer for processing. The print queue can be viewed by opening the printer folder for any individual logical printer.

print server—The computer that hosts the spool file for a printer and is physically attached to the printer.

printer—Typically refers to the logical printer (software component) within the NT environment as opposed to the physical printing device.

printer pool—A collection of identical printers that are served by a single, logical printer.

printing device—The hardware device that creates marks on paper in the pattern dictated by the driver software.

priorities—The method of designating the order or importance of a process to gain processing time.

process tracking—A type of Audit event that records process activities, such as handle duplication, indirect object access, and process termination.

protocol binding—The process NT uses to link network components from various levels of a network architecture to enable communication between components.

protocols—In networking, this is a set of rules that define how information is transmitted over a network.

proxy server—A computer that intercepts network communications attempting to cross defined boundaries. A proxy server also performs the needed operations on behalf of originating clients. A proxy server allows dissimilar or restricted networks to communicate while isolating the identity of the client.

RAID (Redundant Array of Inexpensive Disks)—A standardized method used to categorize fault tolerance storage systems. Windows NT implements Level 0, Level 1, and Level 5 RAID through software.

RAS (Remote Access Service)—A Windows NT service that provides remote network communication for remote clients over telecommunication lines. RAS connections are different from standard, direct-network connections only in relation to speed.

RDISK—The second segment of an ARC name, used with the initial segment of MULTI, to indicate the ordinal number of the physical storage device.

Read access—The ability to view and open a file or document.

redirector—A software component that intercepts and guides I/O requests to the proper server.

Registry—The hierarchical database that serves as a repository for hardware, software, and OS configuration information.

replication—A service of NT that automatically distributes files and directories from one server to multiple servers and workstations on a network.

replicator group—The default group whose members have permissions to access the replication service and directories. This group is exclusively used by the Directory Replication service and the user account created for the service.

Resource Kit—Additional documentation and software utilities distributed by Microsoft to offer added information and instruction on the proper operation and modification of Microsoft products.

rights—Settings that define the ability of a user to access a computer or domain.

RIP (Routing Internet Protocol)—A router protocol that enables communication between routers on a network to facilitate the exchange of routing tables.

router—A device or a software implementation that enable interoperability and communication across networks.

SAM (Security Accounts Manager)—The security database of NT that maintains a record of all users, groups, and permissions within a domain. The SAM is stored on the PDC and duplicated on the BDCs.

SAP (Service Advertising Protocol)—An IPX service that broadcasts services and addresses on a network.

SCSI (Small Computer System Interface)—A standard interface defined by ANSI that provides high-speed connections to devices such as hard drives, scanners, and printers.

security—A manner of protecting data by restricting access to authorized users.

seed router—A Macintosh term that refers to an AppleTalk router (usually a software implementation) that is able to distribute new network addresses to clients.

segment—A division of a network. Usually a single length of cable or a collection of cables and hosts that share a common element or purpose.

Server Manager—The NT administration utility where computer accounts are managed.

server operators—The default group whose members can manage domain servers.

Service Pack—A patch or fix distributed by Microsoft after the final release of a product to repair errors, bugs, and security breaches.

Services applet—The Control Panel utility where services can be started and stopped, and their startup parameters modified.

share-level permissions—The setting of user/group access on a network share. The permissions of a network share must be met by users before access to the object itself is granted.

shares—A network construct that enables remote users to access resources located throughout a network.

SID (Security ID)—A code assigned to users, groups, and computers by NT to identify them. Even when the name of an object changes, NT recognizes the object by its SID. Every SID is unique.

SLIP (Serial Line Internet Protocol)—An older industry standard for RAS communication links. SLIP is included with NT only for establishing connections with Unix systems that do not support the newer PPP standard.

SMP (Symmetric Multiprocessing)—A processing scheme for multiprocessor systems where each CPU can execute any process.

SMS (Systems Management Server)—A Microsoft product used for high-end management and administration of an enterprise-level network.

SMTP (Simple Mail Transfer Protocol)—The Internet protocol used to distribute email from one mail server to another over a TCP/IP network.

SNA (System Network Architecture)—A communications interface used to establish a link with IBM mainframes and AS/400 hosts.

SNMP (Simple Network Management Protocol)—A protocol used to monitor remote hosts over TCP/IP network.

sockets—A Microsoft API used to establish an interface between programs and the transport protocol in use over a network link.

spooler—A software component of the print system that stores print jobs on a hard drive while they wait in the print queue.

SQL Server—A Microsoft product that supports a network-enabled relational database system.

stripe set—A hard disk construct where segments of data are written in sequence across multiple drives.

subnet—A portion or segment of a network.

swap file—Another name for the pagefile used by the Virtual Memory Manager to temporarily store pages of memory on a hard drive.

synchronization—The replication of the domain database between the PDC and one or more BDCs.

System log—The log viewed through Event Viewer where general system information and errors are recorded.

system policy—A setting configuration created through the System Policy Editor that restricts the work environment of users based on a computer, group, or user.

System Policy Editor—The administrative tool used to create and modify system policies for computers, groups, and users.

Take Ownership—The act of grabbing Full Control authority over an object.

tape drives—Devices used for backing up data that employs metal film cassettes for storage.

TAPI (Telephony Application Programming Interface)—An interface and API that defines how applications can interact with data/fax/voice devices and calls.

Task Manager—A utility where applications and processes can be viewed, stopped, and started. Task Manager also offers CPU and memory status information.

TCP/IP—The most widely used protocol in networking today because it is the most flexible of the transport protocols and is able to span wide areas.

Telnet—A terminal emulation utility used to interact with remote computers.

Token Ring—A network topology where computers are arranged in a ring and a token is used to pass the privilege of communicating over the network.

trusts—A link between two domains that enables pass-through authentication so users from one domain can access the resources of another. A trust is only a one-way relationship.

two-way trust—The establishment of two one-way trusts.

UDP (User Datagram Protocol)—A TCP/IP component that transmits data through a connectionless service but does not guarantee the delivery or sequencing of sent packets.

UNC (Universal Naming Convention)—A standardized naming method for networks taking the form of "\\servername\sharename."

Unix—An interactive time-sharing operating system developed in 1969 by a hacker to play games. This system developed into the most widely used industrial-strength computer in the world and ultimately supported the birth of the Internet.

UPS (Uninterruptible Power Supply)—A semi-intelligent, rechargeable battery system that protects a computer from power failures and fluctuations.

user account—The collection of information stored by NT about a specific network user, such as name, password, group memberships, access privileges, and user rights. User accounts are managed through the User Manager For Domains utility.

User Manager For Domains—The NT administration utility controlling account management, group membership, and security policies for a domain.

user name—The human-friendly name of a user account. The user name is one of two items of data used to log on to NT. NT does not recognize an account by the user name, but rather by the SID.

user profiles—The collection of desktop and environmental settings that define the work area of a local computer.

user rights—Settings that define the ability of a user to access a computer or a domain.

users group—This is another term for "group."

VGA (Video Graphics Array)—A PC display standard of 640×480 pixels, 16 colors, and a 4:3 aspect ratio.

VMM (Virtual Memory Manager)—The executive service within NT's kernel that manages physical and virtual (swap or pagefile) memory.

volume set—A disk construct comprised of one or more logical partitions formatted with a single file system.

WAN (Wide Area Network)—A network that spans geographically distant segments. Often the distance of two miles or more is used to define a WAN; however, Microsoft equates any RAS connection as establishing a WAN.

Windows NT Workstation—A Microsoft OS product that is a client version of the NT system. It is the same as NT Server but without the ability to host multiple services and resources for a network.

WINS (Windows Internet Name Service)—A Windows network service used to resolve NetBIOS names to IP addresses.

workgroups—A collection of networked computers that participate in a peer-to-peer relationship.

World Wide Web—An information-distribution system hosted on TCP/IP networks. The Web supports text, graphics, and multimedia. The IIS component of NT is a Web server (which can distribute Web documents).

Write permissions—This setting grants the ability to create or modify files and directories.

XCOPY—A command-line utility used to copy files and subdirectories while maintaining the directory tree structure.

Index

A

Access control lists. *See* ACLs.
Access tokens, 60-61
Account policies, 152-153
Accounts
    adding to domains, 89-90
    default, 65-67
Accounts domains, 20
ACLs, 61-63
Add To command, 229
Address command, 216-217
Address Expression
    dialog box, 211
Addresses, viewing, 216-217
Administrator accounts, 66-67
Alert view, 228, 232
Alerts, 228, 232
AppleTalk
    definition, 162
    routing between subnets,
    175-176
Application logs, 317

Applications
    monitoring.
        See Task Manager.
    nonresponsive,
        terminating, 226
ARC names, 128-129
arp utility, 168
Attributes, object, 61
Auditing
    enabling, 148-151
    event types, 149
    File And Object Access
        events, 149
    overhead, 151-152
    viewing audit logs, 152
Authentication
    Backup Domain
        Controller, 90
    domain controllers, 110
    logon scripts, 90
    and Primary Domain
        Controller failure, 88-89

system policies, 90
user profiles, 90
AutoDial, 301

B

Backing up data, 130
Backing up system configuration, 317-318, 318, 319
Backup Browser, 96
Backup Domain Controller.
See BDC.
Baselining, 233-234
BDC
authentication, 90
definition, 84-85
domain controllers, 110
promoting to Primary
Domain Controller, 88-89
updates, controlling, 86-88
Blue screen errors, 314, 317, 324
Boot disk, contents, 126
Boot failures, 315-316
Boot partitions
on duplexed disks, 120
failure recovery, 127-129
on mirrored disks, 120
on striped disks, 121
Boot up, controlling, 322-323
BOOT.INI file, failure recovery, 127-129
BOOT.INI missing error message, 316
BOOT.INI switches, 322-323
BOOTSECT.DOS missing error message, 316
Broadcast messages, reducing, 165

Broadcasts per second, monitoring, 207
Broadcasts sent, monitoring, 209
Browser service, 96
Buffer Settings command, 217
Bytes per second, monitoring, 207
Bytes received, monitoring, 208
Bytes sent, monitoring, 208

C

Caching user profiles, 92
Callback. *See* RAS callback.
Capture Filter dialog box, 210
Capture Filter SAPs and
ETYPEs dialog box, 210
Capture filters
by address, 211
by data patterns, 212
definition, 209-210
by protocol, 210
Capture Trigger dialog box, 213
Capture triggers, 213-214
Centralized administrative controls, 44-45
Certification tests. *See*
Microsoft certification tests.
Chart view, 228-229, 231
Checking permissions, 63-64
Client applications, 268
Client Service For NetWare.
See CSNW.
Color scheme, configuring, 94
Combination permissions, 71
Complete trust domain model, 23-24

Complete trust model, 37-38
Computer policies, naming, 94
Cross-domain
    permissions, 40-42
CSNW, 254
Custom folders, configuring, 94
Custom shell settings,
    configuring, 94
Customizable user
    profiles, 91-92

D

Data Link Control. *See* DLC.
Dependency failures, 315
Desktops, user profiles for, 92
DEVICE.LOG file, 301-302
DHCP, 165, 190-191
DHCP Relay Agent, 175
Dialog boxes
    Address Expression, 211
    Capture Filter, 209
    Capture Filter SAPs and
        ETYPEs, 210
    Capture Trigger, 213
    Pattern Match, 212
    Virtual Memory, 234
Dial-Up Networking. *See* DUN.
Directed frames sent,
    monitoring, 209
Directory permissions, 67-69
Directory replication
    broadcast interval,
        setting, 114
    configuring, 114
    data types, 111

default export directory, 111
    definition, 111
    description, 113-114
    installing, 112-113
    server wait time, 114
Disaster recovery. *See* Failure
    recovery.
Disk Administrator
    tools, 115-116
Disk Administrator utility, 318
Disk drive letters, 117-118
Disk duplexing, 120
Disk mirroring, 119-120
    and paging files, 235
Disk performance, 230-231
Disk striping
    and paging files, 235
    with parity
        definition, 121-123
        failure recovery, 126
    without parity, 120-121
Disk structure
    drive letters, 117-118
    Master Boot Record, 118
    partitions
        active, 118
        definition, 116-117
    volumes, 117
Diskperf utility, 231
Display filters, 215
DLC, 162
DNS, 191-192, 194
Domain browsers
    Backup Browser, 96
    Browser service, 96
    electing, 97

Master Browser, electing, 97
Potential Browser, 96
and the Registry, 98
resource lists, 97
Domain controllers authentication, 110
Backup Domain Controller
authentication, 90
definition, 84-85
domain controllers, 110
promoting to Primary
Domain Controller,
88-89
updates, controlling,
86-88
failure recovery, 89-90
member servers
definition, 84
Primary Domain
Controller, 110
definition, 84-85
Security Accounts Manager,
84-85, 110
Server Manager tool, 88-89
Stand-Alone servers
definition, 84
switching roles, 84-85
synchronization
definition, 86
forcing during failure
recovery, 89
NT Registry parameters,
86-88
Domain name server, 167

Domain Name Service.
See DNS.
Domains. *See also* Trust relationships.
accounts domains, 20
adding computer accounts,
89-90
capacity, 38
capacity, calculating, 90-91
complete trust domain
model, 23-24
cross-domain permissions,
40-42
definition, 18
global groups,
contents of, 40
local groups, contents of, 40
master domain
model, 20-21
mesh networks, 23-24
multiple master domain
model, 22-23
multiple PDCs, 88-89
resource domains, 20
single domain model, 19-20
size limits, 18
Dr. Watson, 321-322
DUMPEXAM.EXE utility, 325
DUN, 303
Duplexed disks, failure recovery,
125-126
Duplicate account names, 256
Dynamic Host Configuration
Protocol. *See* DHCP.
Dynamic routers, 172

E

Electing a Master Browser, 97
Emergency Repair Disk.
    See ERD.
Encryption, RAS, 299-300
ERD, 319-320
ESDI hard drives, 323-324
Ethernet settings,
    changing, 164
Event Viewer, 316
Explorer access, configuring, 94

F

Failure recovery
    boot partition, 127-129
    BOOT.INI file, 127-129
    disk striping with
        parity, 126
    domain controllers, 89-90
    duplexed disks, 125-126
    floppy boot disk, 126
    mirrored disks, 125-126
    system partition, 127-129
Fault tolerance
    backing up data, 130
    Disk Administrator tools,
        115-116
    failure recovery
        boot partition, 127-129
        BOOT.INI file, 127-129
        disk striping with
            parity, 126
        duplexed disks, 125-126
        floppy boot disk, 126
        system partition, 127-129

Master Boot Record, 118
NT Backup utility, 130
partitions
    active, 118
    definition, 116-117
security
    disk duplexing, 120
    disk mirroring, 119-120
    disk striping with parity,
        121-123
    disk striping without
        parity, 120-121
    hot fixing, 119
    Redundant Array of
        Inexpensive Disks, 123-
        124, 126
    setting level of, 124
    volumes, 117
File And Object Access
    events, 149
File And Print Services For
    NetWare. *See* FPNW.
File permissions, 67-69
File Transfer Protocol. *See* FTP.
Find All Names command, 217
Find Routers command, 217
Firewalls, RAS, 298
Floppy boot disk, contents, 126
404 File not found message, 15
FPNW, 254
FQDN, 192
Frame types, NetWare, 251-252
Frames per second,
    monitoring, 207
Frames received,
    monitoring, 208

Frames sent, monitoring, 208
FTP, 166, 196
Fully qualified domain names.
See FQDN.

G

Gateway Service For NetWare.
See GSNW.
Gateways, RAS, 298
GDI, 271
Global groups, contents of, 40
Gopher, 166, 196
Graphics Device Interface.
See GDI.
Group memberships
Administrator accounts,
66-67
assigning, 65-66
default accounts, 65-67
Guest accounts, 66
multiple groups, 65
Group policies, naming, 94
GSNW
configuring, 252-254
description, 253-254
installing, 254-251
NWLink requirement, 251
Guest accounts, 66

H

Hardware problems,
314-315, 323
Hardware profiles, 95
Hidden drive shares,
configuring, 94

HOST file, 191-192, 302
Host names
displaying, 168
resolving to IP addresses,
191-192
hostname utility, 168
Hot fixing, 119
HTTP, 166, 195
Hypertext Transfer Protocol. *See*
HTTP.

I

IIS, 194-195
Instances, 229
Internet
protocols for, 165-166
RAS security, 294
secure connections, 165-166
Internet Information Server. *See*
IIS.
IP addresses
assigning at startup, 175
displaying, 168
fully qualified domain
names, 192
multiple on IIS, 195
resolving from host names,
191-192
resolving with network
names, 165
sharing across computers,
190-191
specifying, 166
structure of, 192
IP configuration, displaying,
168, 190

IPCONFIG utility, 168-169, 190

IPX addresses, resolving, 189

IPX/SPX
and NWLink protocol, 161-162
pros and cons, 163

K

Kernel Debugger, 324

L

Last Known Good Configuration. *See* LKGC.

LKGC, 317

LMHOSTS file, 193, 302

Local groups, contents of, 40

Log view, 229, 232

Logging, RAS, 301-302

Logging performance data, 229, 232

Logical printers
definition, 270
multiple, 279
ownership, 280
and printing pools, 275
priority, 277

Logon policies, 94

Logoff, forcing, 60

Logon scripts
authentication, 90
replicating, 111

Logon verification, 60-61

Logs, viewing, 317

lpq utility, 168

M

MAC addresses, finding, 208

Macintosh computers
AppleTalk protocol
definition, 162
routing between subnets, 175-176

Mandatory user profiles, 91

Mapping files, 256

Master Boot Record. *See* MBR.

Master Browser, electing, 97

Master domain model, 20-21

MBR, 118, 321

Media errors, 314

Member servers, 84

Memory, monitoring, 230

Memory dumps, 325

Memory use levels, determining, 227-228

Memory:CacheFaults counter, 230

Memory:PageFaults counter, 230

Memory:Pages/sec counter, 230

Mesh networks, 23-24

Microsoft certification tests
Microsoft Training And Certification Web site, 13-14
practice test, 12
reading for comprehension, 8-10
Self Test Software, 16

strategies for
answering, 10-12
test environment, 2-3
third-party providers, 16
Transcender Corporation, 16
typical questions, 4-8
Web sites, as information
sources, 15-16
Microsoft Migration
Tool, 255-257
Microsoft Training And
Certification Web site, 13-14
Mirrored disks
and boot partitions, 120
breaking the mirror, 125
failure recovery, 125-126
finding, 127
MODEMLOG.TXT file, 301
Monitoring network activity.
See Network Monitor.
MP protocol, 294-295
MPR, 171
Multicasts per second,
monitoring, 207
Multicasts sent,
monitoring, 209
Multilink PPP. *See* MP
protocol.
Multiple master domains
definition, 22-23
trust requirements, 36-38
Multiprotocol Router. *See*
MPR.

N

Name resolution
Domain Name Service,
191-192
Dynamic Host Configura-
tion Protocol, 190-191
fully qualified domain
names, 192
HOST file, 191-192
host names to IP addresses,
191-192
and IPX addresses, 189
LMHOSTS file, 193
NetBEUI, 189
NetBIOS, 188-189
Remote Access Service, 302
TCP/IP, 190
TCP/IP networks, 192-193
Windows Internet Name
Service
definition, 192-193
versus DNS, 194
nbtstat utility, 168-169
NetBEUI
definition, 161
installing, 170
resolving names, 189
NetBIOS
definition, 160
names, finding, 217
resolving names, 188-189
status, displaying, 168
netstat utility, 168-169

NetWare
    client service, 254
    Client Service For
        NetWare, 254
    definition, 248
    duplicate account
        names, 256
    File And Print Services For
        NetWare, 254
    file service, 254
    file system, 256
    frame types, 251-252
    gateway service, 254-254
    Gateway Service For
        NetWare
            configuring, 252-254
            installing, 254-251
            NWLink
            requirement, 251
    mapping files, 256
    Microsoft Migration
        Tool, 255-257
    migrating to Windows
        NT, 255-257
    passwords, 256
    print service, 254
    protocols supported, 248
Network addresses
    assigning, 165
    finding, 208
Network command, 217
Network connections,
    testing, 168
Network Monitor
    Address command, 216-217
    addresses, viewing, 216-217

analyzing data from, 206-209
broadcasts per second, 207
broadcasts sent, 209
Buffer Settings
    command, 217
buffer size, 217
bytes per second, 207
bytes received, 208
bytes sent, 208
capture filters
    by address, 211
    by data patterns, 212
    definition, 209-210
    by protocol, 210
capture triggers, 213-214
captured data
    default location for, 209
    displaying, 215-216
capturing data, 206-209
    dedicated mode, 214
configuring, 206
detecting usage of, 215
directed frames sent, 209
display filters, 216
Find All Names
    command, 217
Find Routers
    command, 217
frames per second, 207
frames received, 208
frames sent, 208
installing, 206
MAC addresses, 208
multicasts per second, 207
multicasts sent, 209

NetBIOS names,
  finding, 217
network addresses, 208
Network command, 217
network segments,
  tracking, 217
network utilization,
  percent, 207
passwords, 215
Resolve Addresses From
  Name command, 217
security, 215
Systems Management
  Server, 206
Network segments,
  tracking, 217
Network updates,
  configuring, 94
Network utilization,
  monitoring, 207
NT Backup utility, 130
NT system policies, 93-95
  default location for, 94
  description, 93-94
  priority order, 95
NTDETECT, 323
NTDETECT.COM missing
  error message, 316
NTFS file system,
  permissions, 67-69
NTLDR error message, 315
NTOSKRNL missing error
  message, 315-316
Null modems, 302
NWLink protocol. *See also*
  NetWare.
connecting to NetWare
  networks, 163
definition, 161-162, 248
Ethernet settings,
  changing, 164
installing, 163-164

O

Object counters, 229-231
Objects
  access control lists, 61-63
  attributes, 61
  definition, 229
  services, 61
  types, 61

P

PAGEFILE.SYS file, 235
Paging file, 234-235
Paper sizes, creating, 277
Partitions
  active, 118
  creating, 116
  definition, 116-117
Passwords
  NetWare, 256
  Network Monitor, 215
Pattern Match dialog box, 212
Pausing a print job, 277
PDC
  authentication, 90
  authentication after failure,
    88-89
  definition, 84-85
  domain controllers, 110

failure recovery, 88-89
multiple in one
domain, 88-89
PerfMon utility. *See* Performance Monitor.
Performance charts,
228-229, 231
Performance management.
See Task Manager.
Performance Monitor
Add To command, 229
Alert view, 228, 232
alerts, 228, 232
baselining, 232, 233-234
Chart view, 228-229, 231
counters, 229-231
disk performance, 230-231
diskperf utility, 231
instances, 229
Log view, 229, 232
logging performance
data, 229, 232
memory, monitoring, 230
Memory:CacheFaults
counter, 230
Memory:PageFaults
counter, 230
Memory:Pages/sec
counter, 230
object counters, 230-231
objects, 229
paging file, 234-235
performance
charts, 228-229, 231
performance

reports, 229, 232
PhysicalDisk/
LogicalDisk:CurrentDisk
QueueLength counter, 231
PhysicalDisk/
LogicalDisk:DiskBytes/
Transfer counter, 231
PhysicalDisk/
LogicalDisk:%DiskTime
counter, 230-231
Processor:Interrupts/sec
counter, 230
Processor:%ProcessorTime
counter, 230
Report view, 229, 232
System:ProcessorQueueLength
counter, 230
view types, 228-229
views, saving settings of,
232-233
Performance reports, 229, 232
Permissions. *See also* Rights,
Security.
checking, 63-64
combination, 71
directories, 67-69
files, 67-69
group memberships
Administrator accounts,
66-67
assigning, 65-66
default accounts, 65-67
Guest accounts, 66
multiple groups, 65
NTFS file system, 67-69
and shares, 69-70

troubleshooting, 321
PhysicalDisk/
    LogicalDisk:Current
    DiskQueueLength
    counter, 231
PhysicalDisk/
    LogicalDisk:DiskBytes/
    Transfer counter, 231
PhysicalDisk/
    LogicalDisk:%DiskTime
    counter, 230-231
ping utility, 168
Pinging network
    connections, 168
Point-To-Point Protocol.
    See PPP.
Point-To-Point Tunneling
    Protocol. *See* PPTP.
Policies
    naming, 94
    priority, 95
Potential Browser
    definition, 96
    and the Registry, 98
PPP, 165, 293
PPTP, 165-166, 294
Primary Domain Controller.
    See PDC.
Print auditing, 279-280
Print clients, 269
Print commands, 276-277
Print devices, 269, 271
Print jobs
    definition, 269
    pausing, 277
    purging, 277
    restarting, 278

resuming, 278
    stuck in spooler, 274
Print Manager. *See* Printers
    folder.
Print monitors, 272
Print priorities, 273-274
Print processors, 272
Print queue status,
    displaying, 168
Print queues, 270
Print resolution, 269
Print routers, 272
Print server services, 269
Print servers, 269
Print service, NetWare, 254
Print spoolers
    default directory for, 275
    definition, 269-270
    and NT Server, 272
    restarting stuck jobs, 274
Print spooling
    definition, 273
    enabling, 277
    separate spool files, 274
    stopping/restarting, 274
Print system data types, 276
Printer availability, setting, 277
Printer drivers
    defined, 270
    installing/changing, 276
    and NT Server, 272
Printer settings, configuring, 94
Printer shares, 278-279
Printers
    connecting to, 268
    creating, 268
    definition, 270

multiple, 279
network attached, connecting to, 162
Network Interface Cards, 269
network-attached, 280-281
security, 278-279, 280-281
sharing, 278-279
TCP/IP, 281
Unix, 281
Printers, logical
definition, 270
multiple, 279
ownership, 280
and printing pools, 275
priority, 277
Printers folder, 270-272
paper sizes, creating, 277
pausing a print job, 277
print spooling, enabling, 277
print system data type, 276
printer availability, setting, 277
printer drivers, 276
printing pools, enabling, 276
purging a print job, 277
restarting a print job, 278
resuming a print job, 278
separator pages, 276
Printing, troubleshooting, 320
Printing from
MS-DOS clients, 272-273
Windows 3.x clients, 272-273
Windows 95 clients, 272
Windows NT clients, 272

Printing pools, 275
Printing with NT Server, 270-272
Process priorities, 236
Processes
monitoring. *See* Task Manager.
terminating, 227
Processor:Interrupts/sec counter, 230
Processor:%ProcessorTime counter, 230
Protocol bindings, 170-171
Protocols
AppleTalk, 162
broadcast messages, reducing, 165
Dynamic Host Configuration Protocol, 165
Data Link Control
definition, 162
and network attached printers, 280-281
File Transfer Protocol, 166, 196
Gopher, 166, 196
Hypertext Transfer Protocol, 166, 195
for Internet providers, 165-166
IP addresses, resolving with network names, 165
IPX/SPX
and NWLink protocol, 161-162
pros and cons, 163

Multilink PPP, 294-295
NetBEUI
    definition, 161
    installing, 170
NetBIOS, 160
NetWare networks, connecting to. *See* NWLink protocol.
NWLink
    connecting to NetWare networks, 163
    definition, 161-162, 248
    Ethernet settings, changing, 164
    installing, 163-164
Point-To-Point Protocol, 165, 293
Point-To-Point Tunneling Protocol, 165-166, 294
RAS, binding order, 302
RIP
    definition, 171
    For IP, 172-174
    For IPX, 174
secure Internet connections, 165-166
Serial Line Internet Protocol, 165, 293
SubNetwork Access Protocol, 252
TCP/IP
    default gateway, 166
    definition, 161
    domain name server, 167
    host name,

displaying, 168
    installing, 166-168
    IP addresses, displaying, 168
    IP addresses, specifying, 166
    IP configuration details, displaying, 168
    NetBIOS status, displaying, 168
    network addresses, assigning, 165
    pinging network connections, 168
    print queue status, displaying, 168
    and printers, 281
    routes, tracing, 168
    routing tables, 168
    services, list of, 165-166
    subnet masks, 166
    testing network connections, 168
    utilities, 168-170
    for Unix hosts, 165
    Windows Internet Name Service, 165
    World Wide Web, 166
Pulse parameter, 86
PulseConcurrency parameter, 87
PulseMaximum parameter, 87
PulseTimeout1 parameter, 87
PulseTimeout2 parameter, 87
Purging a print job, 277

Q

Queues, print, 270

R

RAID, 123-124, 126
Randomize parameter, 87
RAS callback
  configuring settings, 94
  definition, 300-301
RAS clients
  Point-To-Point
    Protocol, 293
  Serial Line Internet
    Protocol, 293
RAS Phonebook, 299
RAS
  AutoDial, 301
  callback, 300-301
  definition, 292
  DEVICE.LOG
    file, 301-302
  Dial-Up Networking, 303
  encryption, 299-300
  as a firewall, 298
  as a gateway, 298
  HOST file, 302
  installing, 296-298
  LMHOSTS file, 302
  logging, 301-302
  logon process, 301
  MODEMLOG.TXT
    file, 301
  name resolution, 302
  null modems, 302
  protocols, 292

  protocols, binding
    order, 302
  remembering resource
    locations, 301
  as a router, 298
  security, 299-301
  serial cable connections, 302
  troubleshooting, 301-302
RAS servers
  maximum connections, 293
  Multilink PPP, 294-295
  Point-To-Point Tunneling
    Protocol, 294
  SLIP protocol, 293
Recovery, failure.
  See Failure recovery.
Redundant Array of Inexpen-
  sive Disks. See RAID.
REGEDIT utility, 318
REGEDIT32 utility, 318
Registry
  backing up, 319
  description, 318
  and domain browsers, 98
  synchronization parameters,
    86-88
Registry editing,
  configuring, 94
Remote Access Service.
  See RAS.
Rendering, 270
Replication. See directory
  replication.
ReplicationGovernor
  parameter, 88
Report view, 229, 232

Resolve Addresses From Name command, 217
Resource domains, 20
Restarting a print job, 278
Resuming a print job, 278
Rights, 71-73. *See also* Permissions, Security.
RIP protocol
  definition, 171
  For IP, 172-174
  For IPX, 174
Roaming profiles, 92
Route command, 173-174
route utility, 168
Routes, tracing, 168
Routing between subnets
  AppleTalk, 175-176
  DHCP Relay Agent, 175
  dynamic routers, 172
  IP addresses, assigning at startup, 175
  Macintosh computers, 175-176
  Multiprotocol Router, 171
  RIP protocol
    definition, 171
    For IP, 172-174
    For IPX, 174
  static routers, 172
  static routing tables, configuring, 173-174
Routing tables, 168

S

SAM
  domain controllers, 110
  and domain controllers, 84-85
SAP agents, 252
Screen savers, configuring, 93-94
Security. *See also* Permissions, Rights.
  access tokens, 60-61
  disk duplexing, 120
  disk mirroring, 119-120
  disk striping
    with parity, 121-123
    without parity, 120-121
  hot fixing, 119
  Internet connections, 165-166, 294
  logon verification, 60-61
  Multilink PPP, 294-295
  Network Monitor, 215
  passwords, NetWare, 256
  Point-To-Point Tunneling Protocol, 294
  Redundant Array of Inexpensive Disks, 123-124, 126
  RAS as a firewall, 298
  RAS callback, 300-301
  RAS encryption, 294, 299-300
  renaming default accounts, 66-67
Security Accounts Manager. *See* SAM.
Security logs, 317
Self Test Software, 16
Separator pages, 276
Serial cable connections, 302

Serial Line Internet Protocol. *See* SLIP.

Server Manager tool, 88-89

Server Service, 237

Server settings, optimizing, 237

Services, object, 61

Setup disks, recreating, 321

Shares, permission levels, 69-70

Shell restrictions, configuring, 94

Simple Network Management Protocol. *See* SNMP.

Single domain model, 19-20, 37-38

SLIP, 165, 293

SMS
    and Network Monitor, 206

SNAP (SubNetwork Access Protocol), 252

SNMP
    configuring, 94

Spooling. *See* Print spooling.

Stand-Alone servers, 84

Startup applications, configuring, 94

Static routers, 172

Static routing tables, configuring, 173-174

Statistics, system. *See* Network Monitor.

Stop message errors, 314, 317

Subnet masks, 166

SubNetwork Access Protocol (SNAP), 252

Synchronization, domain controllers
    definition, 86

    forcing during failure recovery, 89

    NT Registry parameters, 86-88

System configuration
    color scheme, 94
    computer policies
        naming, 94
    custom folders, 94
    custom shell settings, 94
    domain browsers
        Backup Browser, 96
        Browser service, 96
        electing, 97
        Master Browser, electing, 97
        Potential Browser, 96
        and the Registry, 98
        resource lists, 97
    Explorer access, 94
    group policies
        naming, 94
    hardware profiles, 95
    hidden drive shares, 94
    logon policies, 94
    network updates, 94
    NT system policies, 93-95
        default location for, 94
        description, 93-94
        priority order, 95
    policies
        naming, 94
        priority, 95
    printer settings, 94
    RAS callback settings, 94
    Registry editing, 94

screen savers, 93-94
shell restrictions, 94
Simple Network Management Protocol, 94
startup applications, 94
user policies
naming, 94
user profile handling, 94
wallpaper, 94
Windows application restrictions, 94
SYSTEM key, restoring, 318
System logs, 317
System partition, failure recovery, 127-129
System performance. *See* Task Manager.
System policies
authentication, 90
replicating, 111
System statistics. *See* Network Monitor.
System:ProcessorQueueLength counter, 230
Systems Management Server. *See* SMS.

T

TAPI (Telephony API), 295-296
Task Manager
information types, 226
memory use levels, determining, 227-228
starting, 226

terminating nonresponsive applications, 226
terminating runaway processes, 227
TCP/IP protocol
default gateway, 166
definition, 161
domain name server, 167
host name, displaying, 168
installing, 166-168
IP addresses, displaying, 168
IP addresses, specifying, 166
IP configuration details, displaying, 168
NetBIOS status, displaying, 168
network addresses, assigning, 165
pinging network connections, 168
print queue status, displaying, 168
resolving names, 190, 192-193
routes, tracing, 168
routing tables, 168
services, list of, 165-166
subnet masks, 166
testing network connections, 168
utilities, 168-170
Telephony API. *See* TAPI.
Tests, certification. *See* Microsoft certification tests.
tracert utility, 168

Tracking system activity. *See* Auditing.

Transcender Corporation, 16

Troubleshooting

Application logs, 317

backing up system configuration, 317-318, 318, 319

blue screen errors, 314, 317, 324

boot failures, 315-316

boot up, controlling, 322-323

BOOT.INI missing error message, 316

BOOT.INI switches, 322-323

BOOTSECT.DOS missing error message, 316

dependency failures, 315

Disk Administrator utility, 318

domain controller communication, 314

Dr. Watson, 321-322

DUMPEXAM.EXE utility, 325

Emergency Repair Disk, 319-320

ESDI hard drives, 323-324

Event Viewer, 316

GPFs. *See* Blue screen errors.

hardware detection, 323

hardware problems, 314-315

Kernel Debugger, 324

Last Known Good Configuration, 317

logs, viewing, 317

Master Boot Record, 321

media errors, 314

memory dumps, 325

NTDETECT, 323

NTDETECT.COM missing error message, 316

NTLDR error message, 315

NTOSKRNL missing error message, 315-316

permissions, 321

printing, 320

Remote Access Service, 301-302

REGEDIT utility, 318

REGEDIT32 utility, 318

Registry

backing up, 319

description, 318

Security logs, 317

setup disks, recreating, 321

STOP message errors, 314, 317

SYSTEM key, restoring, 318

System logs, 317

VGA mode, 323

Windows NT installation, 314-315

Trust relationships.

centralized administrative controls, 44-45

complete trust model, 37-38

cross-domain permissions,
40-42
establishing, 38-39
managing multiple, 42-43
rules for, 34-35
selecting, 42-43
single domain
models, 37-38
three domains, 43-44
User Manager For Do-
mains, 38-39
Trust requirements
calculating, 36-38
multiple master domains,
36-38
Trusted domains, 34-35
Trusting domains, 34-35
Types, object, 61

U

Unix hosts
printers, 281
protocols for, 165
User Manager For Domains,
38-39
User policies, naming, 94
User profile handling, 94
User profiles
authentication, 90
caching, 92
for consistent desktops, 92
customizable, 91-92
default location for, 92
definition, 91
loading on slow connec-
tions, 92

mandatory, 91
replicating, 111
roaming profiles, 92
User rights, 71-73

V

VGA mode, 323
Views, saving settings of, 232-
233
Virtual Memory dialog box,
234
Virtual Memory Manager. *See*
VMM.
VMM, 234
Volume sets, 117

W

Wallpaper, configuring, 94
WAN, 293
Web sites, as information
sources, 15-16
Wide Area Networks. *See*
WAN.
Windows application restric-
tions, configuring, 94
Windows Internet Name
Service. *See* WINS.
definition, 192-193
versus DNS, 194
Windows NT installation, 314-
315
WINS, 165
definition, 192-193
versus DNS, 194
World Wide Web, 166, 195

Order Practice Tests from the
Authors of the *Exam Cram* Series

LANWrights offers diskette copies of practice tests for these MCSE exams:

70-058 Networking Essentials
70-063 Windows 95*
70-067 NT Server 4
70-068 NT Server 4 in the Enterprise

70-073 NT Workstation 4
70-059 TCP/IP for NT 4*
TBD Exchange Server 5.5+
TBD   IIS 4.+

* available 12/97   + available Q2/98   ! available Q2/98

Each diskette includes the following:

√ Two practice exams consisting of 50-60 questions, designed to help you prepare for the certification test. One test automates the test that appears in each *Exam Cram* book; the other is new material.

√ Feedback on answers, to help you prepare more thoroughly.

√ Access to the LANWrights Question Exchange, an online set of threaded discussion forums aimed at the topics for each of these books, where you can ask for help and get answers within 72 hours.

Note: These tests are written in HTML and use Java and JavaScript tools, so you must use Navigator 3.02 or Internet Explorer 3.02 or higher.

Fees for practice exam diskettes:

$25 for single diskette	$100 for any five
$45 for any two	$115 for any six
$65 for any three	$135 for all eight
$85 for any four	All amounts are US$

To order, please send a check or money order drawn on a U.S. bank. Please include complete delivery information with your order: Name, Company, Street Address, City, State, Postal Code, Country. Send all orders to LANWrights Exams, P.O. Box 26261, Austin, TX, USA 78755-0261. For orders from Mexico or Canada, please add US$5; for orders outside North America, please add US$10. For expedited delivery, online orders, or other information, please visit www.lanw.com/examcram/order.htm.

Ordering information:

To complete your order for the Practice MCSE Certification Tests, we will need the following ship-to information:

Name

Company

Street Address

City, State

ZIP/Postal Code

Country

Send a request (you can use this page if you wish) and a check or money order drawn on a U.S. bank in $US to:

LANWrights Exam Orders
PO Box 26261
Austin, TX 78755-0261 USA

For orders from Mexico or Canada, add US$5 to your order fee; for orders from locations outside the United States, add US$10 to your fee. All orders will be shipped as soon as funds clear, and will be sent via the U.S. Postal Service, unless other arrangements are made.

For more information, including telephone orders, processing of purchase orders, licensing of practice tests, or expedited shipment, please visit the LANWrights Exam Cram Web page at: **http://www.lanw.com/examcram/ order.htm.**

If you would like to receive news about new LANWrights books and products, please provide your email address.

If you have any comments or questions, feel free to email us at **examcram@lanw.com. Thanks for your order!**